Environment
and
Buddhism

Environment
and
Buddhism

Dr. I. N. Singh

Prashant Publishing House
DELHI - 110094 (INDIA)

PRASHANT PUBLISHING HOUSE
C-34, 28 Foota Road, Gali No. 3
West Karawal Nagar, Delhi-110094
Phone : 9810396373, 22963970

Environment and Buddhism

First Published : 2011

ISBN : 978-93-80565-12-5

PRINTED IN INDIA

Published by Mr. R. K. Jha M/s. Prashant Publishing House, Delhi and Printed at H.S. Offset Press, Delhi.

Preface

For the last two millennia, human beings never faced a truly serious threat to their existence as a species. But now, as we start the third millennium, the ever-deepening crisis in the global environment raises the real possibility of human extinction. If environmental destruction cannot be reversed, it is more than likely that the earth will degenerate, leaving the global ecosystem in ruins and making it impossible for our species to survive. Buddhists often tend to disregard environment, because the monastic way of life idealized by Buddhism is environmentally very minimalist. Such neglect of comment concerning environmental values is not warranted, however, because the Buddhist scriptures are in fact rich with advice from the Buddha regarding environment values and they are applicable to monastic and lay lifestyles alike.

It will be possible to create an environment conducive to the symbiosis of all living things, including human beings, by recognizing that the world is governed by the principle of dependent origination and by creating a feedback loop of merciful, good 'common karma.' Until now, human refashioning of the environment, it seems, has been single-mindedly directed toward the fulfilment of human desires. For it nurtures an awareness that their environment is something of their own making. That awareness in turn enables people to realize that their environment is an enlarged projection of themselves, hence that they must work hard to protect the health of their environment just as they take care to protect their own health. Also relevant is the contention that products of human desires keep amplifying through the feedback loop of the 'alaya consciousness.' By the same logic, human destruction of the environment ultimately leads to the destruction of the human spirit in its deeper layers.

The book is to tremendous use to students, teachers, environmentalism and general readers.

—*Editor*

Contents

1 Introduction

To live in harmony with nature is a crucial Buddhist practice. When we look at the traditional Buddhist texts there seems to be very little direct reference to what would these days be called environmental or ecological ideas. As we imaginatively enter the world in which the Buddha lived and taught, the reason for this becomes clear. The picture that emerges is one of a culture that lived in far greater harmony with its environment, if sometimes at its mercy, and an 'Environmental Movement' simply wasn't needed.

The strong connection that people felt with nature is illustrated particularly in the story of the Buddha's life, in which all the most significant events occur in the countryside and are associated with trees: his birth at Lumbini as his mother grasped the branch of a sal tree, his early experience of states of meditative absorption beneath the rose apple tree, his Enlightenment beneath the Bodhi-tree, and his Parinirvana (death) between twin sal trees. So in seeking to apply the Dharma to the area of the environment, we have to look for underlying principles that are appropriate to the very different world that we ourselves inhabit.

We don't have to look very far. In the vision of universal interpenetration, one of the Mahayana flowers of the Buddha's teaching of Conditioned Co-production (*pratitya samutpada*), we have a basic insight into our relationship with nature. This vision is exemplified in the simile of Indra's Net: High above in heaven, on the roof of the palace of the god Indra, there hang innumerable jewels interlaced in a great network. As the light reflects off these multifaceted gems not only does each jewel reflect the whole cosmos, but also every other jewel in the net, including all the reflections from all the jewels, the reflections of the reflections, and their reflections.

In this beautiful vision we can begin to connect imaginatively with the mutual interdependence of all processes. Bringing this insight down to earth it becomes clear that by harming nature we are in fact harming ourselves. There are plenty of examples to demonstrate this in the current media: acid rain, the greenhouse effect, the ozone hole, radioactive contamination, to name but a few. These reactions of nature to our carelessness harm us not only physically but also psychologically, as we face the threat of our environment becoming increasingly inimical to healthy human life.

Restating this vision of interpenetration in a positive sense, to improve the quality of our lives we need to live in greater harmony with nature. This may sound like a simple truism, but in fact it is certainly not the way in which our culture approaches nature. In the modern materialist culture, no doubt strongly influenced by the traditional Christian view that God put nature there for people to use for their own purposes, we approach the environment from the viewpoint of resource management. In many cases with large industrial companies this is better termed resource mis-management, as the narrow-minded drive for profit means that huge amounts of toxic substances are pumped into our skies, rivers, and oceans, and scattered across the land where they become 'someone else's problem'.

The 'resource management' approach leads us into difficulties on a more personal level though. In seeing ourselves as the 'managers', and therefore above nature, we can easily lose those very qualities which give us our humanity. Whether it is the immeasurable brutality involved in the slaughter of animals to keep the kitchens of the world constantly supplied with meat, or the killing of the peaceful giants of the sea by wealthy countries such as Japan, these acts degrade the human race as a whole. The Buddhist position, on the other hand, emphasizes a harmonious interaction between ourselves and nature, neither passive nor attempting to dominate, and quite naturally leads us to consider the possibility of vegetarianism.

So this is the vision, but how do we put it into practice? Here we find Buddhist ethics come to our aid, with the basic principle of non-violence (*ahimsa*) or harmlessness. In the statement of the first precept, abstention from harming living beings, we can see how much of the industrial use of resources contravenes the principle; in chopping down a rainforest we destroy a habitat for other creatures and set up the conditions for top soil erosion, which in turn leads to floods and famine thereby incurring untold suffering on others. So to put this principle into practice we also need a high degree of awareness of the consequences of our actions — this is a prerequisite for any truly skilful action.

Often, the actions that we commit in relation to the environment also contravene the second precept, abstention from taking what is not given. This can happen in quite a crude sense or in a very subtle one. How many of us have, while wandering through a field of flowers, plucked some up-more than we needed-as if they belonged to us and without a thought that others will be deprived of the pleasure of appreciating them? The principle of non-violence should not be taken to mean that people should absolutely abandon their use of the earth's resources for fear of harming any living beings whatsoever. After all, we are also part of nature, and need to maintain a healthy concern for our own welfare and that of fellow human beings. We need to use the resources available to free ourselves from the clutches of nature's destructiveness: storms, floods, and famines.

However, with the awareness of the consequences of our actions, we have a great responsibility to use the resources in as harm-free and useful a way as possible. As Sangharakshita has said, 'Right use of nature is part of the spiritual life.' This again leads us to consider the possibility of vegetarianism. At a rough estimate it takes ten times as much vegetable matter te feed a person on a meat eating diet as it does to feed that person on a vegetarian diet. In a world with an ever increasing strain on the food supply the luxury of eating meat seems more and more unethical, quite apart from the slaughter of the animals involved.

If we can begin to deepen our relationship with nature through an understanding of interpenetration, and live more in harmony with our environment using the principle of non-violence, then a growing awareness of nature will begin to feed into our spiritual practice. Our ability to develop as individuals is closely bound up with the environment in which we live; harmonizing that environment will have a positive effect on our spiritual practice. After all, in the natural world we find many of the most inspiring symbols of our potential for development; the blue sky, the great ocean, the lofty mountain peaks. There are many examples of the fruits of inspiration that come from humankind's experience of the beauty and splendour of nature, especially the wildest places. From the scientist to the mystic, individuals have found the mysteries and complexities of nature to be a source of insight and uplift. For this reason alone it is vital that at least some of our wild places remain.

We must beware of over-sentimentalizing nature though; the cycle of life in the natural world can be at times a very harsh one. Our technological development has to some extent freed us from this and a 'back to nature' movement will certainly not solve humanity's problems. With so much at stake every little action counts. Hopefully enough people will wake up to the fact that we urgently need to change our attitudes to nature so that we and future generations may continue to be inspired by the process that is life on earth.

To live in harmony with nature is a crucial Buddhist practice.

When we look at the traditional Buddhist texts there seems to be very little direct reference to what would these days be called environmental or ecological ideas. As we imaginatively enter the world in which the Buddha lived and taught, the reason for this becomes clear. The picture that emerges is one of a culture that lived in far greater harmony with its environment, if sometimes at its mercy, and an 'Environmental Movement' simply wasn't needed. The strong connection that people felt with nature is illustrated particularly in the story of the Buddha's life, in which all the most significant events occur in the countryside and are associated with trees: his birth at Lumbini as his mother grasped the branch of a sal tree, his early experience of states of meditative absorption beneath the rose apple tree, his Enlightenment beneath the Bodhi-tree, and his Parinirvana (death) between twin sal trees.

So in seeking to apply the Dharma to the area of the environment, we have to look for underlying principles that are appropriate to the very different world that we ourselves inhabit.

We don't have to look very far. In the vision of universal interpenetration, one of the Mahayana flowers of the Buddha's teaching of Conditioned Co-production (pratitya samutpada), we have a basic insight into our relationship with nature. This vision is exemplified in the simile of Indra's Net: High above in heaven, on the roof of the palace of the god Indra, there hang innumerable jewels interlaced in a great network. As the light reflects off these multifaceted gems not only does each jewel reflect the whole cosmos, but also every other jewel in the net, including all the reflections from all the jewels, the reflections of the reflections, and their reflections.

In this beautiful vision we can begin to connect imaginatively with the mutual interdependence of all processes. Bringing this insight down to earth it becomes clear that by harming nature we are in fact harming ourselves. There are plenty of examples to demonstrate this in the current media: acid rain, the greenhouse effect, the ozone hole, radioactive contamination, to name but a few. These reactions of nature to our carelessness harm us not only physically but also psychologically, as we face the threat of our environment becoming increasingly inimical to healthy human life.

Restating this vision of interpenetration in a positive sense, to improve the quality of our lives we need to live in greater harmony with nature. This may sound like a simple truism, but in fact it is certainly not the way in which our culture approaches nature. In the modern materialist culture, no doubt strongly influenced by the traditional Christian view that God put nature there for people to use for their own purposes, we approach the environment from the viewpoint of resource management. In many cases with large industrial companies this is better termed resource mis-management, as the narrow-minded drive for profit means that huge amounts of toxic substances are pumped into our skies, rivers, and oceans, and scattered across the land where they become someone else's problem'.

The 'resource management' approach leads us into difficulties on a more personal level though. In seeing ourselves as the 'managers', and therefore above nature, we can easily lose those very qualities which give us our humanity. This is particularly noticeable source.

Whether it is the immeasurable brutality involved in the slaughter of animals to keep the kitchens of the world constantly supplied with meat, or the killing of the peaceful giants of the sea by wealthy countries such as Japan, these acts degrade the human race as a whole. The Buddhist position, on the other hand, emphasizes a harmonious interaction between ourselves and nature, neither passive nor attempting to dominate, and quite naturally leads us to consider the possibility of vegetarianism.

So this is the vision, but how do we put it into practice? Here we find Buddhist ethics come to our aid, with the basic principle of non-violence (ahimsa) or harmlessness.

In the statement of the first precept, abstention from harming living beings, we can see how much of the industrial use of resources contravenes the principle; in chopping down a rain forest we destroy a habitat for other creatures and set up the conditions for top soil erosion, which in turn leads to floods and famine thereby incurring untold suffering on others. So to put this principle into practice we also need a high degree of awareness of the consequences of our actions-this is a prerequisite for any truly skilful action.

Often, the actions that we commit in relation to the environment also contravene the second precept, abstention from taking what is not given. This can happen in quite a crude sense or in a very subtle one. How many of us have, while wandering through a field of flowers, plucked some up-more than we needed-as if they belonged to us and without a thought that others will be deprived of the pleasure of appreciating them? The principle of non-violence should not be taken to mean that people should absolutely abandon their use of the earth's resources for fear of harming any living beings whatsoever. After all, we are also part of nature, and need to maintain a healthy concern for our own welfare and that of fellow human beings. We need to use the resources available to free ourselves from the clutches of nature's destructiveness: storms, floods, and famines.

However, with the awareness of the consequences of our actions, we have a great responsibility to use the resources in as harm-free and useful a way as possible. As Sangharakshita has said, 'Right use of nature is part of the spiritual life.' This again leads us to consider the possibility of vegetarianism. At a rough estimate it takes ten times as much vegetable matter as it does to feed that person on a vegetarian diet. In a world with an ever increasing strain on the food supply the luxury of eating meat seems more and more unethical, quite apart from the slaughter of the animals involved.

If we can begin to deepen our relationship with nature through an understanding of interpenetration, and live more in harmony with our environment using the principle of non- violence, then a growing awareness of nature will begin to feed into our spiritual practice. Our ability to develop as individuals is closely bound up with the environment in which we live; harmonizing that environment will have a positive effect on our spiritual practice. After all, in the natural world we find many of the most inspiring symbols of our potential for development; the blue sky, the great ocean, the lofty mountain peaks. There are many examples of the fruits of inspiration that come from humankind's experience of the beauty and splendour of nature, especially the wildest places. From the scientist to the mystic, individuals have found the mysteries and complexities of nature to be a source of insight and uplift. For this reason alone it is vital that at least some of our wild places remain.

We must beware of over-sentimentalizing nature though; the cycle of life in the natural world can be at times a very harsh one. Our technological development has to some extent freed us from this and a 'back to nature' movement will certainly not solve humanity's problems. With so much at stake every little action counts. Hopefully enough people will wake up to the fact that we urgently need to change our attitudes to nature so that we and future generations may continue to be inspired by the process that is life on earth.

THE TIBETAN BUDDHIST VIEW OF THE ENVIRONMENT

For centuries, Tibetans lived in their vast, sparsely populated country in perfect harmony with their environment. It was not simply due to a small population and plentiful resources, but the result of an attitude of respect for all living creatures, fostered by the Tibetan Buddhist outlook.

The backbone of Buddhism is the theory of karma and rebirth, the law of cause and effect. Buddhists believe not in a creator, but in beings fashioning their destiny by their own actions.

In the course of their lifetime, living creatures perform virtuous or non-virtuous actions (karma) which create predispositions for rebirth in any of the six realms of cyclic existence. Virtuous actions bring about pleasant rebirths in the upper realms of gods, demi-gods and men and non-virtuous deeds, suffering and rebirth in the animal, hungry ghost and hell-beings' realms.

When beings have exhausted the karma which caused their rebirth in a particular realm, in dependence on other accumulated karma, they take rebirth in another realm, wandering endlessly within the limits of cyclic existence until they find a way out to liberation or the state of Buddhahood- the ultimate goal of Buddhist practice.

Among all the creatures of the six realms, humans are the most fortunate, and have the best opportunity for attaining the ultimate achievement.

Gods and demi-gods dwell in immeasurable happiness, exhausting the fruits of their positive karma, and are too distracted with worldly pleasure to seek liberation from cyclic existence. Hungry ghosts and hell beings are too disturbed with suffering and animals are too dumb. Humans, who enjoy both pleasure and pain are the only ones who can seek liberation.

The driving force of this aim for the attainment of Buddhahood is motivation, of which there are three types; motivation of beings of small, middling and great capacities. Though the ultimate goal of all three is happiness and freedom from suffering, the extent of their goals is immeasurably different. The being of smaller capacity's virtuous acts are aimed at securing a rebirth away from the hells, and his basic rule of conduct for achieving this is avoiding the non-virtuous actions which bring about lower rebirths. These are: killing, stealing, sexual misconduct, lying, slander, harsh speech, idle gossip, covetousness, harmful intent and wrong view.

The being of middling capacity seeks to go one step further and achieve liberation from cyclic existence by realizing the Four Noble Truths: true sufferings, which are like an illness, sources, the internal and external conditions that bring about that illness, cessations, the state of being curedo the illness and paths, the medicine which brings about the cure. In order to realize these Four Noble Truths, one must realize

(1) the suffering of cyclic existence, like a sick person identifying his ailment,

(2) that the origin of suffering is karma and defilements, like a patient identifying the cause of his illness,

(3) the existence of a remedy to suffering, like a patient knowing that his illness can be cured,

(4) that engaging in the paths will bring about freedom from suffering, like a patient realizing the benefit of medicine.

Buddhahood- in order to liberate all sentient beings from the sufferings of cyclic existence. The sufferings of beings are so infinite they cannot be alleviated by an ordinary person. To attain his purpose, the practitioner must strive to become a Bodhisattva, by training his mind in the six causes and one effect.

These include practices such as thinking of all sentient beings as one's mother, remembering their kindness, thinking of ways to repay this kindness, immeasurable love, compassion, resolute thought and bodhisattva mind as well as equating oneself with others, exchanging oneself with others, etc. With Bodhisattva mind firmly planted within his continuum, the practitioner is ready to engage in the six perfection of giving, ethics, patience effort, concentration and wisdom.

In practising virtue in this unique and immeasurable way, he will not only be able to help beings but will accumulate the immense merit necessary for attaining the state of Buddhahood.

The motivation of the being of great capacity is the core of Mahayana Buddhism, which is the Buddhism of Tibet. Knowing this, it is easy to understand how respect for the environment and for all creatures naturally became not only a norm of social behaviour, but the core of policies formulated by the Tibetan government as far back as the 7th century. At that time, King Songtsen Gampo promulgated religious laws, based on the ten virtues (opposite of the ten non virtues) and temporal laws, including sixteen rules of social conduct. From the time of the Fifth Dalai Lama Ngawang Gyatso, in the 17th century, the Dalai Lamas and regents promulgated the Rilung Tsagtsig, or decrees that the protection of animal life and the environment, which were issued every year in their names.

These not only forbade the killing of wild animals, such as animals of hill and forest, birds, fish and otter, but also that of domestic animals on certain days, such as the 8th, 15th and 30th days of each month. They also forbade the sale of fresh meat in Lhasa during the fourth month, the holiest month of the Tibetan calendar. The edicts commanded village heads, governors and officials of all districts in Tibet to ensure that these orders were enforced and to personally prevent the killing of all wild animals. They were read out by village heads to their assembled populations, and stuck on notice boards where they remained displayed throughout the year. Breaking of Tsagtsig was punished by law. The government also organized a great many rituals for inducing rain, to ensure the well-being of animals domestic and wild, good crops and plentiful trees and flowers.

In the social sphere, though domestic animals were slaughtered, efforts were made to avoid meat eating on certain holidays and In the fourth month of the Tibetan calendar. Buying back animals from the butcher and setting them free was also a common practice. Tibetans were not adventurous in their gastronomical habits and ate mostly yak meat. Survival on the high plateau required protein, but it was considered more ethical to live off the meat of larger animals than on that of many small ones, of which many more would have to be killed. Thus, consumption of fish and chicken was rare and the idea of eating snakes, chibis (prairie dogs) ducks and wild ass, as practised later by the Chinese, totally repulsive. In this way, most wild animals had little to fear from humans.

Though some people in remote areas indulged in hunting, it was considered neither a sport nor a pleasure, but more like poaching, practised by individuals who felt they could get round the law and social conventions. Fishing for fun was something unheard of, except in the case of naughty children who did it behind their parents' backs, and poachers, who sold their catch in Lhasa as 'water radish'. Sports such as cock, dog or bull fights and any other games involving cruelty to animals were never seen in Tibet, and their mention to Tibetans nowadays inevitably arouses incredulity and disgust. Every effort was made to avoid unnecessarily disrupting bird and insect life by digging and cutting trees.

The views and norms described above are very similar to those of most animal and wildlife protection agencies. The difference with the Tibetans, however, is that the same criteria was extended beyond the animal world, taking into account all beings of the six realms. Though men and animals are the only tones ordinarily perceived by humans, others such as demi-gods and hungry ghosts are believed to be present in the humans realm greatly influencing many aspects of animal life. There is a saying in Tibetan that 'Gods, demons and men all have the same attitude'. All three, being within cyclic existence, strive for pleasure and avoid pain, and likewise enjoy good treatment and react negatively to harm inflicted by others. Thus, they should be treated equally.

As a result of these views the Tibetan government limited mining and exploitation of natural resources to avoid disrupting not only the animal life and ecological system, but the unseen creatures believed to dwell there. Moreover, it officially organized a great many rituals, which sought tit please the local deities and ensure harmonious natural conditions.

In formulating these edicts and performing these rituals, the Tibetan government sought to achieve both immediate and ultimate purposes: the first was to keep all the potentially dangerous natural forces pleased and satisfied, thus ensuring their good will, or at least, their non-interference, in helping the country achieve peace and prosperity. The second was to uphold the principles of the Buddhist doctrine, which set the conditions for the general population to acquire personal and collective merit by refraining from non-virtuous acts and benefit from the resulting positive karma.

Unseen forces are believed to be as numerous as those we can see: in every pond, forest, tree, house, dwell creatures big and small, important and humble which occasionally appear to humans in various forms, as well as in visions and in dreams.

All these creatures are believed to be ruled by the protectors of the ten directions. These deities include gods from the Hindu pantheon such as Brahma and Indra. They are gods, and though they are immensely powerful and believed to control all the forces of the universe they are not beyond the wheel of cyclic existence and thus cannot be an object of refuge for humans aspiring for liberation. They may or may not be sympathetic to the Buddhist doctrine, but their help and cooperation can be cultivated and is considered essential, since they control all other non-human creatures, gods, demi-gods and ghosts. Tantric rituals always include an offering to them at the beginning to assure their non-interference.

The creatures dwelling in individual places are called Sa-dag or land owners, or guardian deities. They belong to the realm of demi-gods or ghosts- not all ghosts are miserable creatures, some are wealthy and powerful demons. They may appear to people as ghosts, demons, or in dreams in an infinite variety of forms, including the human one and may either help or harm depending on their disposition. Many of the creatures in lakes, ponds and rivers are nagas, or serpent beings who belong to the animal realm. They sometimes appear in the form of snakes, or as half snakes and half humans with elaborate jeweled crowns. They are believed to be infinitely wealthy and to owe their present form to a previous life of unethical generosity.

Human activity is bound to encroach on the well being of living creatures including those of other realms. Coming to a plot of land and inadvertently building a house, cutting trees or mining and digging natural resources will upset nagas and sa-dags just as it does animals and insects in such a situation. It is said that sa-dags and nagas equate the unauthorized use of land and natural resources they occupy to pilfering their personal possessions. The weaker ones among them will undergo great hardship or die off, while the more powerful will react with anger and strike back at the offenders, inflicting disease, death, and sudden catastrophe.

They will not necessarily strike at the humans having committed the harm, as most cannot identify the actual offenders, but at any human they see, and innocent people may fall ill or die for no apparent reason, or the whole area be affected with epidemics or cases of leprosy. The following story was related by a Dema Locho Rinpochey, from Drepung, and occurred in the 1950s in Tibet. One day, one of the monks who was responsible for having the trees in the debating square watered, developed a large sore on his thigh. Suspecting it was caused by harm from nagas, he asked Rinpochey to consult an oracle in a nearby village- a nun who was possessed by nagas- to find out the cause of his illness. The naga, speaking through the oracle admitted having caused the harm: 'Yes, it was I who struck at that monk.' When Rinpochey asked the reason, it replied: 'I was angry at humans for other reasons and I saw this monk's luck I was down and that he was vulnerable, so I caused him to develop this sore'.

Humans are most vulnerable to nagas and sa-dags when their luck is low, as it is said that any weakness is immediately apparent to these other-worldly creatures. In order to avert unlucky circumstances which may bring on harm, people hang up strings of different prayer flags bearing the image of a horse. The 'wind-horse' or Lung-ta is the symbol of one's luck. The Tibetan expression 'His wind-horse is running' or 'is broken' refers to this luck, and the prayer flags fluttering in the wind, a tradition of Bîn origin, is believed to give the upper hand to one's wind-horse.

Since humans cannot survive without some form of land exploitation and building, Tibetans take certain measures to prevent unnecessary mishaps. While the hanging of prayer flags is like a general preventive measure, that of avoiding harm which has no direct cause, more particular measures are sought when any kind of digging is involved. Whenever choosing a site for building, whether for a mandala, temple or house, a lama is consulted as to the method by which the nagas and sa-dag on the site might be appeased and treated. The lama will know something about them either through dreams, divination or clairvoyance. According to Buddhist tantric practice, there are other ways of performing rituals. These are: peaceful, increasing, forceful and wrathful. The methods that apply to pacifying creatures of other realms are peaceful and wrathful, and the rituals used are extremely varied, in type as well as in tradition.

Generally, in either case, a ritual based on sutra called Tashi Sojong is performed, to bring good luck and please the dwellers. If performing tantric rituals, the lama will offer tormas to the Sa-dag or nagas abiding on the land. Tormas are conical-shaped offering cakes which have been blessed in three ways by a highly realized being by mantras, where they are purified from any defilements of ordinariness, by meditational stabilization, by which they are made infinite and by gestures, or mudras, which ensure that the recipient is satisfied. The idea of this ritual is to offer gifts to the sa-dag and nagas in exchange for use of their land.

It is a deal, a give and take situation like selling a house, and if the 'sellers' are satisfied, things will proceed smoothly. There are some situations, however, where the land may be owned by particularly powerful sa-dags, who will not want to give in to humans and will do their utmost to create obstacles and harm. Such places are known as 'rough'. The spirits and demons inhabiting them it will be unyielding in their views and generally delight in causing harm to human trespassers causing illness and bad dreams. If the lama examining the land sees such a situation, he will either declare the site unfit for building, or deal with the situation using the wrathful method.

Through the possibilities are vast, the most commonly used wrathful method for clearing a site from negative forces, is the 'throwing of ritual cakes' which is like using a bomb to send harmful creatures to another existence. The motivation of the lama is one of compassion, and knowing that the purpose of the project is beneficial one and that the being causing the harm is accumulating negative karma, he will actually help it by transferring its consciousness to another realm where it will be of less harm to other beings. Only a person with a higher level of realization is qualified to perform such a ritual. When obstacles are removed, the Lu Thaye, a very powerful naga believed to be constantly moving under the ground is dealt with. Sudden digging would disturb him, but his movements in a particular spot can be plotted astrologically, and a spot on the plot can be found where no part of his body would be present at the time of the first, symbolic digging. This would be followed by offerings of ritual cakes to pacify him. This done, the building could proceed without further interference.

In some cases, sa-dags and nagas not only take offense at encroachment on their land, but at harm inflicted on certain animals they feel are their own. The following is a story which took place about eighty years ago in a remote area of Kham. The head of a group of nomads, feeling he was above the law against hunting wild animals which prevailed in his land, one day decided to go shooting. He went off with his rifle and spotted a beautiful stag. He aimed at it, and saw something like a golden stirrup between its antlers.

He put down his rifle and stared, but could see nothing. He aimed and put down his rifle two or three times, seeing the stirrup appear and disappear, hesitated, and finally shot. The stag was hit by the bullet but escaped, leaving a trail of blood. That night, the man returned home, unable to find the carcass of the animal he had hoped to kill and suddenly became very ill. As he lay dying, he related to his kin the incident with the stag, regretting he had shot it and mumbling he should have known better, seeing such an unusual object as a golden stirrup between its antlers. He died that very night and his family concluded he was the victim of a revengeful sa-dag to whom either the stag belonged to or of which he had taken the form.

Incense and vase-offering rituals, which were routinely performed by the Tibetan government and also by private individuals and lamas were not only meant as a remedy in case of drought or other calamities, but also as a regular preventive measure to bring about positive conditions. Non-human creatures were known for their liking of fragrant smells, and the tradition of sang-so, which was originally practised by the Bîn to appease and please local deities, was later practised by Buddhists for the same purpose. In the case of vase-offering rituals, vases were filled with different precious metals and cereals, blessed by mantras, meditative stabilization and gestures and placed in lakes or other places throughout the country where nagas were known to dwell, as a boon to them.

These gifts could be likened to presents offered by the king of one country to that of another, aimed at pleasing the recipients who reciprocated with timely rain, pure water and a disease free environment. They had ways of showing their liking in particular ways. Dema Locho Rinpochey recalls a time when Drepung Loseling college decided to renovate a small retreat house on one of their estates, a few hours from Lhasa. The place had a spring and was known for its important naga and sa-dag population. The college called on Rinpochey to perform a ritual to keep the nagas out of the way during the time of the restoration work.

This involved attracting them into a mirror which was transformed, by the lama's concentration, into a very pleasant abode in which they were asked to remain, as honoured guests, until their usual dwelling was once more fit to stay in. Rinpoche also offered a bathing ritual to the spring, purifying any defilements it would have undergone during the work. He said that the next morning, the caretaker pointed out that the water was much more abundant than usual, a sign that the nagas who dwelled in it were pleased.

Likewise, some spirits liked to return gifts. Once, a merchant was traveling to Lhasa from Kham, with a caravan of yaks laden with tea bricks. This man had a great liking and faith in the guardian spirit of the mountain, the Nycuchen Thanglha, whom he believed helped him on his journeys and his success in business. When he came in sight of the mountain, which stood isolated on the plain and could be seen from a great distance, he unloaded a large bundle of tea and looking towards it, dumped it on the side of the road, his offering to the deity. His companions, who were aware of his gift thought he was really quite simple minded- how would the spirit, from this distance, know the gift was intended for him? The next morning, the merchant went off to relieve himself and saw something like a chibi's hole full of small black and white stones. He took a closer look and found it was a large quantity of zi- the striped and pierced agate stones believed to date back to prehistoric times- and which are highly prized in Tibet as jewelry. He was not a greedy man. He knew it was a gift from the mountain spirit and only picked one from the bunch, never revealing his discovery to his companions. Later, it was said this was an exceptional zi.

Many non-human creatures were dedicated to the Buddhist doctrine and strove to protect and help those who were its living embodiment; lamas and highly realized beings. They could appear to them in different forms and offer assistance in difficult situations or sometimes simply chose to express their faith and appreciation with offerings which materialized in the most unusual ways. The following tent occurred about fifty years ago, near the same mountain, in Central Tibet. A lama, Ari Rinpochey was traveling from his native Amdo to Lhasa.

It was his habit, every evening, whether at home or traveling, to offer a butter lamp in front of his altar. When he came to the mountain and set up camp there, he lit his evening butter lamp as usual. He noticed that a little black ball had formed on the wick and was surprised, when it fell, to hear a little 'tac' sound, like something heavy falling into the lamp. Knowing that soot has no weight he was intrigued, and the next morning, asked his steward to check the butter lamp. The steward looked and saw a blue spilt in the hardened butter. He extracted it and held it up in the daylight it was a small bright blue turquoise. Ari Rinpochey, who knew of the powerful spirit of the mountain realized it was his gift.

Nowadays, the environmental situation is deteriorating rapidly in Tibet with deforestation and the depletion of the fauna. Diseases and calamities previously unheard of are now common in many parts of the country. Whatever the causes are, the effects are present and need to be remedied. Although, due to the political situation, little can be done at present, Tibetan Buddhist principles which state that all beings have an equal right to exist, are the basis for the preservation of the environment.

2 Mahayana Buddhism and Environmental Ethics

In this chapter we will describe Buddhist views of nature and environment, and the contribution of the Consciousness-Only doctrine of Buddhist psychology to solving environmental problems. In particular, we emphasize an important role of the alaya consciousness in the deeper layer of our minds from the perspective of the Consciousness-Only doctrine. The alaya consciousness is the root entity that forms the framework of all existences, i.e., our own bodies, our minds, and our environments. To put its important role concretely, the concept of alaya consciousness is able to give accounts of the enlargement of human desires as the cause of environmental problems, responsibility as environmental ethics, and the effects of products of science and technology on our minds. Finally, I discuss a methodology for reforming the alaya consciousness through social movements and the bodhisattva way, and the solution of environmental problems at its most basic source.

INTRODUCTION

For the last two millennia, human beings never faced a truly serious threat to their existence as a species. But now, as we start the third mil- lennium, the ever-deepening crisis in the global environment raises the real possibility of human extinction. If environmental destruction cannot be reversed, it is more than likely that the earth will degenerate, leaving the global ecosystem in ruins and making it impossible for our species to survive.

Tremendous efforts have been made over the past 50 years to try to control problems in the environment, and some of those problems, e.g. Minamata disease and ouch-ouch disease that are local problems in Japan, have been solved or at least alleviated. The irony is, however, irrespective of such efforts that we have created new problems, e.g. destruction of ozone layer and exogenous endocrine disrupters, one after another, so that now the environmental picture is, on balance, worse than ever before.

Together, environmental problems such as the green house effect, marine pollution and destruction of rainforest are expanding in scale and growing more serious in nature.

How are we ever to break the hold of this vicious circle? One thing is clear, and that is the need for a fundamental reappraisal of the material civilization that has been propelled onward by science and technology. Buddhism has much to offer in the quest for answers to the environmental crisis. This approach is gradualist, through a human revolution. Like reform through education, the Buddhist method may seem circuitous, but it seeks to get to the heart of the problem.

Recently, I described the natural and environmental views of Bud- dhism and summarized several points addressing Buddhist issues on environmental problems (Yamamoto, 1998a, 1998b, 1999). In additon , Kawada (1994), Harvey (2000) and Keown et al.(2000) discussed gen- erally Buddhist thought and Buddhist ethics in relation to global prob- lems.

The relation of Buddhism to ecological ethics is discussed in detail by Schmithausen (1991a; 1991b; 1997; 2000). In this article, alongside summarizing several points dealing with Buddhist perspectives on the environment, we would like to examine some of the ways Buddhism can contribute to solving the environmental problem by focusing on the doctrine of 'Consciousness-Only (*yui- siki*)' (terms in single quotation marks are Buddhist terms, and italic terms are Buddhist terms in Japanese) by Vasubandhu (*Sesin*), which is often referred to as the Buddhist version of psychology. The 'Con- sciousness-Only' teachings which were expounded by Asanga (*Mujaku*) and Vasubandhu in fourth or fifth century of India are called the 'Yogacara School (*Yugagyo-ha*) (Harvey, 1990).'

HUMANITY, SOCIETY, AND THE NATURAL ENVIRONMENT FROM THE PERSPECTIVE OF THE 'CONSCIOUSNESS-ONLY' DOCTRINE

As we described before (Yamamoto, 1998a), the essences of Buddhist environmental thoughts and their meanings for solving environmental problems are summarized as follows.

(1) Principle of Symbiosis: Concepts of nature and environment which are seen in the doctrine of 'dependent origination' in Buddhism are similar to concepts of ecology. Everything is somehow connected. Therefore, the very principles of bio-diversity and symbiosis of nature and living things are primary in maintaining our world.

(2) Principle of Circulation: The concept of cycles or cycling that birth and death is repeating in the universe is important for considering the system of cycling in soci- ety. Moreover, the concept of 'transmigration of life' and 'rebirth of life' is significant for cultivating views of environmental ethics, because oneself in the future is determined by behaviors of oneself at the pre- sent.

(3) Perspective of Recognition of the World: In Buddhism all phenomena are understood basically in terms of 'dependent origination,' the idea of the interdependence and interaction among all existences. Perception of them takes place in the context of the three areas set forth by the doctrine of the 'three realms of exis- tence': the area of mind vs. body; the area of the self vs. others (i.e., human society); and the area of human race vs. natural ecosystem.

(4) Relationships of Subject and the Environment: The environmental view of Buddhism is a life-centric one, and is life-independent or anthropo-independent too. Both subject and its envi- ronment have a mutually interdependent and an interconnected relation- ship.

(5) Intrinsic Value of Nature: The doctrine of 'dependent origination' shows that everything in the ecosystem is equal in value. Because all living things and non-living things have the Buddha-Nature, they are regarded as having an equal dignity and an intrinsic value.

(6) The Rights of Nature: Though environmental ethics will be expanding the concept of rights from human rights into the rights of nature, the doctrine of 'dependent origination' in Buddhism argues that human rights are based upon the rights of nature.

Buddhism holds, however, that if we grasp the above concepts at the superficial level of consciousness we lose sight of their essence, for underneath consciousness is a vast realm of unconsciousness, and essence lies in that deeper layer, according to the doctrine of 'Con- sciousness-Only.' This Buddhist idea is the doctrine of 'Consciousness- Only' which had been expounded by Vasubandhu and others in the 'Consciousness-Only school (*yuishiki-ha*)' of Mahayana. Therefore, I think that the doctrine has a significant meaning for understanding the Buddhist thoughts.

This doctrine is developed by his meditation, which is summarized to a short sentence of *Thirty Verses* (*Yuishiki-sanju-ronju*) by Vasubandhu (in modern edition of Taisho-Shinshu-Daizokyo, 1970). The feature of the 'Consciousness Only' doctrine will be described from the next sec- tion. It is manifested that the consciousness which appears on the sur- face always affects the depths on the basis of dependent origination, and the surface consciousness and the subsurface consciousness are always changing fluidly. In the same way, subject and its environment have close relation still more at the depths as well as relation which appears as phenomenon at the surface. Therefore, the phenomenon and the consciousness, which appear at the surface, are only the tip of the iceberg floating on the water. There is a vast world that extends under the surface of the water. That vast world is developed with the depths of the consciousness and the phenomenon in Buddhist thought.

The 'First Five Consciousnesses,' the 'Mind Consciousness' and the 'Manas Consciousness'

According to the 'Consciousness-Only' doctrine, the uppermost stratum of human 'consciousness (*shiki*)' is composed of the 'first five con- sciousnesses (*zen-go-shiki*)' that correspond to the five sensory organs (eyes, ears, nose, tongue, and body), plus the 'sixth (*roku-shiki*),' which is the 'mind consciousness (*i-shiki*).' The 'first five consciousnesses' means discernment of the human sense organs, i.e. the 'eye conscious- ness (*gen-shiki*),' the 'ear consciousness (*ni-shiki*),' the 'nose con- sciousness (*bi-shiki*),' the 'tongue consciousness (*ze-sshiki*)' and the 'body consciousness (*shin-shiki*).' The 'mind consciousness' includes reason and integrates the perceptions of the five senses into coherent images. In contrast to these six layers of 'consciousness,' or six 'con- sciousnesses,' that deal with the external world, the 'seventh (*nana- shiki*)' or the 'manas consciousness (*mana-shiki*)' discerns the inner spiritual world. Basic awareness of self originates at this level. The 'passionate attachment (*shuuchaku*)' to the 'ego (*ga*),' which functions to create 'evil karma (*aku-go*),' is also the working of this 'seventh con- sciousness.' These 'karma' include 'self-stupidity (*ga-chi*),' which leads to ignorance of true nature; 'self-pride (*ga-man*),' which can turn into arrogance; 'self-biased views (*ga-ken*),' which more often than not are false views; and 'self-love (*ga-ai*),' which is the source of greed. The 'manas consciousness' is, indeed, the root ego that sustains self- consciousness.

Then, the 'manas consciousness' is also called the 'consideration consciousness (*siryo-shiki*).' The object that is considered is the 'alaya consciousness (*araya-shiki*)' in the depths of the 'manas conscious- ness,' and the 'alaya consciousness' is regarded as an entity. Buddhism understands that various suffering and 'evil passions (*bon-no*)' are caused there. Attachment to the entity results in clinging to the thought of the existence of the self.

The 'Alaya Consciousness'

Located in the layer deeper than the 'manas consciousness' is the 'eighth (*hachi-shiki*)' or the 'alaya consciousness.' This is also known as the immortal consciousness, as it is regarded as that which undergoes the cycle of birth and death. It is the root entity of individual existence that underscores the Buddhist idea of 'transmigration of life,' that is, eternal, continuous change of life. According to Yokoyama (1976), the 'alaya consciousness' has two distinct characteristics. First, the 'alaya consciousness' is the root entity that forms the framework of all existences. It generates and influences the workings of the 'first seven consciousnesses (*zen-nana-shiki*).' One's own body and its environment, as well as the 'first seven con- sciousnesses'—all arise from what the 'alaya consciousness' is trans- formed.

Second, all the experiences of life that take place through the 'first seven consciousnesses'—both physical and mental activities—are accu- mulated as 'seeds (*shuji*)' in the 'alaya consciousness.' The 'seeds' thus imprinted and stored there grow and mature to give birth to new exis- tences (the environment, body, and the various consciousnesses). The 'seeds' registered in the 'eighth consciousness' through the 'three kinds of human acts (*san-go*)'—'bodily (*shin*),' 'verbal (*ku*),' and 'mental (*i*)'—are together called the 'name and word seed (*myogon-shuji*),' because those that are conceptualized through language leave especially strong imprints.

There are morally 'good (*zen*),' 'evil (*aku*),' and 'neu- tral (*muki*)' seeds, and of these, good and evil ones are called 'karma seeds (*go-shuji*).' Buddhism attaches particular importance to the con- scious acts of the 'first six consciousnesses (*zen-roku-shiki*),' hence whether such physical and mental acts are good or evil is clearly imprinted in the 'alaya consciousness' as 'karma seeds.' Therefore, the 'eighth consciousness,' 'alaya consciousnes' is called the 'store con- sciousness (*zo-shiki*),' because this 'consciousness' stores the 'karma seeds' of all consequences of 'karma' action. Moreover, the 'alaya consciousness' is dyed with 'good' or 'evil karma seeds' though the 'alaya consciousness' is originally ethically 'neutral,' as a blank sheet of paper. The 'good' and 'evil karma seeds' will decide a condition of the 'alaya consciousness' in the future world.

'Common Karma' and 'Individual Karma'

There are two kinds of 'karma seeds' that are imprinted in the 'alaya consciousness': those that are common among members of a family, an ethnic group, or a society and those that are specific to individuals. The former are called 'common karma seeds (*gugo-shuji*),' and the latter, 'individual karma seeds (*fu-gugo-shuji*).' A person's body and mental activities are by nature individual, hence they are formed by 'individual karma (*fu-gugo*).' By contrast, the natural environment and social milieu do not belong to one person but are common to the members of a group or an area, hence they are formed by 'common karma (*gu-go*).' It is described in the text of Abhidharma-nyåyånusåra (*Abidaruma-Jun- shori-ron*) by Hsuantsang (*Genjo*) (in the modern edition of Taisho- Shinshu-Daizokyo, 1962) that "mountains, rivers, the earth and so on are born from 'common karma,' and sentient beings are born from 'individual karma'."

'Common karma' applies at different levels. The 'common karma' of a family, for example, informs its family consciousness and a particular familial environment, while that of an ethnic group informs the ethnic consciousness and a particular ethnic environment. Thus, 'common karma' informs not only the outer layer of the social consciousness of a family, an ethnic group, a nation, and humankind as a whole, but their subconsciousness as well. 'Common karma' also extends vertically, affecting both our ancestors and future generations. In this point of view, the relations between an individual and its mind, between an indi- vidual and society, and between human and the nature, which relations are aspects of the world recognition in Buddhism, will be supported by the standpoint of the doctrine of 'Consciousness-Only.'

'Dependent Origination of the Alaya Consciousness'

Like the 'first five consciousnesses' that correspond to the five sensory organs, the 'alaya consciousness' has its own objects of cognition. Whereas the 'eye consciousness' discerns form, among other things, and the 'ear consciousness' discerns sound, among others, the 'alaya consciousness' discerns the seeds, the environment, and the 'first five' through the 'first seven consciousnesses' that are its own making. The 'alaya consciousness' has its own unique mental functions by which to discern them. Its discernments are reflected in 'bodily,' 'verbal,' and 'mental acts,' which are in turn imprinted as 'seeds' in the 'alaya consciousness.' This is called the 'dependent origination of the alaya consciousness (*araya-shiki-engi*).' According to the Wei-shih-san-shih-lun (*Yuisiki-sanju-ronju*) by Vasubandhu, he expressed that the 'alaya con- sciousness' is always changing and is like a torrent.

In applying this concept of dependent origination to the environmental problem, we must keep in mind that the 'alaya consciousness' functions to affect individual, society and the natural environment. As the 'individual karma seed' imprinted to the 'alaya consciousness' makes an individual body and the 'first seven consciousnesses,' the perception, discernment, and conception by the 'first five consciousnesses' and the 'mind consciousness' always imprint new 'seeds' to the 'alaya consciousness' in the individual. As a result, when 'three kinds of bodi- ly, verbal, and mental acts (*shin-ku-i-no-sangou*)' newly express them- selves, 'individual karma seeds' will be accumulated again. The 'alaya consciousness' always changes by thus accumulating new 'individual karma seeds.' A feedback loop of the 'individual karma' of the 'alaya consciousness' in the individual will be formed here.

The concept shows that the 'common karma' imprinted in the 'alaya consciousness' always maintain dynamic relationships with society and the natural environment, and undergo constant change, thereby leading to the accumulation of new 'common karma,' which eventually mani- fest themselves, becoming phenomena. In other words, a feedback loop of 'common karma' of the 'alaya consciousness' is formed involving society and the natural environment. It goes without saying that 'indi- vidual karma,' too, when shared by many members of the group or area, can potentially become 'common karma.' Hence, the feedback loop at the individual level and the one formed involving society and the natural environment can be closely interconnected.

PERSPECTIVE OF THE 'CONSCIOUSNESS-ONLY' DOCTRINE TO ENVIRONMENTAL PROBLEMS

It will be possible to create an environment conducive to the symbiosis of all living things, including human beings, by recognizing that the world is governed by the principle of dependent origination and by cre- ating a feedback loop of merciful, good 'common karma.' Until now, human refashioning of the environment, it seems, has been single-mind- edly directed toward the fulfillment of human desires.

Human desires vis-à-vis the environment have manifested themselves in automobiles, chemicals and other industrial products and material substances, as well as in the transformation and destruction of nature through deforestation, depletion of natural resources, and development projects. What is important to note here is that the consequences of unbridled human desires appear in concrete form in the environment. As mentioned earlier, the 'Consciousness-Only' doctrine holds that whatever is manifested in the environment and what kind of environ- ment is created reflect the 'common karma.' In other words, what is internal in humans, such as desires, transform themselves into compo- nents of the external environment. These products of externalized desires stimulate not only human responses to the objects of perception by the five sensory organs-form, sound, smell, taste, and texture, but also stimulate the 'evil passions' lurking in the 'seventh consciousness,' the 'manas consciousness.'

Initially, the 'common karma' as a totality was small in scale, but through the feedback loop of the 'alaya consciousness' involving soci- ety and the environment, the products of human desires further stimu- lated popular craving for more, and they amplified the 'common karma' over time until it has grown to constitute the 'common karma' of humankind as a whole. In our world today we see greed expanding apparently boundlessly via the feedback loop that originates in the 'alaya consciousness.' And we see the environment saturated with things to satisfy human desires, an environment changing into the kind that corresponds with the 'common karma' of our time.

The 'Consciousness-Only' doctrine thus sheds light on how humans have formed the environment and how the environment has affected humans. Particularly relevant here is the idea that the nature of the envi- ronment depends on the 'common karma' of the people who make up the particular society.

For it nurtures an awareness that their environ- ment is something of their own making. That awareness in turn enables people to realize that their environment is an enlarged projection of themselves, hence that they must work hard to protect the health of their environment just as they take care to protect their own health. Also rele- vant is the contention that products of human desires keep amplifying through the feedback loop of the 'alaya consciousness.' By the same logic, human destruction of the environment ultimately leads to the destruction of the human spirit in its deeper layers.

Let us examine more closely the destructive impact on the environment by science and technology and their products. From the perspective of the 'Consciousness-Only' doctrine, gigantic machines that destroy nature, chemical substances that contaminate many forms of life and nature itself, and pesticides and herbicides designed to kill plants and animals are all functions of the 'common karma.' Products of science and technology may be divided into two categories in terms of the 'Consciousness-Only' doctrine.

Machines used to destroy nature and agricultural chemicals applied to kill pests and weeds fall in the first category—products made for pur- poses of destruction and/or killing, which are evil acts. In Buddhism, producing things with the conscious purpose of evil acts is considered especially conducive to the accumulation of evil 'karma seeds.' Put another way, the science-technology products of the first category are none other than manifestations of the evil 'common karma.'

Thus, products of evil 'common karma seeds' lead through the feedback loop to further accumulation of those 'seeds' in society. As evil 'common karma seeds' pile up in the 'alaya consciousness' of people, good 'com- mon karma seeds' diminish and become less powerful, and at some point the margin opens for unmerciful acts to be committed uncon- sciously. When that point is crossed, people are no longer aware that it is evil to kill life and destroy nature. That is why it is so critically important not to manufacture products of science and technology whose intended purpose is to destroy and kill.

Most products of modern science and technology fall in the second category; they are not originally intended to kill or accomplish other evil objectives. In fact, they are made to serve some useful purposes in human society. Yet it is quite possible for many of these products to end up destroying nature, contaminating or even killing living things, or harming human health. In terms of the 'Consciousness-Only' doctrine, this bespeaks the human inability to accurately forecast the effects of certain products on the environment and failure to understand the relationship of 'dependent origination.' Those human failings can be attrib- uted to the state of the 'manas consciousness.'

As long as the 'seventh consciousness' is obsessed with the root ego, it is exceedingly difficult for a person to understand that this world is governed by the principle of 'dependent origination' and that all existences in it are mutually dependent and in constant interaction. Failure to carefully consider in advance the possible effects of scientific-technological products on other beings makes people realize later that even those intended to serve human society and fulfill human desires can in the end bring about the destruction of nature, contamination of plants and animals, and have hazardous effects on human health. The examples are the earth warming by the emission of green house gases as carbon dioxide, the destruction of ozone layer by chlorofluocarbon, contamination and harming health of living things and people by agricultural chemicals, polychlorobiphenyl and exogenous endocrine disrupters.

Human knowledge of nature is still inadequate, hence it is perfectly understandable how difficult it may be to prevent beforehand all adverse effects of scientific-technological products. Precisely because of that, it is all the more important for us to understand clearly that human beings are not really capable of perceiving this world as one of 'dependent origination' insofar as greed thoroughly permeates the root ego in the 'manas consciousness.' Once we grasp that condition, we will be aware that we have been making many scientific-technological products primarily to fulfill our desires to satisfy our five senses and part of our mind. Meanwhile, we have not thought hard enough or been wise enough about the possible consequences of our productive activi- ties on the natural ecosystem.

MEANINGS OF THE ENVIRONMENTAL MOVEMENT AND THE WAY OF BODHISATTVA

As I described above, the 'alaya consciousness' is a root entity that makes the surface and subsurface human mind, and plays an important work for the formation of a sense of social responsibility, too. The 'alaya consciousness' is in constant flux and is always changing. But the changeable nature itself of the 'eighth consciousness' also makes reforms possible. The question now is how to change the 'alaya con- sciousness.'

Let me discuss the methodology of reform from two different angles. One approaches the reform of the deeper layers (the 'manas' and the 'alaya consciousness') by starting at the dimension of the 'first five con- sciousnesses' and the 'sixth (mind).' The other seeks to get at the deep- er layers directly. I will call the former "reform from the social dimen- sion," and the latter, "reform from the religious dimension."

This approach corresponds to what is known as environmentalism or the environmental movement. The movement focuses on the reform of 'consciousness,' which, from the perspective of the 'Consciousness- Only' doctrine, can be interpreted in the following way. The environmental movement consists of programs in environmental education and ethics, as well as exhibitions, publishing, lectures, dia- logues, and other practical activities. In terms of the 'Consciousness- Only' doctrine, these can all be received via the 'first five consciousnesses,' especially those of the eyes, ears, and body. The significance of the environmental movement carried out through the surface layers of 'consciousness' is internalized in the 'sixth,' or the 'mind consciousness.'

The more deeply imprinted in the 'mind,' the greater the impetus for further action. From the Buddhist point of view, also, this kind of movement has great significance, for the 'alaya consciousness' is the source of these 'first six consciousnesses,' which are, in turn, objects of cognition for the 'eighth consciousness.' Thus, whatever is perceived by the five sensory organs and is integrated in the 'mind' (the 'sixth consciousness') is also discerned by the 'alaya consciousness.' Most representative of the 'seeds' imprinted in the 'alaya consciousness' is the 'name and word seed.'

As explained earlier, many 'seeds' are formed and imprinted through language. Environmental education, dialogue, lectures, publishing, exhibitions, and so forth are conducted through the medium of language, hence everything one has learned in the environmental movement is imprinted as the 'name and word seed' in the 'alaya consciousness.' Because 'seeds' relating to moral goodness and evil are imprinted as 'karma seeds,' one's wishes for solutions to the environmental problem, symbiosis with other forms of life, coexistence with other nations and ethnic groups, a feeling of gratitude toward nature are all registered as good 'karma seeds.' The 'seeds' thus imprinted are eventually reflected as 'karmic' effects in actions via the feedback loop of the individual. If these 'karma seeds' are imprinted through the feedback loop of society as good 'common karma,' then, vertically, they will affect future generations, and horizontally, the whole human race in all its ethnic, racial, and national diversity, as well as all other forms of life. Thus, the environmental movement is truly meaningful in the context of Buddhist philosophy.

REFORM FROM THE RELIGIOUS DIMENSION

'Evil passions' of an individual spring up from the deeper layer of unconsciousness, hence it is extremely difficult to control them on the level of the 'sixth', the 'mind consciousness.' Similarly, the 'common karma' that forms the environment and social consciousness cannot be so easily elevated to the level of the 'mind consciousness.' For these reasons, Buddhism seeks solutions to the environmental problem through religious practices aimed at direct reforms of 'evil passions' and 'common karma' themselves. How, then, does Buddhism suggest going about it?

The 'alaya consciousness' is sometimes called the 'bodhisattva con- sciousness (*bosatsu-shiki*),' and the way of reforming the 'alaya con- sciousness' itself is the 'way of bodhisattva (*bosatsu-do*).' The basic spirit of the 'bodhisattva way' is expressed in the 10th chapter of the 'Lotus Sutra,' The 'Teacher of the Law (*Hosshi-bon*),' as 'compassion (*jihi*),' 'maintaining patience (*nin-niku*),' and 'emptiness (*kuu*).' 'Com- passion' is extended equally to all human beings, animals, plants, and even non-life matter, regardless of whether they are good or evil.

By 'maintaining patience' one can develop the true strength with which to withstand any and all difficulties, and also put the principle of 'satisfaction with little desire and a little gain' into practice, thereby exercising moral control over greed. Finally, the 'view of emptiness (*kuu-gan*)' nurtures global life consciousness that stresses the relationship of 'dependent origination' among all forms of life and seeks human coexistence with other living creatures. It also enhances the sense of gratitude and the spirit of repayment for the entire ecosystem, which is by nature interdependent. The 'way of bodhisattva' refers to practice based on these spiritual qualities. 'Wisdom (*chie*)' inherent in the 'bodhisattva consciousness' is capable of not only discerning the feedback loop formed by 'dependent origination of the alaya consciousness,' but also directing all the 'individual' and 'common karma' toward solution of problems confronting society as a whole.

By injecting the energies of 'wisdom' and 'compassion' in the 'way of bodhisattva' into the layers of 'consciousness,' from the 'eighth' to the 'first,' it is possible to equip each layer with 'wisdom.' In Buddhism there is a term 'pravrtti-vijñåna (*tenjiki-tokuchi*),' meaning "transform the four layers of consciousness into the four-fold wisdom." This is the approach of the 'bodhisattva way' to reform of the 'alaya consciousness.' Whereas the social approach to reform discussed earlier starts out from the upper layers of 'consciousness,' the 'bodhisattva way' goes directly to the deeper layers, hence it is more fundamental.

Accumulation of the energies of 'wisdom' and 'compassion' through practice of the 'way of the bodhisattva' leads to accumulation in the 'alaya-consciousness' of good 'common karma.' As more and more 'good karma (*zen-go*)' is imprinted there, the 'alaya consciousness' evolves into 'the great, perfect teaching-wisdom (*dai-enkyo-chi*),' wisdom which reflects all phenomenal things clearly, as if in a bright mirror. Springing forth from this 'wisdom' of 'dependent origination' is the sense of gratitude and repayment for all phenomena and existences that have had a part in its birth. Also arising naturally therefrom is global consciousness for symbiosis and coexistence.

The other seven layers of consciousness that derive from the 'alaya- consciousness' each are transformed into 'wisdom.' The 'seventh,' the 'manas consciousness' turns into the 'wisdom of equality of all things (*byodo-sho-chi*),' the 'sixth,' the 'mind consciousness' into the 'wisdom of wondrous observation (*myo-kanzat-chi*),' and the 'first five layers of consciousness' become 'the wisdom of accomplishing what is to be done to benefit sentient beings (*josho-sa-chi*).' The 'wisdom of equality of all things' makes it possible for the 'manas consciousness' to free itself from the 'obsession (*shuuchaku*)' that it embodied the 'alaya consciousness' and that it was the seat of the root ego. Liberation from an 'obsession' with the 'small self (*sho-ga*),' hence from 'self- love (*ga-ai*)' and other 'evil passions' that generate human desires, will be achieved.

The 'wisdom of equality of all things' also enables people to understand all phenomena in terms of 'dependent origination' and to embrace all existences as equal in their intrinsic value. The Buddhist idea of 'compassion' comes into play here. Then the 'wisdom of won- drous observation' and the 'wisdom of accomplishing what is to be done for the benefit of sentient beings' enable people to free themselves from 'evil passions,' act according to the dictates of reason, and make correct judgments and accurate inferences. As a result, they can display their physical abilities as their 'consciousness' commands. By virtue of all this, people will finally be able to overcome their inordinate material desires now dominating their first layers of consciousness and the 'mind consciousness.'

The two approaches to the reform of the 'alaya consciousness'—religious and social—combine to bring about changes in both 'individual' and 'common karma.' Eventually, these changes will lead to the solution of the environmental problem at its most basic source.

3 Buddhist Ecology of Compassion—Caring for Creation

What does Buddhism say about nature, the environment, and ecology, about caring for creation? A brief understanding of its history helps answer this question. Siddartha Gautama, the son of a royal family in Northern India, founded Buddhism 2600 years ago. His lifelong contemplative nature led him at the age of 29 to forfeit his inheritance to the throne and leave his family to search for a way to end suffering, not only for himself but also for all beings. He wanted everyone to experience the bliss and compassion of enlightenment, or in Christian terms, the grace of God and the peace that surpasses understanding.

He studied with India's two most revered Hindu masters, learning their teachings so thoroughly that he was asked by both to become their successors. But he declined because neither was able to explain fully what caused suffering and how to end it. He also practiced with other spiritual aspirants the severe austerities, including virtual starvation, commonly felt to facilitate spiritual growth. But he concluded that these only caused more suffering. So he left his teachers and fellow seekers to meditate alone in the forests of India. And six years after he began his quest, sitting all night beneath the fabled Bodhi tree, after wrestling with the temptations of lust, greed, anger, power, and pride, he attained full enlightenment. And for the next 45 years he taught what he called the Four Noble Truths and the Eightfold Path or the middle way to end suffering.

Buddha, the name given him after his enlightenment, meaning "awake" or "aware," taught that suffering would end only when one realizes that true happiness, contentment, and peace must transcend and can never depend upon external or internal conditions. He taught that the four divine virtues of lovingkindness, compassion, joy, and equanimity were innate but were obscured by the inevitable suffering caused by three basic conditions:

(1) Our endless pursuit of physical and mental pleasures,

(2) Our tendency to react with anger and aversion to physical pain and frustration of desires, and

(3) Ignorance of our interconnectedness with all physical and mental phenomena, resulting in an illusory sense of having an independent, autonomous, and separate self or ego that can control its own destiny.

Buddha taught meditation, mindfulness, and other practices that would lead to the wisdom, compassion, and insights necessary to end these causes of suffering.

From a Buddhist perspective, then, failure to care for creation, to be compassionate for the animal, plant, and mineral kingdoms, results when we separate ourselves from these domains of life. When we exploit them in the pursuit of satisfying our selfish needs and desires, and when we deny our connectedness to and interdependence upon them.

Genuine caring for creation is an ecology based on compassion and is a natural, spontaneous result of understanding that everybody and everything is connected and interdependent, that Thou art That, in Hindu terms. To hurt, harm, exploit, neglect or cause suffering to any living being, or to our natural resources, environment, or the planet is simply to hurt, harm, exploit, neglect, and cause suffering to ourselves.

This recognition has led to the development of what contemporary Buddhist scholars call engaged Buddhism. They recognize that to ultimately end our individual and collective suffering, we must consciously confront the suffering that exists on all levels: physical, mental, social, as well as ecological. I would like to quote from a couple of books: (1) *The Path of Compassion: Writings on Socially Engaged Buddhism*, edited by Fred Eppsteiner, Parralax Press, 1985, and (2) *For a Future to Be Possible,* by Thich Nhat Hanh, Parallax Press, 1993. Zen master Philip Kapleau says, "A major task for Buddhism ... is to ally itself with religious and other concerned organizations to forestall the potential catastrophes facing the human race: nuclear holocaust, irreversible pollution of the world's environment, and the continuing large-scale destruction of non-renewable resources. We also need to lend our physical and moral support to those who are fighting hunger, poverty, and oppression everywhere in the world" (1, pg. xii)." He said this in the early 1980's.

Nobel Peace Prize nominee, poet, and Vietnamese Buddhist Master Thich Nhat Hanh is unexcelled in adapting Buddhist teachings to modern society. He advocates practicing compassion and reverence for all life by learning ways to protect the lives of, not just people, but of animals, plants, and minerals. He urges us all to resolve not to harm, let others harm, or support any act of harming in the world, in the way we think, in the way we speak, and in the way we act.

And he advocates practicing lovingkindness and generosity by becoming "aware of the suffering caused by exploitation, social injustice, stealing, and oppression" and learning "ways to work for the well-being of all people, animals, plants, and minerals".

The Dalai Lama says "because the individual and society are interdependent, one's behavior as an individual is inseparable from one's behavior as a participant in society".

Author Kenneth Kraft suggests that a Buddhist "awareness of interdependence fosters a sense of universal responsibility". Engaged Buddhism, according to Zen Buddhist and Poet Gary Snyder, can lead to specific acts of "civil disobedience, outspoken criticism, protest, pacifism, voluntary poverty, and even gentle violence if it comes to a matter of retraining some impetuous crazy".

Engaged Buddhism is a practical manifestation of caring for creation. It is a Buddhist ecology of compassion. Once we realize the interconnected nature of all people, all beings, and all things, that everything is a manifestation of God, we will recognize our involvement in the conditions we deplore and become empowered to do something about them. Until then, until we realize that everything is God, we will continue to hurt God. Thich Nhat Hanh reminds us that: "We need a person to inspire us with calm confidence and to tell us what to do. Who is that person? ....You are that person. If you are yourself, if you are your best, then you are that person. Only with such a person—calm, lucid, and aware—will our situation improve".

INTRODUCTION

Buddhism and Deep Ecology explores the ecological and environmental teachings of Buddha, particularly Dhamma (nature) and their relationships with Deep Ecology as well as with effective public participation. In the context of this book, Dhamma (also known as Dharma by many Buddhists) is nature, natural truth, natural law and the teachings of Buddha. Lack of effective communication and citizen participation in environmental affairs, especially between Westerners and the peoples of Asia, has been the cause of needless environmental, societal, and economic problems and costs. Buddhism, especially through Dhamma and Deep Ecology offers a means to secure that participation in the decision-making process in both Buddhist and non-Buddhist nations.

Technical experts offer countless opinions, pro and con, on developments that may change forever a stream, stand of rain forest, or other fragile ecological setting. But although technical comment abounds, it is, unfortunately, for sale or hire by the highest bidder. Public opinion is scarcely heard over the cacophonous chorus of vested interests. The Author trusts that Buddhism and Deep Ecology will bring some harmony to the discordant voices of all those concerned with the life on this planet. The World Community declared at the United Nations 1992 conference in Rio de Janeiro, Environmental Issues are best handled with the participation of all concerned citizens, at the relevant level. At the national level, each individual shall have appropriate access to information concerning the environment . . . including information on hazardous materials and activities in their communities, and the opportunity to participate in decision-making processes. States shall facilitate and encourage public awareness and participation by making information widely available. Effective access to judicial and administrative proceedings, including redress and remedy, shall be provided.

Much of Buddhism and its Dhamma, along with Deep Ecology, contains values, awareness, and concepts which could be incorporated into public participation efforts. Buddhism and its Dhamma is a spiritual, philosophic approach based on acceptance and compassion for all living things. Deep spirituality and deep ecology are philosophic sisters. Those who shy from the notion of "spirituality" should note that the enemy is a secular and anthropocentric religion of never-ending technological progress, unlimited materialism, and uncontrolled development which pays only lip service to the health of this planet and welfare of all living things.

In his book, Earth in Balance: Ecology and the Human Spirit, Al Gore states, "The more deeply I search for the roots of the global environmental crisis, the more I am convinced that it is an outer manifestation of an inner crisis that is, for lack of a better word, spiritual . . ." But what other word describes the collection of values and assumptions that determine our basic understanding of how we fit into the universe? Buddhism is a spiritual approach which emphasizes ecological values through a reverence and compassion for all beings or all forms of life.

This approach, along with Deep Ecology, points toward the development of a spirituality, a higher consciousness or awareness (Buddha means "the awakened one") which would recognize and integrate spiritual values toward nature. The formulation of positive ecological and environmental values as the basis for assuming a wise stewardship role toward the earth is becoming increasingly important, if not critical, especially between peoples of diverse cultures.

Buddhism and Deep Ecology focuses on the Buddhist view of "One" world that is home to all known life. While living with Buddhist Forest Monks in Thailand, the author found a strong concern among them for nature and forest protection . The monks translated that concern into action that included holding regional conferences on protecting rainforests from illegal logging and poaching and ordaining trees. While Buddhism is an ancient and complex belief system, consciousness of the threat of global environmental destruction is relatively new.

The author hopes this volume will stimulate discussion of a new consciousness in the light of an ancient wisdom as well as integrate it with Deep Ecology. At this point, it is appropriate to examine Buddhism's diversity. It has been called the most mystical and the least mystical of all religions. Some seekers call it the most spiritual religion. Others insist it is a philosophy and not a religion at all. In fact, Buddhism does not lend itself to a precise, unequivocal and unified definition in Western terms.

There are many schools of Buddhism, all of which stem from the original Theravada School. All accept the basic teachings of that school, yet they differ in various ways and interpret the original inspiration by their own lights. While Theravada Buddhism (the Old Wisdom School) is basically ethical and non-mystical, Mayahana Buddhism (the New Wisdom School)has a different complexion with its numerous divisions. It is considered to be more speculative, more cosmic, and more mystical.Some writers consider Mayahana Buddhism more responsive to society and nature (Badiner, 1990).

But much of the direction of both Theravada and Mayahana Buddhism on the environment is subject to varied interpretation in differing local situations. For example, the International Network for Engaged Buddhism, an NGO active in social and environmental concerns, contains members of both schools from a number of countries. Theravada ('School of the Elders' or 'Lesser Vehicle'),that is, orthodox Buddhism, is followed in Thailand, Myanmar (Burma), Laos, Cambodia, and Sri Lanka. Mahayana ('Greater Vehicle') developed relatively later and is followed in China, Japan,Tibet and Mongolia.

Although these schools differ in certain beliefs,practices and observances, they agree upon the most important and basic teachings of Buddha. The Dalai Lama has said the basic teachings of Buddhism should remain culture-and country- free. The teachings of Buddha also have "Oneness," egocentric, and spiritual orientations with loving and compassionate concern for all living beings. These teachings are very correlated and compatible with

Deep Ecology and its orientations. Thus both teachings can contribute to each other for holistic and deeper approaches toward various ecological and environmental issues. This book will deal with Buddhism and Deep Ecology on a general and overall basis so that both Buddhists and non-Buddhists with ecological and environmental interests will find it a refreshing, valuable, and insightful approach to their labor of love.

BUDDHISM AND VALUES

The immortal British naturalist Charles Darwin hiked with a friend through an English countryside. "There's an abundance of clover here," observed Darwin. "This district must have many widows." The two strolled on, Darwin enjoying the country air, his friend lost in deep contemplation. At last, the friend tugged the great scientist's sleeve. "What has clover to do with widows?" he asked. Darwin smiled and explained, "An abundance of clover needs many healthy swarms of bees to pollinate it. Thriving bee hives mean there are few rats to raid and ravage them. A scarcity of rats spells an abundance of cats. Who keeps and feeds packs of cats? Widows, of course."

Darwin, who shook Christendom with his discoveries, would have made a good Buddhist. He understood and explained to the Western world the interconnectedness of nature's realm. Centuries before Darwin, sages of the Orient found this truth self-evident. They knew nature to be part of humanity and humanity a part of nature. Unfortunately, Darwin's truth was relegated to the narrow realm of biological study. His 19th Century homeland and the other burgeoning and aggressive Western Industrial nations shared a different view. Infected by the doctrine of Manifest Destiny, capitalists and adventurers, politicians and pioneers joined in a brotherhood that viewed Nature as the enemy and themselves as those chosen by God to conquer her.

The legendary Paul Bunyan, slayer of trees, became the model of American heroes. America's folk heroes were deer slayers, bear killers, tree fellers and the Indian fighters who waged genocide on natives living in harmony with nature. At the height of its hubris, America created a Bureau of Reclamation to dam its free flowing rivers. Thus, a Christian nation set out to "correct" God's errors and alter a vast portion of the North American continent. The same evangelistic spirit swept the rest of the industrial world. Conquerors and colonial powers marched to the beat of a new theology, "taming" rivers, clearing forests, breaking prairies, claiming the Earth for "God's chosen few." We find ourselves in the 11th hour of this technological, materialistic fanaticism. Moderating this self destructive, earth-devouring dogma will not suffice. Only a new world view can save us and the planet we share with all known forms of life. Buddhism's ancient wisdom may prove to be post- industrial man's salvation.

The following is a brief introduction to Buddhism's application to the environment and ecological concerns: Buddhism is the teaching of the Enlightened one. A Buddha is an individual who knows the truth about all things. A Buddha knows "what is what" and how to behave appropriately in respect to all things. According to Ajahn Buddhadassa , a famous master teacher/scholar of Thailand, Buddhism is based on intelligence, science, and knowledge. Its purpose is the extinction of suffering and the source of that suffering. Liberation from suffering requires examining things closely, understanding their true nature and behaving in a way appropriate to that true nature. (Buddhadassa, 1989).

Buddhism views people as a part of nature. If the environment is destroyed or degraded, people cannot survive or have a quality life. By abusing the environment, people abuse themselves and their descendants as well as future generations of all life. This basic Buddhist concept bars "unskilled" behavior which is inappropriate, incorrect, and abusive toward the environment and its variety of living things. The environment can be defined as the aggregate of all surrounding things (biotic and a biotic) and conditions that influence the life of individual organisms or populations, including humans. It is the sum of all external things (living and nonliving),conditions, and influences that affect the development and, ultimately, the survival of an organism.

Buddhist teachings recognize that all things are interdependent and conditional upon each other. Every condition follows another and all are part of an orderly sequence of cause and effect. A tree falling in the forest changes the life of a banker in the city. As the

English poet John Donne wrote, "No man is an island, entire of itself. Every man is a part of the Continent, a part of the Maine; If a clod be washed away by the sea, Europe is the less." Like his countryman, Darwin, Donne understood.

The Western world view, which considers humans separate and superior to the rest of nature, can only lead to environmental crisis and destruction. Aldo Leopold, pioneer ecological philosopher, said, "a thing is right when it tends to preserve the integrity, stability, and beauty of the biotic community. It is wrong when it tends otherwise." Noting that environmental awareness dawned slowly and apart from the ethics of society, he continued, "There is as yet no ethic dealing with man's relation to land and to the animals and plants which grow upon it . . . the land relation is strictly economic, entailing privileges but not obligations."

People inflicted with the Western disease of "progress" find it difficult to accept ethics that might limit their pursuit of materialism and techno-scientific advances. They seek only technical solutions to environmental problems with no thought of ecological morality. At the root of our environmental problems is an ethical dilemma: To conquer or coexist. Attempting conquest can lead to the kind of logic expressed by a U.S. Army officer during the Vietnam war after leveling a hamlet with artillery and flame throwers: "We had to destroy the village to save it." We have a choice. We can wait until the last hectare of rain forest is cleared, the last river polluted, channelized and dammed, the last tract of virgin prairie plowed.

Or, we can learn to live in the Eden in which Homo Sapiens evolved. Buddhism offers a spiritual solution, a life of harmony with nature. Western materialism and blind faith in technology is the cause of the current global environmental crisis, not its salvation. Only an elevated consciousness can save our planet from unregulated technology. Buddhism offers a direct path to harmony with nature. Technology, coupled with greed and ignorance, is the beast bent on destroying our home planet in its fervor to improve it.

Chatsumarn Kabilsingh, scholar of Buddhist environmental philosophy, notes that Buddhism is not a dogma that binds all adherents to a single regime. Buddhism encourages individual perceptions, even questions and challenges on the part of each practitioner. But the braided paths of individual seekers wind in a common direction. Teachings emphasize the importance of coexisting with nature, rather than conquering it.

Devout Buddhists admire a conserving lifestyle, rather than one which is profligate.(Kabilsingh, 1987) Over 2500 years ago, Buddha was born in a forest. As a youth, he meditated under Jambo trees, studied among the Banyans, and found enlightenment beneath a great Boddhi tree. A denizen of the woods for the next 45 years, he died beneath a pair of Sal trees among his disciples. Buddhism budded and was born in the company and protection of a great life form: the forest. Buddhist teachings give rise to an environmental ethic with a concern for nature of which man is a part.

Buddhism begins with reverence for life and its recognition of the interdependence of all life. The Buddha taught that all sentient beings might attain Nirvana, the cessation of suffering and the liberation from the wheel of birth and death. Mahayana, a radical reformation movement in Buddhism around the beginning of the Christian era, stressed the possibility of liberation to greater numbers of beings. In the Gaia view, the earth itself is considered as a sentient being. Silva quotes Gauthama Buddha, "Just as with her own life a mother shields from hurt her own, her only child, let all embracing thoughts for all that lives be thine." Protection of all life is a Buddhist tenent. A Buddhist Monk's first vow is, "I abstain from destroying life."

One of the most illustrative influences of Buddhist thought on nature conservation is its doctrine of rebirth and reverence of special trees. This doctrine holds that a human being after dying can be reborn as an animal, or an animal upon dying can be reborn as a human being. In reverence for special trees, Buddhist literature lists 2l species of tree under which 25 Buddhas attained enlightenment. Veneration and protection of these species is a natural consequence of this belief. Kabilsingh notes, "Wherever Buddhism is influential, studies will usually show some direct benefit for the natural world.

In Sri Lanka, for example, Buddhism has had the largest single impact on the conservation of flora and fauna with conservation measures beginning in the third century.Formal government measures for protection of nature required acceptance by the people, with the recognition that effective conservation needs to be based on deep value convictions."(Kabilsingh, 1987) Without public acceptance based on deep value convictions, many governmental measures to protect the environment cannot be successful. Studies of national parks in Thailand revealed large amounts of poaching and illegal logging might be stemmed only through an appeal to the values of Buddhism. Buddhist forest monks in Thailand, with their strong concerns for nature protection are the strongest voices for conservation in these areas. Buddhist forest monasteries (or Wats) are naturally more concerned with forest protection than monasteries in urban areas.

There are approximately 700 Buddhist forest monasteries in Thailand. These monasteries are often located in the last remaining forest lands in their area. Some are located near national parks and wildlife refuges. Without the influence of these monks over the centuries, there would be no forests to preserve in many areas. The Buddhist forest monasteries have a strong concern for the welfare of the residents of nearby villages. The villagers, in turn, revere and respect the monks. The monks, by example and teaching, influence all aspects of the villagers' lives. More understanding of Buddhist environmental teachings and values is generally needed by many monks at this point. Thus there is a great potential for environmental education through the monasteries which can also serve as a communication "bridge" between national parks, wildlife refuges, and villagers.

The main concern of Buddha was to find a reason and remedy for the suffering involved in the corruptibility of all living beings. He regarded all abstract philosophical and theological speculations as sterile on the grounds that no satisfactory and demonstrable answers were possible. Thus it was not necessary to enter into them in order that his main purpose of extinguishing suffering might be achieved. On religious and philosophical issues, he maintained a "noble silence" or answered in paradoxes when questioned. Buddhist doctrine's acute analysis of the world promotes tolerance, compassion and love for all creatures. The Buddhist goal is the realization of Nirvana and cessation of Dukkha (trouble) through the Noble Eightfold path. The teachings are subtle and filled with paradox.

The basic principles of Buddhism can be summed up in the Three Signs of Being, the Four Noble Truths, and the Noble Eightfold Path or Middle Way to Nirvana. The Three characteristics of Being are suffering impermanence, , and Anatta (no soul). The doctrine of Anatta is particularly difficult to interpret. The doctrine holds that a person consists of the Five Aggregates: matter, sensations, perceptions, mental formations, and consciousness in a perpetual state of flux. This view leaves no room for "soul" or "self." There is, consequently, no "I" or "Me" which is a doer of anything. It is the senses that move among various objects.

The deeds are there, but there is no doer. It is merely aggregates in process without a self or soul. This world-centered view regards man as part of nature, not the conquistador born to subjugate it. First of the Noble Truths is the impermanence and insubstantiality of life, its suffering, sorrows, its imperfections and dissatisfaction. In brief, it is a doctrine of acceptance of suffering. The second is the Origin of Dukkha. The Buddha taught that Dukkha is "desire," or attachment, the source of all passions, suffering, and defilement. The third is the realization of the Cessation of Dukkha which is found through non-attachment or release from all attachments. The fourth is the Noble Eightfold Path, which leads to the realization of Nirvana. Buddhism is the light to wither the greed and ignorance that drive the engines of mindless development. Buddhism teaches that the desire which cannot be sated can be extinguished. It assures its adherents that detachment is joy.

Finally, it leads the seeker down the Eightfold Path to:

(1) Right Understanding,

(2) Right Thought,

(3) Right Speech,

(4) Right Action,

(5) Right Livelihood,

(6) Right Effort,

(7) Right Mindfulness, and

(8) Right Concentration.

The detachment that is incomprehensible to a materialistic mind becomes a comfort to the Buddhist who believes attachment is the cause of suffering. Greed cannot thrive in a cosmos where nothing is permanent and self does not exist.

The Four Noble Truths are based on the fundamental Buddhist doctrine of dependent co-arising or dependent origination. The doctrine teaches that existence of any single thing is conditional to the existence of all other things. This concept does not permit the division of nature into creatures that have instrumental or intrinsic value. In contrast, the notion that things have independent existence leads to the false idea of a real self that can attain its fulfillment by appropriating real things which, in turn, is the cause of suffering or Dukkha.

If nothing exists as an independent entity, nothing can possess intrinsic value by itself or be ecologically isolated. Values are essential to environmental perception because they influence an individual's objectives and behavior. Much of the Dhamma teachings of Buddhism dwells on what we recognize as environmental values. Solving conflicts and problems associated with the natural environment requires sacrificing some values for the sake of others. Further, no one can realistically be expected to assume a role of value-neutrality or of a "value free" approach. Even physics, along with other sciences, now recognizes the role and influence of values and biases held by researchers in their subject matter and investigations. Values are conceptions of worth, importance, or desirability. Values also include judgments and degrees of what is "good" or "bad", "right" or "wrong".

The Western pursuit of happiness through consumerism and materialism and Buddhism's trek toward Nirvana are not the same, but this ancient philosophy of the Orient can illuminate the dilemma of Western materialism. The answer begins with the simple principle of detachment. Westerners will be happy with what they have when they stop chasing what they do not have.

This may sound tautological. Westerners could be happy with their lot if they were only happy with their lot. However, we need not be trapped by circular reasoning if we realize that our addiction is both the cause of our unrest and the monster that threatens any chance of finding the happiness we seek.

Unfortunately, the West has done a better job infecting the East with its disease than the East has done in teaching the West a better way. As old values crumbled and new were formed in the headlong rush toward materialism and what Westerners thought would be a "world made better through science," a snobbery of "progress" was born. The conquest, at first by arms, then through dollars, pounds, franks and marks, continues. It is difficult for conquerors to accept that subject peoples have anything to offer. Is a culture that produces a million electric washing machines better than one that treasures children and has no word for "orphan?"

Is the culture that produced the harried businessman superior to the one that provides children with a father who is friend, teacher and spiritual instructor? In the Amazon rain forest a Cofan Indian elder conversed with a "gringo" from the "world beyond the forest." The elder's knowledge of the rain forest surpassed that of biologists holding PhD's who came to study there. His was a practical knowledge. He is able to find and identify more than 140 plants his people used for medicinal purposes. He knows where the peach tree grows and when its fruit attracts the brilliant blue gold macaw.

In addition to his knowledge, the elder has access to a great research library. Each volume is a friend. That woman over there, she knows all there is to know about marital discord and how to insure a household's harmony. That old man walking beneath the trees, he talks to the God of Creation. The brothers fishing along the strand, they are the heads of a family that has built the best boats on the river for many generations. The elder's material possessions are scant and include a machete from upriver and two cloaks from the city. His wife owns several spoons and a metal pot. Aware of the village school, run by a Jesuit priest, the visitor asks, "Do any of your children go on to high school in the city? Do any seek a university education?" The old man shakes his head. There is too much to be learned at home. "It takes many years to learn to be a Cofan," he says. His gaze drifts across the river, then returns to the gringo. "My heart aches for you," he says. "For me?" replies the gringo. "Why?"

"Because you are so poor. We in the forest have all we want. You gringos want for so much you do not have." The Dalai Lama says, "If we develop good and considerate qualities within our own minds, our activities will naturally cease to threaten the continued survival of life on Earth. By protecting the natural environment and working forever to halt the degradation of our planet we will also show respect for Earth's human descendants—our future generations—as well as for the natural right of life of all of the Earth's living things." (Badiner, 1990).

The Dalai Lama continues, "It is important that we forgive the destruction of the past and recognize that it was produced by ignorance. At the same time, we should re-examine, from an ethical perspective, what kind of world we have inherited, what we are responsible for, and what we will pass on to coming generations . . . We have the responsibility as well as capability, to protect the Earth's inhabitants—its animals, plants, insects, and even micro- organisms. If they are to be known by future generations, as we have known them, we must act now. Let us all work together to preserve and safeguard our world.(Badiner, 1990) Many values, like wildlife and scenery, are intangible and therefore difficult or impossible to define or assign monetary values.

Consequently, they are not given proper weight. Tangible values such as board feet of timber or tons of a given mineral can be quantified, described, and equated to money benefits, and therefore often will be given more emphasis and weight in decision making for the natural environment. Intangible values also recognize that a given species of plant or animal has a right to life for its own sake, to carry on its struggle for survival. In considering these unique environmental values, we must recognize that conservation, like development, is for people. While development aims to achieve human goals through use of the biosphere, conservation aims to achieve them by ensuring that such use can continue on a sustainable basis with consideration for all forms of life. The ethical imperative or belief here implies, "we have not inherited the earth from our parents, we have borrowed it from our children."

Conservation is management of human use of the biosphere so that it may yield the greatest sustainable benefit to present generations of all life while maintaining its potential to meet the needs and aspirations of future generations. Conservation is positive, embracing preservation, maintenance, sustainable use, restoration, and enhancement of the natural environment. Living resources conservation is specifically concerned with plants, animals, and microorganisms, and with those non-living elements of the environment upon which they depend. (IUCN, 1980). Development can be considered the modification of the biosphere and the application of human, financial, living, and non- living resources to satisfy human needs and improve the quality of life. For development to be sustainable, it must take into account social and ecological factors, as well as economic ones, of the living and non-living resource bases and of the long term as well as the short term advantages and disadvantages of alternative actions (IUCN,1980).

Value articulation is an effective way of linking environmental and development theory with practice to widen perspectives and develop insights into values systems. Value definition demonstrates that value awareness, change, and clarification are interrelated. It involves the exposure to values which may be relatively new and unfamiliar or neglected. Consequently this approach is innovative and responsive to the needs and interests of the participants as they move into new areas of learning about the environment, as well as how Buddhism relates to it.

Value awareness can help people establish "lines of demarcation" between technical expertise and broader value judgments. As values are clearly identified, more efficient and comprehensive judgments and decision-making would emerge in terms of both environmental and societal value considerations on a broader basis. In the field of law, it is common procedure to prohibit experts from testifying on value opinions and judgments. For example, an expert witness who is a psychologist would not be allowed to present his opinion on an accused individual's guilt or innocence in a court trial. With value judgments, no one is really an expert. The use of professional images and technical or expert autonomy to profoundly affect value judgments and decisions serves to discourage or cloud the values and alternatives available.

Values are subject to change. Our global crisis demands change. Change requires the re-education of people locked into old attitudes and attached to values no longer functional. The insights of Buddhism provide an excellent point of departure.

4 Dhamma, Deep Ecology and Environment

A blind elephant crashes through the forest, leaving trampled bushes and broken trees in his wake. Emerging from the forest he lumber through a village, destroying several homes in his passage. Two Buddhist monks drawing water at a well observe the great beast's progress. "What a fearsome, powerful creature," exclaims the first monk. "What a pitiful, helpless animal," says the second. And the "elephant" (science) continues to blunder through the forest. Harnessed and cared for, the beast could be a servant of great worth, but blinded by materialism, it wastes its strength in self-defeating confusion. The teachings of Buddha center on Dhamma (also spelled Dharma). The Buddhist teachings of Dhamma will be considered in the present chapter; Dhamma in its application to nature and Deep Ecology will be taken up in chapter three.

SOCIETY AND MORAL CONTEXT

Science and technology have given humankind powerful means for research and development. Yet much of science and technology has been used to promote industrial development for mass consumption and military use with little responsibility for ways that might be beneficial to all living beings and the environment. Within the last fifty years, science and technology have had dynamic and profound influences on life styles, economics, and the environment worldwide. These influences defy assessment or prediction concerning their effect. In spite of benefits, uncontrolled change, rapid consumption, and serious ecological impacts continue to be important consequences of science and technology.(Henning and Mangun, 1999). In this star-wars era, science can no longer claim value neutrality for the environment or any other area. Thus, moral considerations which ought to apply to the management of technology often become involved with political and governmental issues. Moreover, many environmental problems simply have no scientific or technical solution, despite the tendency to seek such solutions.(Henning and Mangun, 1989). An ad in the Bangkok Post (March 28, 1993) declares, "Technology for a better environment.. How to reduce your problems.. It's time man should concentrate on developing technologies to secure his life and this beautiful world with both hands."

Western civilization has been trying to find solutions in science and technology and has dropped Christian ethics in favor of progress and materialism associated with conquest. Yet, Einstein and Jung have observed that Buddhism is the religion most compatible with science and their own views. As Bhavilai notes, The materialism of science inevitably leads to an ethic of irresponsibility because when people believe that everything in their lives end with death, they are not really responsible for their deeds. At best, they may control their behaviors only for the sake of good and smooth relationships with their fellow men while they are alive.

This materialism is certainly contributing to moral decay and hosts of problems in the present world. We need a much broader and deeper understanding about the world and life than science can offer. Buddhism can answer this need.(Bhavilai, n.d.). Snyder writes, The mercy of the West has been social revolution; the mercy of the East has been individual insights into the basic self/ void. We need both. Both are contained in the traditional three aspects of the Dhamma path: wisdom (prajna), meditation (dhyana),and morality (sila). Wisdom is the mind's intuitive knowledge of love and clarity that lies beneath one's egodriven anxieties and aggressions. Meditation is going into the mind to see this for yourself over and over again, until it becomes the mind you live in. Morality is bringing it back out in the way you live through personal example and responsible action, ultimately toward the true community (sangha) of 'all beings.' (Snyder, 1985)

And Dr. Mustafa Tolbra, the past executive director of the United Nations Environment Protection Programme (UNEP) writes: "Governments have faced the reality that man is both creature and molder of his environment and that the power afforded him by scientific and technological advances has given him a new capacity to alter his planet's life support system in significant and irreversible ways.

The same power carries with it the concomitant responsibility to act with prudent regard for environmental consequences."

Progress and materialism are greatly influenced by science and technology. Consumer goods are produced in speed and quantity far beyond the real needs of people, as well as machines that replace manpower. In many countries, the value of progress and materialism in any form is unquestioned. The underlying premise is a short term orientation that is principally concerned with quantity, economic benefits, newness, and expediency, rather than with long- range quality or environmental considerations. Advertisement and promotion media try to enhance the desire or craving within society for a variety of goods and throw-away products.

Gore considers modern civilization and society to be dysfunctional and addictive in terms of the environment. As he notes, The disharmony in our relationship to the earth, which stems in part from our addiction to a pattern of consuming ever-larger quantities of the resources of the earth, is now manifest in successive crises, each marking a more destructive clash between our civilization and the natural world; whereas all threats to the environment used to be local and regional, several are now strategic . . . such as rainforests, ozone layer, climatic balance, species extinction, etc . . . all these suggest the increasing violent collision between human civilization and the natural world. (Gore, 1992)

Much of this collision is based on uncontrolled economic models of unlimited growth and progress, along with mounting anthropocentric world views. Rejecting these models, a workshop of the International Network of Engaged Buddhists outlined a Buddhist economic counterculture that would strive to find a balance between human needs, communities, and the environment. Such a program would require an economic model based on interconnectedness, sustainability, and non-accumulation. Other basic Buddhist values such as compassion, loving-kindness, and altruism combined with respect for all life, including future generations, would figure very prominently in this Buddhist economy.(INEB, 1993)

In recognizing some of these economic, societal, and technological issues for current environmental conditions, the Foundation for Deep Ecology notes the following root causes without placing them into a hierarchy of degrees of importance:

1. The assumption of human superiority to other life forms as if we were some sort of royalty over nature; the idea that nature is here to serve human will.
2. Overpopulation in both the "developing" and "developed" worlds.
3. The prevailing ethic of western society that holds that economic growth, the market economy, and lifestyles committed to commodity accumulation are desirable and possible on a finite planet.
4. Technology worship; the prevailing paradigm that technological evolution is invariably good and that problems caused by technology can be solved by more technology.
5. The loss of an ethic of behavior informed by an understanding and appreciation of the sacredness of the natural world and the appropriate role of human beings within that.
6. The domination of mass media by viewpoints that serve the interest of the technocratic-industrial world and the suppression of alternate views to keep them from public consciousness.
7. The concentration of power in an industrial elite, and the consequent loss of democratic empowerment which has been profoundly detrimental to human beings as well as nature.

TWO APPROACHES TO ECOLOGY

Scientific ecology involves the scientific study of the interrelationships between species and their environment. In this approach, the relationship of the detached observer is separate from the object of study. The focus is on measurable data "out there" which is collected by experts who know their facts and figures. Yet this approach often neglects the role of values and biases of, for example, industrial ecological consultants in their "scientific" ecological approaches. Expression: "How interesting as I study the pond of life as a scientific, detached observer".

DEEP ECOLOGY: Experiencing ourselves as part of the living planet (Gaia) and finding our role in protecting the earth and its life. In this approach, the relationship is more of an involved participation as one who feels connected with as well as a part of the world surrounding the self. It recognizes and involves the role of values and biases in the overall picture of society and environment. This approach is for everybody, not just for scientifically trained experts, with each person being moved by their values experience and feelings to do their bit for the world around them. Expression:

> "I am immersed in and involved with the pond of life and must therefore protect it". The term Deep Ecology was first introduced by the Norwegian activist and philosopher Arne Naess in the early 1970's. However, Aldo Leopold, an American forester (and later wildlife professor in the 1930's) developed many of the concepts behind it, such as the land ethic and the idea of people as mere members of the total living community or web of life. Eco-philosopher Naess developed the term Deep Ecology in stressing the need to go beyond superficial responses to the social and ecological problems we face. He proposed that we ask deeper questions and really look at the way we live and see how this fits with our deeper beliefs, needs, and values (see Deep Ecology platform). Asking questions like "How do I live in a way that is good for me, other people, and our planet with its various forms of life?" may lead us to deep changes in the way we live.

Deep Ecology can also be seen as part of a much wider process of questioning basic assumptions that may lead to a new way of looking at science, economics, politics, education, spirituality, health, etc. Because this change in the way we see things is so wide ranging, it has been called a new world view. It tends to emphasize the relationships between different areas holistically and bring together personal and social change, science and spirituality, economics and ecology.

Deep Ecology applies this new world view to our relationship to the earth. It challenges deep- seated assumptions about the way we see ourselves. It moves us from seeing ourselves as individuals toward seeing ourselves as part of the earth along with other living beings. This, in turn, increases our sense of belonging in life and our tendency to act for life, wanting to protect other life as we would our own. Deep Ecology workshops were strongly influenced by John Seed, Joanna Macy and others with the aim of deepening our sense of connection with life and strengthening our ability to respond to global environmental problems.

These workshops bring people together with the intention to heal our relationship with the earth. They provide an opportunity to explore our emotional responses to world problems of the environment and may offer "despair and empowerment" methods to use the energy of these emotional responses in our work for earth recovery. The workshops introduce the Deep Ecology which includes working with ideas, feelings, spirituality, and personal action planning; sometimes, even singing, drumming, dancing, meditating, and communication exercises that offer nature-connecting experiences and non-dogmatic explorations of the role of ritual.

IDEAS: The basic idea of Deep Ecology is that we are part of the earth and not apart or separate from it. This idea is in contrast with the dominant individualistic thought of our culture in which we see ourselves as separate from the world, which makes it too easy not to be bothered by what is happening beyond our immediate self- interests: "If I am separate from the rest of nature, what happens out there is not my problem". In this century, two key ideas have emerged in our scientific thought which support the view of ourselves as part of the earth: Systems Theory and the Gaia Concept. In Systems Theory, we see our world in terms of systems where each system is a whole that is more than the sum of its parts, but also itself a part of the larger systems. For example, a cell is more than just a pile of molecules and itself is a part of larger systems, e.g., an organ. An organ is on one level a whole in itself, but on another, it is part of a system at the level of an individual person. A family and community can both be seen as systems where the parts are people. Systems Theory can also be correlated with energy flows between the various parts of the system in terms of inter-and intra-relationships.

The Gaia hypothesis takes Systems Theory still farther and applies it to the whole planet. All of life on earth can be seen as a whole that is more than the sum of its parts but is also itself a part of larger systems with this whole being like a huge super-life form which we call Gaia (after the name for the ancient Greek Goddess of the earth) with a collective intelligence. Living systems have a tendency to keep themselves in balance but also adapt and evolve over time. Scientists have found that the earth also has these tendencies with feedback mechanisms to keep in balance the temperatures and oxygen levels of the atmosphere just as our bodies maintain the temperature and oxygen levels in our arteries. Thus the Gaia hypothesis states that the earth is alive and that we are part of it. This is something that many cultures have known for centuries. For example, Indian Chief Seattle of North America (1854) has stated, "We are part of the earth and it is part of us".

FEELINGS: In trying to face the scale of social and ecological crises in our world today, we can be left feeling numbed, overwhelmed, and powerless. Yet there is often little place for such feelings in conventional politics or in our society. The dominant response is to deny or distract ourselves from any uncomfortable feelings about the state of the world and to carry on with business as usual. If we see ourselves as part of the world, it becomes impossible to see that such uncomfortable feelings may serve a valuable function. Just as it hurts when we put our finger over a flame, pain for the world alerts us to the injuries of the world and can move us to respond with compassion and action. By allowing ourselves to feel for our world, we are also opened to a source of energy and aliveness and to a strength that comes from connection to something more than just our narrow selves.

SPIRITUALITY: Spirituality has to do with our inner sense of connection and/or interrelationship with something larger than ourselves and with our relationship with what we see as sacred. This can give our lives a sense of meaning and purpose beyond material success, and those special moments when we feel that connection more deeply can provide an important source of strength and perspective during difficult times.

If we see ourselves as a part of the tree of life and the interconnected web of living beings we call Gaia, then a Deep Ecological approach to spirituality might emphasize our relationship with this larger whole. We may look at life itself as being sacred and see possibilities for the larger force of life acting through us for earth recovery. Thus this life-saving spirituality can be an important source of inspiration to face and respond to environmental/societal problems of our world.

ACTION: When we integrate our beliefs, values, and ideas into our behavior, we bring them alive and give them power to influence our world. If, however, we see ourselves as separate from the world, it is easy to dismiss our actions as irrelevant or unlikely to make any difference. But from a Deep Ecology perspective, we are a part of the world and every choice we make will have ripples which extend beyond us. What may seem tiny and insignificant by itself actually adds up to a larger context. Thus every time we act for life and the earth, we put our weight and strength behind the shift toward a life- sustaining environment and culture.

Much of Deep Ecology, in turn, asks deep questions of society and its relationships to life. Thus, in the words of professor Arne Naess: "...in Deep Ecology we ask whether the present society fulfills basic human needs like love and security and access to nature. We ask which society, which education is beneficial for all life on the planet as a whole, and then ask further what we need to do in order to make the necessary changes."

A fur trader making contact with the Crow Indians in 1805 offered beads, mirrors, tobacco, guns and ammunition in exchange for beaver hides. The next week, to the trader's delight, the Indians brought him 40 prime pelts. He paid them in trade goods and returned to the fur company's fort. The next month, the trader sought out the same band, eager to do business once again. He found the men of the tribe had taken not a single beaver in his absence. "I expected to buy more hides," he said. "You have enough," the chief said. "But I will pay you handsomely in trade goods," the fur company agent protested. "We have enough," the chief said. Phra Debvedi writes,

One important point that must be stressed is that the economic results that we seek are not ends in themselves. They are means, and the end to which they must lead is the development of the quality of life and of humanity itself. Consequently, it is the view of Buddhism that economic activity and its results must provide the basis of support for a good and noble life of individual and social development. Buddhism considers economics to be of great significance this is demonstrated by the Buddha having the peasant eat something before teaching him . . . after eating the peasant listened to Dhamma and became enlightened. We must ensure that the creation of wealth leads to a life in which people can be creative, develop their potentials, and endeavor to be good and noble. It is in short the quality of life that we are talking about.(Phra Debvedi, 1992)

For many people, shopping has deteriorated from a daily routine to purchase the basic food and household-necessities to an addiction or intense craving as a kind of entertainment to compensate for the emptiness and frustration within, caused by lack of value, of spiritual meaning, and of inner peace. Rahula holds that the Buddha considered economic welfare as a requisite for human happiness, " . . . but he did not recognize progress as real and true if it was only material, devoid of a spiritual and moral foundation." (Rahula,1990) Buddhadasa also emphasizes that the abandonment of selfishness and its clinging and craving desires is a major point in Buddhism (Buddhadasa, 1989).

Sulak writes, "For the new generation in Asia, we need to articulate a value system that reflects . . . our needs for leisure, contemplation, love, community, and self realization. We also need to describe the economy within its social and ecological context." He observes that development policymakers and experts generally fail to take into account of the big picture, quality of life, or "what is a human being and what should a human being be?" Consequently, they measure results rather simplistically and quantitatively with little attention to what the people really need from development. (Sulak, 1992)

Sulak further points out that (from a Buddhist perspective) Development must aim at the reduction of craving, the avoidance of violence, and the development of the spirit rather than materialistic things. (in Buddhism) the goal of increasing the quality of life is understood differently. From the materialistic standpoint, when there are more desires, there can be further development. From the Buddhist standpoint, when there are fewer desires, there can be further development . . . Only a religion that puts material things in second place and keeps the ultimate goals of development in sight can bring out the true value in human development.(Sulak, 1992).

Silva sees pollution of the environment and pollution of the mind as being two aspects of the same problem and emphasizes the importance of viewing possible solutions to the problem "under the primacy of values over technology," as "ethical claims have an independent appeal to human dignity and responsibility." (Silva, 1990) Boonyanate observes, "Our conduct is influenced and, to a large extent, is determined by the way we perceive the world in relation to ourselves. If we see the world merely as a storehouse of resources for our own use , then that is exactly how we are going to treat it." (Boonyanate, 1992). Many of the traditional approaches to nature are based on anthropocentric or man-centered views which place people at the center of the cosmos.

Nature is considered a world of separate things which are valued only in terms of their use by human beings. This is in contrast to the ecocentric view of Deep Ecology (closely correlated with Dhamma) which views people as a part of a holistic nature which is interdependent and integrated. A uniquely American strain of this philosophy emerged in the United States more than a half century ago. Leopold wrote, "A thing is right when it tends to preserve the integrity, stability, and beauty of the biotic community. It is wrong when it tends to do otherwise." (Leopold,

1966). Rights, in this sense, are extended to all species as well as the land. As Boonyanate notes, However, there is a rider: man has to make this moral decision to include the other orders.

The other orders are unable to make any claim on their own behalf . . . The holistic view of both the Buddhist position and Leopold's stance subscribe to the same practical conclusion: the dissolution of an anthropocentric system of value in regard with nature. Although Leopold's center of value clearly lies in the well-being of the biotic community, Buddhist metaphysics does not place the center anywhere, as everything is metaphysically one under the same ultimate law. (Boonyanate, 1992). Much of Buddhist/Dhamma metaphysics and teachings are based on the unique concept of anatta or non-self which involves an awareness of total interconnectedness with all life in nature.

Nonself is the understanding that the idea of self is an imaginary, false belief which has no corresponding reality in nature and that it produces harmful thoughts of "I, Me, and Mine," which, in turn, produce craving, attachment, desire, aversion, and other defilements that are the sources of troubles in the world. In short, this false view of self can be traced to all the evil in the world.(Rahula, 1990). Drug addicts are universally afflicted with an egocentric view. The world exists for them. Anything that does not go their way is a personal affront. In their manipulation of persons and events to satisfy their cravings, they discard all morality and trample their own principles.

In this respect, the conspicuous consumer in his overpowered car and opulent house is the soul-mate of heroin junkies in the gutters from Bangkok to New York. Goenka points out that without the practice of sila/morality, including respect for all living beings, "there can be no progress on the path because the mind will remain too agitated to investigate the reality within . . . without sila one can never liberate the mind from suffering and experience ultimate truth. (Goenka, 1987).Khantipalo states, "The moral code of Buddhists is not an end in itself but is practiced as a stepping stone to reach enlightenment." (Khantipalo, 1989).

Like Christianity, Islam and Judaism, Buddhism's ideal can be far removed from its practice. Buddhism is a universal and missionary religion that has penetrated the most remote corners of Asia. In its spread, it did not enter a vacuum. Cults, animism, and ancient beliefs linger as encrustations upon the practice of unlearned Buddhists.

Ignorance of the teachings lead to the subjugation of women and a belief that Buddha's doctrine of "impermanence" is a license to degrade the environment. As the gender that spends much of its time working and living in the natural environment, Buddhist women in Asia obviously need much more of a voice in public participation and decision making for its care and for their concerns of its sustainability and protection. Yet Buddhist nuns and laywomen traditionally play a very insignificant role in Buddhism and environmental affairs in Asia.

Much of the future of the natural environment depends on the morals of any society. In the case of Buddhism, there may be a two-edged sword toward the future in some cases. In Thailand, for example, many Thai attitudes toward nature are based on Buddhism which certainly can be considered a strong, but not fully tapped, force for conservation. Many of Thailand's 700 Forest Monasteries offer protection for plants and animals while thousands of monks and nuns serve as examples of compassion for all living beings (Gray,Piprell, and Graham, 1991).

These attitudes would certainly seem to involve concern for the future of the natural environment. On the other edge of the sword, social scientist Juree Vichit- Vadakan states, "The Thai people are notorious for indulging in the immediate gratification of needs. Perhaps it is the Buddhist concept of impermanence and transience that has motivated Thai people to live more in the present than in the future. Thai people are reluctant to sacrifice the present for the future. The planting of forests for future generations is far more difficult than the felling of trees to build a house." (Vichit-Vadakan, 1993).

As Phra Paisal Wisalo, a Buddhist Monk involved with environmental causes , notes, "Before, nature had a life and spirit of its own. The trees, skies, and rivers were living spirits. Now we are only concerned how they can serve us." (Gray, Piprell, and Graham, 1991). Snyder goes a step further in his observations of the antagonism between the ideal of Buddhist ethics and its practice as religion. "Institutional Buddhism has been conspicuously ready to accept or ignore the inequalities and tyrannies of whatever political system it found itself under. This can be death to Buddhism because it is death to any meaningful function of compassion." (Devall and Session, 1985)

It should be kept in mind that the following concepts can only represent Buddhist values in their basic idealistic and all encompassing nature. They do not always find their match or correlation in the way they are understood or rehearsed even by predominantly Buddhist societies. Buddhism consists of Morality, Concentration, and Wisdom as explained in the Noble Eightfold Path which, in turn, is based on the Four Noble Truths. A summary/review of the Four Noble Truths of the Buddha's enlightenment or Dhamma involves concepts of

(1) Suffering: attachment to whatever is born and subject to decay, results in dissatisfaction and/or suffering;

(2) Cause of Suffering- dependent origination: ignorance in contact and the arising of attachment conditions of birth, decay and death,

(3) Cessation of Suffering—the realization that the chain of suffering can be broken through not reacting to feelings with craving/aversion and attachment, and

(4) Path to Cessation of Suffering—the Noble Eightfold Path with the three characteristics of:

   (a) Morality,

   (b) Mental Discipline and

   (c) Wisdom which follow:

(a) MORALITY (sila) (encompasses the three factors of Right Speech, Right Action and Right Livelihood of the Noble Eightfold Path). In this context, morality is focused on the Five Precepts (panca sila) of the Noble Eightfold Path of the teachings of Dhamma. In considering the "five moral precepts," Sulak says, "all Buddhists accept the five precepts (paca sila) as their basic ethical guidelines. Using these as a handle, we know how to deal with many of the real issues of our day." (Sulak, 1992) The concept of morality manifests itself in the five basic precepts underlying the rules for monastic life and for laypeople's conduct respectively:

1. not to kill any living being (often interpreted as "not to harm");
2. not to take what is not freely given by the owner (stealing);
3. not to indulge in sexual misconduct;
4. not to lie; and
5. not to consume intoxicants that lead to carelessness.

Instead of the traditionally bland recital of the above precepts, Buddhadasa unites all five precepts under a theme of non- violence. Thus, for Buddhadasa, the five precepts require their adherents to abstain from doing violence to:

(1) the life and body of people, animals, and other living beings;

(2) other people's property;

(3) that which is dearly loved by others;

(4) other people's rights and identities, and;

(5) one's own conscience and intellect. (Khantipalo,1989).

First Precept: I undertake the training to refrain from killing. General: Khantipalo states, "life is easily taken but impossible for us to give. As we do not enjoy dying ourselves, it is unwise to use our knowledge to destroy others." (Khantipalo, 1989). Non-violence does not only mean the absence of violence, but the presence of care, of good will, of mindfulness, and charity toward other beings. Non-violence shows itself in compassion and the sense of appreciation concerning the happiness and well-being of others. Environmental Aspects: In the first precept, Sulak notes, "we promise not to destroy, cause to destroy, or sanction the destruction of any living being. Through accepting this precept, we recognize our relationship to all life and realize that harming any living creature harms oneself. The Buddha said, 'Identifying ourselves with others, we can never slay or cause to slay.'"(Sulak, 1992)

The first precept on refraining from killing and its meaning of non-violence (ahimsa) not only refers to directly taking the life of a living being through intentionally destroying its body. It also refers to indirect actions and non-actions. For example, the removal of natural habitat from wildlife and other living beings will destroy or harm these beings. The pollution of bodies of water will result in the dying or suffering of fish and other aquatic life, including other forms of land life which feed on water life. Also by not taking measures to prevent these indirect actions, one is involved with non- action when possibilities may exist to stop the killing of other living beings. Buddha's mindfulness about the environment created a variety of rules and precepts for the lives of forest monks, e.g., not to cut branches of trees, not to wear sandals made from palm leaves or young bamboo, not to eat fruit containing seeds and seeds that still grow, not to use toothwood of certain sizes, etc. He provided rules about how to urinate, how to use water, etc. which were remarkable in their environmental consciousness.

Second Precept: I undertake the training to refrain from stealing. General: The second precept involves more than simply not stealing. Careless borrowing, for instance, would be included here when, subconsciously, one does not have any intention to return the item. Also, embezzlement, fraudulent business dealings, adulteration of food (by some merchants) should be included. (Khantipalo, 1989). Stealing involves the discounting of other beings and a lack of respect for their dignity and rights as individuals. In this sense, stealing can be considered violence against people and their property.

Environmental Aspects: Unwise, inappropriate, and uncontrolled developments, marketing, and consumption steal from present and future generations of all life. This is particularly true when options and heritages are irreversibly removed from future generations. It becomes stealing from the unborn while ignoring their rights and needs to life in the future. By not doing one's part to ensure appropriate and wise use in the development, marketing, and consumption of goods and services, one may be turning one's back on the moral act of stealing from present and future generations of all life.

This precept also raises the question of possession of living things. For example, who is the owner of a tree? The person who planted it? The birds and insects who are inhabiting it? The people who live under its shade and who nurture and protect it? The person who owns the forested area? The country which includes the tree in its boundaries? Nobody really owns the tree, but earth, nature or Dhamma itself, which grew a tree according to its own laws. A tree, if undisturbed, lives its life according to Dhamma, the very law of nature. Whoever comes in contact with a tree may sit in its shade, eat some of its fruit, find shelter under its branches when it rains, and breathe its oxygen freely without ever being asked for anything in return. These are the gifts that nature presents us through every tree. If we cut the tree down, we take away these gifts from other beings who might come the same way. A tree belongs to itself. Seeing the tree only in terms of its usefulness to gain material wealth is a selfish and delusive act of stealing from other beings.

The Cedrus of Buddhism recognize that the main cause of theft, immorality and violence is poverty. While all social systems recognize the theory that any of the above should be met with punishment, the Kutadanta-sutta explains that punishment will not change society. In order to stop crime, Buddha suggests that economic conditions of people should be improved. (Rahula, 1990). These Cedrus apply to current problems of illegal logging and poaching in national parks and forest reserves throughout Asia.

A recent study of the Dọng Yai Forest and Taplan National Park in Northeastern Thailand showed clear evidence that the poor farmers in surrounding villages are encouraged to do illegal logging by lumber and furniture companies. Much of the available agricultural land in this area is used for eucalyptus plantations by the paper industry and hence is unavailable to farmers. It should also be recognized that "professional" loggers and poachers will also undertake these illegal activities without adequate law enforcement measures.

The concept of the Earth as mother is universal. African Bushmen, the ancient Greeks and Native Americans paid homage to the Earth Mother in one form or another. Even modern Westerners, who like to think of themselves as sophisticated intellectuals, talk of "Mother Nature."

Third Precept: I undertake the training to refrain from sexual misconduct. General: Sulak notes, "Like the other precepts, we must practice this in our own lives, refraining from exploiting or hurting others. In addition, we have to look at the global structures of male dominance and the exploitation of women."(Sulak, 1992). The Dhammapada (215, 251) states, "There is no fire like lust . . . From lust arises grief, from lust arises fear. For him who is free from lust there is no grief, much less fear. (Rahula, 1990). Environmental Aspects: The third precept of morality towards sexual behavior should be extended to the complexities of exploitation of the natural environment which is a form of rape and violence.

Nature is being raped, including the rapid and obvious destruction of tropical forests in Asia, with little consideration toward its fragile and non-regenerative character. Greed, craving, ignorance, and aversion are the basic forces for exploitation. With a deeper understanding of the third precept, the natural environment cannot be made an object of one's selfish and desirous behavior because of the realization that using the environment to satisfy one's greed will only result in suffering.

Due to lack of attention to birth control, the population of Asia is expected to double in the next 25 years. This increase will increase pressures for exploitation of the remaining forested areas. The third precept would reasonably include birth control measures to limit the size of families. As Clausen points out, An alcoholic denies he drinks too much. His wife, unable to confront the traumatic truth of her husband's alcoholism, tells friends and relatives, "He is under stress" or "He works awfully hard and needs to unwind." Fear of Fetal Alcohol Syndrome (the poisoning of babies in the womb) prompts a young woman to deny her pregnancy to continue drinking. Only ruthless honesty will save the alcoholic. The same is true of a race inflicted with addictive materialism. (Clausen,1994)

Fourth Precept: I undertake the training to refrain from false speech.

General: This is considered to be one of the most difficult precepts for people to keep since it includes not only lying, but harsh speech, backbiting, and idle gossip. (Khantipalo, 1989) The fourth precept is much more than not telling lies. It implies that one speak the truth only, to not engage in idle talk, and to not use unfriendly words or unwholesome phrases. It calls for skillful, thoughtful, and truthful use of our oral and written communications. It also calls upon us to recognize the dignity, rights, and identities of all living beings and not to lie to them or to manipulate them and to deceive ourselves in the process.

As Sulak states, Truth is ultimately unknowable and inexpressible. For a Buddhist, being in touch with truth is being grounded in a deep critical doubt about all beliefs and prejudices. Having seen through the practice of meditation, the arising of illusion within oneself, one holds all views more loosely. Wisdom can only be achieved through the free and open exercise of the critical intellect. We need to look closely at the mass media, and the patterns of information that condition our understanding of the world . . . It will only be possible to break free of the systematic lying endemic in the status quo if we undertake this truth-speaking collectively. (Sulak, 1992).

Environmental Aspects: Lying or not telling the truth can be both gross and subtle. Often, public and private sectors involved in the environment and development will pay only lip service to conservation and ecological values and considerations. Public relations or information programs often do not present the real issues, facts, and alternatives beyond glossy brochures and biased approaches which strive to present a good organizational image to the public. As a result, the public trust and dignity is violated and the public cannot effectively participate in decisions that affect their lives for lack of essential information and alternatives. Thus they are deprived of the human right to determine their own futures.

In Thailand, natural forests are sometimes illegally logged so that they come to be considered damaged or degraded forests in need of reforestation. The "reforestation," however, often involves plantations of eucalyptus by large companies for sale as paper and pulp commercially. With three or four year cycles for eucalyptus trees, the "crops" of these trees eventually deplete the soil, removing nutrients and water. There is also the difference between the language and approach of everyday life and the spiritual life of Dhamma. This difference may neglect certain truths. Everyday language is based on physical things and on experiences accessible to the ordinary person.

With its basis on the physical rather than the spiritual, it serves only for tangible and concrete things perceived under ordinary, everyday experience. By contrast, Dhamma language has to do with the mental world which is intangible and non-physical. In order to be able to speak and understand this Dhamma language and approach, one needs to gain insight into this mental world (Buddhadasa, 1991).In not taking this insight and approach, one may miss the "truth" which includes the intangible and spiritual as well as the tangible and concrete needs of the environment. Rites, rituals, and use of ordinary and Dhamma language are needed to help lay-people in everyday life understand some of the higher goals and ethics of Buddha's teachings toward life and the environment.

A poor farmer in the rain forest regions of Laos can earn $600 tending a small field of opium poppies. His small production translates into $50,000 worth of heroin on the streets of Los Angeles, London or Paris. The War on Drugs, led by the United States and joined by other Western nations, funds national opium eradication efforts. Lao drug agents and regional officials insist that policing demands roads built into the remote hill country. Loggers and poachers follow the roads Development follows degradation.

Thus, junkies in cities thousands of miles away threaten a fragile environment that is wondrous beyond their opium dreams.

Fifth Precept: I undertake the training to refrain from substances that intoxicate and lead to carelessness. General: This precept refers both to refraining from consuming any intoxicating substances such as alcohol and drugs as well as avoiding involvement in their production and trafficking. It is also concerned with the immediate and long-term effects of intoxicating substances. The Buddha says to Sigala, "There are six dangers of drink: the actual loss of wealth; increase of quarrels; susceptibility to disease; an evil reputation; indecent exposure; ruining one's intelligence," (Rahula, 1990). Environmental Aspects: According to several agricultural extension agents, alcohol consumption by Thai farmers involved with cash crops such as casawa sometimes results in large decreases in funds available to families with consequent loss of nutritional foods for children. This is in contrast to subsistence-type farming where the food goes directly to the families.

Social workers working with poor fisherman in the fishing industry have found very high rates of drug use, particularly opium. These alcohol and drug pressures can contribute to illegal acts and overexploitation in order to obtain needed money for continued use as well as regular living expenses. The use of narcotic drugs not only proves hazardous to the physical and mental well-being of its consumer and his relatives but also causes great damage to nature by its production. The United Nations Drug Control Program notes, " One significant contributor to forest removal, water and soil pollution in these (tropical forest) regions, however, whose impact has gone virtually unnoticed by scientists and journalists, has been the cultivation of illicit narcotics crops—cannabis, coca, and opium poppy. (UNDCP, 1992).

The UNDCP further notes, Cultivation of illicit narcotics not only accounts for an increasing share of tropical deforestation, it is also the cause of some of the most severe environmental damage. Growers commonly plant their illicit crops in fragile forest environments in remote areas . . . The more severe environmental degradation to tropical forests by illicit narcotics cultivators largely results from the rapid and damaging techniques used to clear land. Even today, the most widely used forest removal method of manual clearing, commonly known as 'slash and burn' agriculture, where trees are rapidly felled and destroyed by fire, leaving no vegetative matter to stabilize or replenish soils . . . Chemicals used by many growers at all stages of illicit drug cultivation and production likewise have a substantial negative impact upon tropical ecosystems and on human populations. (UNDCP, 1992)

The Buddha said, "O Bikkhus, there are two kinds of illness. What are those two? Physical illness and mental illness. There seem to be people who enjoy freedom from physical illness even for a year or two . . . even for a 100 years or more. But, O Bikkhus, rare in this world are those who enjoy freedom from mental illness even for one moment, except those who are free from mental defilements." (Rahula, 1990).

MENTAL DISCIPLINE (Samadhi) Encompasses the three factors of Right Effort, Right Mindfulness, and Right Concentration of the Noble Eightfold Path. General: Basically, Samadhi, concentration, or mental activity means the cultivation of mastery over the mind by means of practicing mindfulness and one-pointedness. Samadhi should be grounded on good moral conduct. If the mind is preoccupied with the continuation of immoral acts such as killing or stealing, it will be too agitated for meditation and right concentration and its result—panna/wisdom.

Much of samadhi or mental discipline deals with awareness/concentration in the present moment. Thich Nhat Hanh notes, "You should be as awake as a person who walks on high stilts, any misstep could fling him to his death. You should be like a medieval knight walking weaponless in a forest of swords. You should be like a lion, going forward in slow, gentle and firm steps. Only with this kind of vigilance can you realize total awakening." (Thich Nhat Hanh, 1989). The Thai Buddhist Monk, Phra Prachak, considers trekking through the forest a form of meditation for keeping mindful in the present moment and for not dwelling on the past or future. Getting scratched or tripping in the trail often indicate that one needs to be more mindful and alert in the present through trekking meditation. This trekking/meditation process contributes to making one more ecologically attuned to the present environment. Besides the formal meditation practices of sitting, walking, standing, and lying, Bhavilai points out that one can constantly meditate in all activities by observing with awareness and concentration the vibrations, sensations, emotions, etc. which one experiences throughout the day.

The key is to stay in the present moment rather than dwelling on the past or future moments or experiences. Both formal and informal meditation can, in turn, lead to the realization of non-self and impermanence, letting go of defilements and selfishness along with associated negative values and behavior. (Bhavilai, 1993). The mind is purified by meditation, which is the contemplation of reality or the penetration of the true nature of phenomena by focusing all one's awareness on the present moment with no accompanying subjective feelings, opinions, or judgments.

This, of course, is not easy. For example, seeing is difficult. When seeing, people make an aesthetic evaluation of beauty or the lack of it. This act is often pervaded by thought and memory, associations with the object being seen or viewed. This same difficulty applies to other senses, such as hearing, smelling, tasting, feeling, etc. To overcome this difficulty requires infinite patience and a sincere wish to remain mindful of the constant rising and falling (impermanence) of mental phenomena and of nonself.(Inwood, 1981)

The ability for seeing as seeing, hearing as hearing, etc., the recognition of reality, and the resultant state of samadhi is made possible by a comprehensive and individual selection of meditation practices. These practices develop an awareness of unconscious motives and impulses so that, once recognized, they can be cast aside or let go to allow for the progressive purification of the five senses and the mind. With this concentration and mindfulness, the complementary use of Insight (vipassana) emerges for the purified and peaceful mind associated with nibbana (Inwood, 1981). Such a mind would obviously be free from greed, aversion, and delusion which are the bases of our environmental problems.

Environmental Aspects: Various aspects of the natural environment can be cited as a subject for meditation to understand Dhamma or nature. Because people and the natural environment are made up of the same elements, meditating on the composition of the body, mind, and emotions in relation to nature can be very helpful for general concentration practice as well as preparing the ground for the arising of panna, wisdom. The rising and falling away of impermanence, for example, is associated with the human body as well as the tree/forest in the natural environment.

The most practiced meditation in Buddhism is said to be "mindfulness with breathing" (Anapanasati) in accordance with the Satipatthana Sutta. Here the mind first becomes concentrated through the observation of the most natural rhythm, the meditator's

Greek death: to the end of the classical period—Charistophir Souvino Infell.

own breath. Sitting under a tree for this meditation, one may become aware that, through this very breath of life, one is truly interconnected with the tree by breathing in the oxygen that the tree provides. When one is breathing out carbon dioxide, the tree will breathe this in and turn it into oxygen which it will breathe out to renew the cycle as one again breaths in the oxygen during anapanasati/ meditation. Such practices certainly aid one's understanding of "oneness" and interconnectedness. According to Gore, the same oxygen molecules from the time of Buddha are still present on the earth. Thus it would be possible for some meditators to breath in oxygen from Buddha's own breath when they are meditating.(Gore,l992)[1]. Buddha praised forests as the best place for those seeking to practice Dhamma.

The first Buddhist Monastery was a forest temple which was named "Weruwanaram" or the bamboo temple. A number of his teachings reiterate that he always praised and encouraged his followers who had chosen to live and practice meditation in the forest. By their choosing this way, he knew that peace and solitude would help them to gain concentration and to contemplate their minds. As he says to one of his followers, "Bhikku, for those forests, those bases of trees and those unoccupied houses, you should contemplate your mind in those places and undoubtedly, (of your practice) the grand success resulting in the first level, the middle, and the end which means liberation." (Anapana-sati Sutra) The forest provides natural, undisturbed, and peaceful surroundings which are agreeable and most appropriate to those who seek solitude and quiet for the practice of meditation.

As noted in chapter one, the life of the Buddha was spent in forests. He was enlightened while meditating under a Bodhi tree. His instructions to monks: "Here, O Bhikkhus, are the roots of trees, here are empty places: meditate," can be considered a categorical imperative of Buddha as well as a symbol of the Buddhist way of life. It would naturally follow that Buddhism would be concerned about the protection of natural forests for meditation as well as for Buddha's teachings on love and compassion for all living things.(Kabilsing,et.al., l988). WISDOM (Panna) Encompasses the two factors of Right Understanding and

1. Algore-Earth in Balance: Ecology and Human Sprit, 1922.

Right Thought of the Noble Eightfold Path. Rahula writes: When wisdom is developed and cultivated according to the four noble truths, it sees the secret of life, the reality of things as they are. When the secret is discovered, when the truth is seen, all the forces which feverishly produce the continuity of samsara in illusion become calm and incapable of producing any more karma formations, because there is no more illusion, no more 'thirst' for continuity. It is like a mental disease which is cured when the cause or the secret of the malady is discovered and seen by the patient. (Rahula,1990).

The Four Noble Truths, as delivered in the first sermon after his enlightenment to the five ascetics in the deer park of Isipatana (today's Sarnath). When he left the palace, the aim of young Prince Siddhara Gautama was to find the ultimate remedy for the suffering of all living beings. A young commander of a British regiment fighting in Africa exhorted his men to plunge into the battle. "What are you waiting for? You owe God a life." A grizzled and battle-weary Scottish sergeant rose from the trenches to lead his troop into the fray. "Aye, lads, let us go. God owes us a death." (1) First Noble Truth-Dukkha (or suffering) encompasses a range of feeling from mild irritation to traumas of grief and sorrow. Buddhism is particularly concerned with the kind of suffering based on the clinging to self. In the spiritual sense, feelings of being incomplete, yearnings for inner peace, and desires for purification are all motivated by the omnipresence of Dukkha.

This concept does not deny happiness, joy, or laughter but recognizes that life's impermanent states are conditioned with inevitable suffering.(Inwood, 1981). Thus suffering is to a certain degree inherent in the existence of all living beings, as coming into existence conditions old age and death. Whatever is born is bound to decay. There is no way to escape this natural law of impermanence, neither by trying to satisfy each and every desire that is born in one's mind, nor by choosing between them. There are many kinds of delusive happiness, but they do not last. Whatever we perceive through our physical senses and our minds is determined and bound to pass away.

1. Rahula Walpole: What Buddha Taught (1990)

Environmental Aspects: Dukkha or the First Noble Truth applies to the natural environment with the recognition that nature is suffering as a whole and that serious environmental crises are appearing locally and globally everywhere. These crises range from loss of tropical forests and their plant and animal species to global warming. With the recognition that life is suffering, exploitation and insensitivity toward the living environment cannot make humankind escape the natural law of impermanence.

- ***Second Noble Truth (Samudaya):*** This truth explains the cause of suffering, as everything in the world falls under the law of cause and effect. Buddhist teachings see the cause of all suffering in desire, aversion, and delusion, all of which emerge from people's ignorance and clinging. In order for suffering to occur, there must be attachment or clinging to a certain object of desire, aversion, or delusion. Suffering is often self-inflicted by grasping after the illusions of an "I, me, and mine." Buddhism recognizes that there is no real self, but that man mistakes an illusory self to be real in his ignorance. Thus it is the illusory self, not a real self, that clings and causes the suffering. Environmental Aspects: Phra Debvedi considers these fundamental principles:

- Everything in the universe is subject to the law of cause and effect. Every act of man has an effect on the universe. Thus man is part of the process and subject to the laws of nature, including impermanence and suffering along with other beings;
- Recognizing this fundamental principle, people should be friends with other living beings, and should protect the living environment, and should share some of the suffering through lovingkindness. (Phra Debvedi, 1993)

However, the above principles are dependent on development of the conventional self through freedom and happiness rather than through moral imperatives or other means, such as the acquisition of wealth. This requires knowing the laws of nature before one can be free from fear, suffering, or the tendency toward harming nature through unwise acts and unsound practices. It also requires knowing the causes of suffering and the crises of nature in order to solve these problems, particularly as they relate to people. (Phra Debvedi,1993) Those causes include ignorance and desire, which require looking within oneself rather than for outside factors to blame. Ignorance of the chain of suffering leads one to attempt to compensate for dissatisfaction through external activities such as development for development's sake, mindless "use" or exploitation of natural resources, and consumerism. Wisdom helps one cut through the vicious cycle of desire-exploitation-suffering. Tanha— desire or craving—is the major cause of materialism with its increasing pressures on the natural environment. Phra Debvedi observes also that most people are undeveloped and try to achieve happiness by acquiring more and more things from nature and by dominating it. However, they lose their freedom by getting more things from outside themselves and become more dependent upon these things as they acquire them. In reality, what they need is to become less dependent on material things through self-development, so that they can be free to be happy within themselves rather than dependent on so many externals. With the victory of inner freedom and happiness over underdevelopment and ignorance, there is the possibility for greater balance, moderation, and harmony between people and the living environment. (Phra Debvedi, 1993)

The Third Noble Truth (Nirodha) or the law of cessation of Dukkha shows how the chain of dependent origination can be broken, so that contact between the six sense organs (eyes, nose, ears, tongue, body, and mind) will not lead to feelings that cause craving or aversion. As a result, the arising of attachment, becoming, birth, and death, with their consequent suffering will not take place. Thus the third noble truth is the realization that people can transcend Dukkha or mental pain and grief. Just as a flame expires without fuel, Dukkha similarly becomes extinct if its fuel of cravings is consumed. (Inwood, 1981). With the recognition that suffering is caused by certain conditions, the removal of these conditions causes suffering to cease.

When one is free from the illusory self with its attachment and clinging, then one has broken the bondage that bound him or her and is freed or liberated.(Kabilsingh,et.al., 1988) Environmental

1. Buddhist Economics.

Aspects: When it is possible to identify the causes of environmental problems, it then becomes possible to look for the ways to reduce or eliminate environmental problems. This requires that people realize their ignorance of nature and to rightfully understand that they are a part of the natural environment along with other living beings. (Kabilsingh, 1981)

The Fourth Noble Truth (Magga) explains the path that leads to the cessation of dukkha or suffering/unsatisfactoriness. Although Buddhism teaches that the world is full of suffering, it also provides the means to overcome this suffering.(Kabilsingh, et. al, 1988) Thus the fourth noble truth offers the way of liberation. By avoiding extremes, Buddhism presents "The Middle Way"— a path which rejects asceticism and sensuality, is tempered by a logical attitude toward morality, and is devoid of dogma, ceremony, and ritual. The "Path" prescribes purity of spirit, love, and noble deeds as the basis of the way to supreme happiness. (Inwood, 1981) The Noble Eightfold Path consists of: Right Understanding and Right Motives or Thoughts (the Wisdom Group); Right Speech, Right Action and Right Means of Livelihood (the Virtue Group); and Right Effort, Right Mindfulness, and Right Concentration (the Concentration Group).

Environmental Aspects of the Eightfold Noble Path follow:

(1) From Right Understanding Proceeds Right Thought: This path implies that one must possess the right knowledge of self and one's place in nature. It encompasses the capacity to realize that life is suffering and that exploitation of the environment in order to satisfy desires that spring from craving/aversion/ignorance of people are a part of this natural law. However, wise protection of the natural environment will lessen the suffering for oneself and other beings.

(2) From Right Thought Proceeds Right Speech: This path means right attitude of mind with freedom from thoughts of lust, ill-will, and cruelty. It also means a resolution to change things and their consequent suffering, particularly ignorance, greed, and craving. In awareness of the four noble truths, thought becomes wholesome, caring, and understanding toward the interconnectedness of human

beings, other living beings, and nature, resulting in right speech to support wise action toward protecting the natural environment.

(3) From Right Speech proceeds Right Action: This path would include the five precepts with both physical and mental abstention from killing, stealing, lying, sensuality, and intoxicating drugs and alcohol. However, it would also include positive and wholesome measures to protect and restore the natural environment. Right action(s) would encompass the raising of consciousness toward the importance and issues of the natural environment and toward active participation in the protection process.

(4) From Right Action proceeds Right Livelihood: This path requires avoidance of harmful or undesirable conduct. Poaching of wildlife, illegal logging, unwise clearing of natural forest for exploitation, and other negative livelihoods that impact the natural environment are not considered right actions or livelihoods in terms of the environment/Dhamma. In some countries, past poachers and ex-loggers were hired as park and forest guards and they were quite successful in their new careers as protectors of the forests.

(5) From Right Livelihood proceeds Right Effort: This path demands the exertion of will to overcome evil states of mind and to continue to grow in such good that already exists. Right effort is needed as craving and ignorance are very deeply rooted in the human mind and have the tendency to overpower one if right livelihood and right effort are not practiced.

(6) From Right Effort proceeds Right Awareness: This path requires training the mind so that it does not wander from thought to thought and so that one can be mindful in the present moment, avoiding the condition of "monkey mind" which constantly flits from thought to thought. The mind should be a useful tool of man and not his master. "The mind is very hard to perceive, extremely subtle, flits wherever it lists. Let the wise man guard it; a guarded mind is conducive to happiness." (Dhammapada, 36).

Right awareness encompasses mindfulness of one's own attitude toward nature as well as one's own behavior, in not destroying or degrading the natural environment, as well as by taking measures to protect and enhance it. This attitude includes keeping mindful of opportunities and challenges to stay on course for good and just causes such as environmental protection.

(7) From Right Awareness proceeds Right Concentration: This path encompasses a tranquil state of mind from which negative thoughts have been banished and have been replaced by awareness. The Buddha taught that the mind is where all acts arise and that good or evil issue from the mind. The fruits of mindfulness are right concentration with higher insight into the law of nature which removes ignorance, the source of suffering.

(8) From Right Concentration proceeds Right Wisdom: The understanding of the law of nature is pure wisdom. This results in loving care towards all living beings and their natural environment, and from right wisdom proceeds right liberation or Nibbana.

GENERAL ENVIRONMENTAL ETHICS/VALUES

The following represent some general ethics/values that are commonly associated with Buddhism and are applicable to the natural environment:

Compassion (Karuna): The Dalai Lama states, "Usually I tell people that compassion, warm heartedness, is something we can call universal religion. It is valid whether we believe in reincarnation or not, believe in God or not, whether we believe in Buddha or not." (Dalai Lama, 1991)[1]

Care is not a question of conflicting religious dogmas or different cultures. There is no such thing as Buddhist care, Christian care, Moslem care, or Thai, Chinese, or American care. Care, if it springs from real compassion, good will, and warm heartedness, is universal. The challenge of the environment concerns all life on planet earth and not one culture or religious group is excluded.

1. Dalai Lama. Path to Bliss, 1991.

This challenge includes our changing from selfishly exploiting our natural environment to care and compassion for all living beings on a united basis. Snyder notes, "Institutional Buddhism has been conspicuously ready to accept or ignore the inequalities and tyrannies of whatever political system it found itself under. This can be death to Buddhism, because it is death to any meaningful function of compassion. Wisdom without compassion feels no pain." (Devall and Sessions, 1985).

Compassion is for all living beings who are suffering, in trouble, and/or affliction. Compassion represents love, charity, kindness, tolerance, and similar noble qualities on the emotional side. In Dhammapada 3, the Buddha states, "Hatred is never appeased by hatred in this world; it is appeased by love. This is an eternal law." (Rahula, 1990). Khatipalo observes, "Compassion is taking note of the sufferings of other beings in the world. It overcomes callous indifference to the plight of suffering beings, human or otherwise.It must be reflected in one's life by a willingness to go out of one's way to give aid where possible and to help those in distress. It has the advantage of reducing one's selfishness by understanding other's sorrows . . . It is the Buddha's medicine for cruelty, for how can one harm others when one has seen how much they suffer already?"(Khantipalo, 1989).

The counterpart of love can be considered compassion with its wish that all beings be separated from suffering and the causes of suffering. Although one may not be certain that this wish is possible, it is still beautiful to hold in mind. It can be all the more moving if one amplifies it with the thought: "I will free beings from suffering." (Hopkins, 1984). (Mahayana bodhisattas vow to help all living beings become enlightened before they may attain Nirvana themselves.)

Loving Kindness (metta): The loving kindness experience is expressed by the Pali word, metta, which, in turn, is derived from the word, mitta, meaning "friend." Loving kindness means true friendliness toward the earth. This love and compassion means freedom for the earth and ourselves. By strongly loving the earth, one releases one's sadness and gains freedom in spirit for joy, efficiency, and abandon, regardless of any odds. (Badiner, 1990).

1. Deep Ecology, 1985.

Phra Debvedi says love or loving kindness toward nature comes from experiencing it and being a friendly to it. He notes that everyone wants to be happy and that love toward nature emerges from true happiness and freedom which is dependent on internal rather than outside things.

With happiness inside, the developed self is in balance and love with nature while the undeveloped self with its external clinging is not. (Phra Debvedi, 1993) Bhavilai also notes that; after one has reached a certain realization in Dhamma, one does good deeds out of love and wisdom for oneself and nature rather than out of moral imperatives; i.e.,one does good things for the environment or restrains from doing bad things because one has loving kindness and compassion toward oneself and other living beings.

When the thought is good and associated with loving kindness and Dhamma, then good deeds for nature result for their own sake.(Bhavilai, 1993) Loving kindness is an unselfish and unconditional love which can be extended to every living being. The quality of loving kindness becomes an integral part of one's character through absorbed concentration. Although this love without attachment is inconceivable to many people, such a love is much superior to the attached kind. Without attachment, it can become infinite and need not be confined to any group of beings nor leave any group outside of it. (Khantipalo, 1989).

Loving kindness and compassion are considered to be holy or unbounded states of mind which are to be cultivated by everyone during meditation and in daily life. Loving kindness radiation is considered to be compulsory for all Buddhists. (Kabilsingh,et.al.,1988).In Buddhism, the spreading of loving kindness is the power of the mind because it makes the mind bright and clear (Sanong, 1992). Cultivating loving kindness allows the mind to find pleasantness in relation to every living being. The simple fact that every living being possesses a Buddha nature and is a sentient being who was previously your mother is sufficient cause to find him or her pleasant. (Hopkins, 1984).

By realizing that human beings are not owners of nature, and that they interconnected with other beings who all share suffering and happiness, people practice loving kindness for all living beings and for their care and protection of the natural environment. This type of loving kindness permits people to extend their love beyond the limited and secular love of their immediate circle of people.

Loving kindness may be seen as a spiritual and ecological love of concern, hope, and care to and for all beings.

Effort/Responsibility (Viriya): The Buddha encouraged everyone to develop oneself and to work out one's own emancipation from all defilements of the mind toward complete liberation from the concept of worldly suffering. All humans are supposed to have the power to free themselves from all bondage through their own personal efforts and intelligence. Merit cannot be passed on to somebody else and Buddha only taught the way without interfering with anyone's personal path of freedom or enlightenment.

The Buddha said, "By oneself alone is evil done, by oneself is one defiled. By oneself is evil avoided, by oneself alone is one purified. Purity and impurity depend on oneself. No one can purify another." (Dhammapada, 165). Still, as Phra Prachak observes, "One can feel responsible, but one does not need to carry the responsibility. It is like drinking water. You drink it but you do not feel that you are carrying it. It is not like carrying a log. But it is good sometimes to know that you carry it." (Prachak, 1993) An essential part of Buddha's teaching responsibility is illustrated in the Kalama Sutta: on self- Yes, Kalamas, it is proper that you have doubt, that you have perplexity, for a doubt has arisen in a matter which is doubtful.

Now, look you Kalamas, do not be led by reports, or tradition, or hearsay. Be not led by the authority of religious texts, nor by mere logic or inference, not by considering appearances, not by the delight in speculative opinions, nor by the idea: 'this is our teacher.' But, O Kalamas, when you know for yourselves that certain things are unwholesome (akkusala) and wrong, and bad, then give them up . . . And when you know for yourselves that certain things are wholesome (kusala) and good, then accept them and follow them. (Rahula, 1990).

Equanimity (Upekkha): Equanimity may be seen as the mind coming into harmony with the laws of nature and of impermanence. Basically, equanimity is accepting that one cannot make permanent what is impermanent. It is an acceptance that the world will not conform to what we want it to be. (Weissman, 1990). Goenka states, "In every situation, one understands that the experience of that moment is impermanent, bound to pass away. With this understanding one remains detached, equanimous." (Goenka,1987). Equanimity is being " . . . able to face life in all its vicissitudes with calm of mind, tranquillity, without disturbance." (Rahula,1990).

The cultivation of equanimity does not mean that one tries to become indifferent to all living beings. Rather, it means reflecting on the fact that all living beings want happiness and do not want suffering and that each and every sentient being throughout space has been our mother many times in the past. It is also a recognition of the deeper nature or Buddha nature in all living beings, regardless of their present form and situation. Equanimity thus opens the door for loving kindness and compassion for all living beings on an equal basis as well as for their care through protection of the natural environment. (Hopkins, 1984).

Charity (Dana): Khantipalo states, "Worldliness talks about 'getting,' The Way talks about 'giving'. . . . In the practice of giving one should never expect any return, the only return being that one's own heart is purified, for one rejoices in a wholesome action and the heart then becomes flexible and one's ways more easy to train. What greater return could there be than this?" Attachment to money one earns and to possessions one owns results in the development of ego and selfishness and does not permit one to go along a spiritual path. (Khantipalo, 1989).

In modern society, the amount of input into something is often measured by its expected income as in a business transaction. Real charity is giving for the sake of giving without expecting anything in return; it is only beneficial giving if it is entirely unconditional and free from any craving for fame, wealth, or power. Charity does not have to be financial. It can be selfless service, such as cleaning up polluted beaches, assisting in the protection of a forest and its wildlife, and so forth. Much of the effort for environmental protection involves this kind of selfless giving where one can give on a volunteer basis for the welfare of all living beings, including the unborn.

This type of giving also frees one on his or her spiritual path. As Phra Debvedi notes, "Helping others also helps us to develop good qualities in ourselves. The mind tends toward skillful reactions in its everyday contact. In this way, the practiser sees the relationship between his own personal practice and the practice of relating to the world. One sees that all beings are related and so deals with them with metta, goodwill and koruna, compassion, helping them in their need." (Phra Debvedi, 1990).

Humility (Nivata): In contrast to the arrogance and possessiveness that some people have toward living beings and the natural environment, humility assumes a meek and modest approach. The term humility actually comes from the Latin word Humus for soil which is the lowest part of the forest as well as its life support as the medium for water and nutrients. Humility is also the recognition that all beings, including human beings, are basically powerless before the laws of nature or Dhamma. In this sense, humility would subscribe to the will of Dhamma being done rather than the will of one's own ego. The concept of anatta or non- self and humility are closely related since humility arises when the consciousness of I, me, or mine diminishes.

Humility also teaches us that we cannot really own anything in any absolute sense. We can only temporarily own or use something so that we can be merely good stewards in any given moment. (Kalbilsingh, et.al., 1988). Human beings, like other beings, belong to Dhamma or nature and are subject to its laws. Thus, Phra Debvedi states, " . . . we understand that all other beings are afflicted with the same illness as we are. Therefore it is proper that we learn to help each other as fellow travelers on the path of practice." (Phra Debvedi, 1990)

It is necessary to see the Buddha nature in the person or living being before us. By practicing this mindfulness regularly, a change will occur in us through the development of humility and by the realization that our abilities are boundless. In knowing how to respect other beings, we will also know to respect ourselves.

(Thich Nhat Hanh, 1990). Roberts notes, " Meditation and mindfulness give character to our actions. They prevent us from being engulfed with panic when our actions fail or from being too driven in the pursuit of success. Since they show that no action is final, they keep us from taking ourselves too seriously." (Badiner, 1990)

Buddhadasa observes, "Living close to nature makes it easier to understand, to know, and to practice in harmony with nature. Please learn to enjoy and be contented with plain and simple living together with nature. This will benefit and support your study and practice." (Buddhadasa, 1988).

Gratitude/Thankfulness (Katannu-katavedi): After his enlightenment, the Buddha stood for one week gazing at the Bodhi tree to show his gratitude and appreciation to the tree that had sheltered and nurtured him. Gratitude in and for nature shows our appreciation and thankfulness for blessings and gifts, both tangible and intangible, which have been given to us whether we have asked for them or deserve them. Often, we forget our "life support systems" and interdependencies with nature as well as its rich gifts and blessings through other beings and through the natural environment. We owe our lives to nature which created us and which sustains us moment by moment.

And we owe much of our humanity and spirituality to contact with nature and its natural forms of beauty and life. This would also include respect for nature or Dhamma as the giver. As Weissman notes, "Gratitude and respect are so closely related that it is hard at times to tell whether one comes before the other or whether they arise together." (Weissman, 1990) It is this type of gratitude, thankfulness, and appreciation that motivates and inspires one to do what he or she can to protect and enhance the natural environment so that present and future generations of all living beings can continue to live in nature and to receive its gifts and blessing, particularly the gift of life and living. In this sense, we belong to Dhamma or nature and have a duty of appreciation to express our gratitude toward it through environmental service.

Non-self (Anatta): Goenka states, "Within the physical and mental structure, there is nothing that lasts more than a moment, nothing that one can identify as an unchanging self or soul. If something is indeed 'mine,' then one must be able to possess it, to control it, but in fact one has no mastery even over one's body; it keeps changing, decaying, regardless of one's wishes." (Goenka, 1990).

Mindfulness (Sati) Right-mindfulness is to be diligently aware, attentive, and mindful of activities of the body, sensations or feelings, activities of the mind, and ideas, conceptions, thoughts, and things. (Rahula, 1990). When considering ethical conduct, mindfulness acts as a gatekeeper whose job is to keep his eyes on people passing in and out, permitting entrance and exit to those for whom it is proper and forbidding entrance to those for whom it is not.The mind with sati possesses the qualities of purity, radiance, spaciousness, joy and freedom as an unconstricted and untarnished mind. (Phra Debvedi, 1990)

Right-mindfulness enables the observer to look at things objectively, the way they are, not as one likes them to be. Mindfulness involves one's only taking note or observing mental and physical phenomena and not reacting according to one's past conditioning, emotions, or thought-concepts of liking or dislike. Thus one becomes capable of purer actions in harmony with Dhamma, the law of nature, in the sense of not relating them to oneself. Once there is seeing through mindfulness, there needs to be acting or the seeing becomes meaningless. Thus, seeing environmental problems through mindfulness means taking action for the solution of these problems.

Thich Nhat Hanh notes, "We are making the earth an impossible place to live for ourselves and for many generations of children. If we live our present moment mindfully, we will know what to do and what not to do, and we will try to do things in the direction of peace." (Thich Nhat Hanh, 1991).

Interrelatedness/ interbeing (paticca samuppada—dependent origination): Buddhadasa notes, "Dependent origination is in the middle between the ideas of having a self and the total lack of self. It has its own principle: Because there is this, there is that; because this is not, that is not." (Buddhadasa, 1992). It is recognized that each of the factors of dependent origination is conditioned as well as conditioning. Consequently, they are all relative, interdependent and interconnected, and nothing is absolute or independent. Thus, no first cause is accepted by Buddhism (Rahula, 1990) With interrelatedness, "the emphasis is on harmony between individuals, communities, and nature. It involves an inner spiritual work of cultivating ecological consciousness, a process of becoming aware of the being of rocks, trees, and rivers . . . learning how to listen with an appreciation that everything is connected." (Badiner, 1990)

It also means recognizing that ecological elements are codependent. If damage occurs to one of these ecological elements, then it affects the entire ecological system, i.e., one cannot do one thing without its consequences to other things in nature. Internally, the concocting and attaching process of dependent origination through the ego also brings about craving, aversion, and delusion in people which, in turn, affect outside relationships and other living beings and the environment. Hence, awareness and wisdom are needed to prevent this process at the very beginning.

5

Dhamma, Deep Ecology, Ecology and Tropical Forests

This chapter will deal with Dhamma as nature, natural truth, and natural law as it applies to Deep Ecology, ecology, and tropical forests. Shallow ecology (and conservation, resource management, etc.) assumes that it is possible to go on with business as usual if we do things more carefully while increasing our human populations, technology, and economies. By doing things more carefully to nature, we will not have to question ourselves, our values, or our world views in terms of controlling nature. In contrast, Deep Ecology, such as that inherent in Buddhism, assumes that we cannot continue business as usual. Deep Ecology begins with the recognition that one group of human beings has neither more nor less worth than any other, and that each kind of natural being has intrinsic worth, is valuable for its own sake. (Drengson, n.d.).

Like Dhamma or nature, Deep Ecology goes far beyond the study of relationships between organisms and their environments; it points to a fundamentally new way of looking at our relationships to ourselves, to one another, and to the world. It represents, while timeless and perennial, a "new" type of consciousness that is emerging within the collective psyche of humankind. It involves a consciousness of synthesis, integration, and non-dualism with corresponding values in the world, i.e., that all things are part of an interrelated continuum of wholeness and diversity. (Taylor, 1990).

The Foundation for Deep Ecology is also named Ira-hiti , which refers to the annual Karuk ceremonies whereby certain Native Americans "fix the world" by bringing all natural forces back into balance. It recognizes that there is an ancient Earth-based knowledge, philosophy, and system of practice among traditional native peoples that still exists today. This knowledge and practice informs human beings about how to live on planet earth in reciprocal, cooperative, and healthy relationships with other living beings for the survival and quality of all present and future life. (Ira- Hiti, 1991)

The basic premise of Ira-hiti consists of the recognition that life on earth has entered its most precarious phase, with serious threats to all forms of life as well as to the health and viability of the biosphere. Many scientists now predict, conservatively, massive plant and animal diebacks on planet earth within three to sixty years. Ira-hita also recognizes the precipitous world-wide decline in the quality of life for human and other forms of life. Such awareness is the motivational basis for Ira-hiti's programs.

Thus, the Foundation for Deep Ecology in Ira-hiti is defined by the following quotation: Deep Ecology, partially rooted in native thinking, is a new movement among westerners that rejects the prevailing anthropocentric (human centered) paradigm of technological society, in favor of a biocentric ethic and practice. Deep Ecology abandons the notion that the natural world exists as a "resource" in service to human beings, but that forests, oceans, wildlife, and the natural world have intrinsic values, and the right to exist for their own sakes. Both as a philosophy and a new form of activism, Deep Ecology considers the survival of natural systems and the capabilities of the planet for self-renewal to be of primary importance and not to be compromised.

("IRA-HITI, Foundation for Deep Ecology," 4th draft of missions statement, [unpublished handout 6/20/91]) As a new natural philosophy, some of the key tenets of Deep Ecology are as follows:

- Contrasts with "shallow" or "reform" environmentalism, which takes up with environmental problems, such as resource depletion and pollution, form the Prevailing technocratic worldview, and seeks primarily to further the health and affluence of the world's dominant and technologically developed nation states.

- A practical, normative philosophy (not ecological sciences, though in part inspired by such science) that leads to changes in our vision and practice, our actions, our forms of life.
- Takes the biggest historical perspective. For example, technological civilization is only about 10,000 years old at most, perhaps beginning with agriculture. The human species is 3-4 million years old; (think of all the knowledge in our genes; dinosaurs lived for 150 million years, etc.) This perspective helps liberate one to act, and even gives ground for hope.
- Biological egalitarianism (vs. homocentricism): in principle, all beings are created equal, and have an equal right to live and blossom (Naess). This requires care and the minimization of impact on others of all sorts, but it also mitigates alienation from participation in the world.
- Stresses the internal (vs. external) relatedness of beings. If two things, A and B, are internally related, then the relation belongs to the constitution of both, so that neither would be what is apart from its relation with the other. A and B are part of one another—for example, human and nature, self and others. We are all part of each other, and contribute to the unity of the whole. Thus when the bell tolls for another species, it also tolls for us.
- Importance of diversity, symbiosis, and complexity in both human cultures and the world at large. This requires emphasis on coexistence and cooperation (vs. domination, oppression) both as an obligation and as the most effective survival strategy.
- Recognition of the necessity for wildness and wilderness, not simply for their ecological value, but also as essential to ethical-spiritual practice and thus to the vitality of human forms of life as well as to the life of the world.

Deep Ecology is also known as "ecosophy" which means ecologically wise actions and ecological wisdom. Thus it refers to both a practice and a state of being. This term, along with Deep Ecology, was also introduced by Arne Naess, the Norwegian philosopher, who used the expression, "deep and shallow ecology." Ecosophy comes from the Greek words, ecos, meaning "household place," and sophia, which means "wisdom." Thus, ecosophy is ecological wisdom which is manifested in actions which are ecologically harmonious.

In contrast, the assumption of shallow ecology is that we can go on with our business as usual with major changes if we clean up our act by doing things more carefully. We can continue to increase our numbers and technological power without questioning our world view, values, and aims.

There is no need for fundamental change or redefinition of progress or in our attempts at the unlimited control of nature. Professors Drengston and Inoue observe, So-called corporate (shallow) environmentalism still dominates the mainstream. It advocates continuous economic growth and environmental protection by means of technological innovation (such as catalytic converters), "scientific resources management" (such as sustained yield forestry) and mild changes in life styles (such as recycling). It avoids serious fundamental questions about our values and worldviews; it does not examine our sociocultural institutions and our personal lifestyles.

This mainstream technological approach has to be clearly distinguished from the Deep Ecology approach, which in contrast aims to achieve a fundamental ecological transformation of our sociocultural systems, collective actions, and lifestyle. (Drengston and Inoue, 1995) Consequently, the Deep Ecology or Ecosophy approach recognizes that we cannot continue with business as usual, but must face a deep crisis in the kind of culture and character which threatens the earth, and ask ourselves how we might live so as not to destroy the earth and all its living beings.

Thus, Deep Ecology is a global movement toward a diversity of ways for achieving ecosophic relationships with the earth. It is a radical (get at the roots) philosophy of life wherein each kind of natural being has intrinsic worth. Ecosophy or ecological wisdom involves deepening our ecological sensibilities and practices for ecological harmony. This involves an awareness of one's relationships with the processes of life that flow around, through.

and between all beings. (Drengston, n.d.) In this sense, Deep Ecology does not separate humans from the natural environment, in contrast to "shallow" ecology which is anthropocentric. The latter considers humans as above or outside nature, and that they are the source of value with their instrumental or utilitarian uses of natural resources. Deep Ecology sees the world as a network of phenomena that are fundamentally interconnected and interdependent. It views human beings as just one particular strand in the web of life. (Capra, 1995)

This deep ecological awareness recognizes that nature and the self are at a "oneness" with values inherent in all living beings, including trees and other plants, and is therefore basically a spiritual awareness. The human spirit is concerned with finding one's place or consciousness within the universe so that the individual may feel connected and at one with the cosmos rather than separate and isolated. Thus ecological awareness can be considered spiritual; Deep Ecology and Deep Spirituality are essentially one and the same. Not surprisingly, this sense of oneness with nature is consistent with the expression of religious feeling all over the world, from Christian mysticism to Native American, African, and Asian spiritual traditions to the feminine spirituality of the women's movement. (Capra, 1995)

There is beginning to be a greater recognition paid to how societies relate to the environment and the world in general through their religious beliefs and practices. As a result, more people are looking at the potential for finding spiritually-based solutions to problems which arise from ignorance, superstition and greed. These solutions must include a paradigm shift in values and ways of thinking and behaving—from anthropocentric ("human-centered") to ecocentric ("total-life centered").

And perhaps the route to this new consciousness is through a recognition of the wisdom and understanding of nature that has been with us in lesser and greater degrees since primordial times, the buried sense of oneness with the cosmos and all the life it contains. The "oneness" of deep spirituality and Deep Ecology is particularly reflected in Buddhism. As the spiritual dimension of the environmental movement, the worldview of Deep Ecology is highly compatible with Buddhist teachings and practices.

The restating and interaction of Deep Ecology with Buddhist principles and ethics greatly contributes to one's understanding, imagination, and reinvigoration for activism and education. Deep Ecology reflects an awareness and concern about the intrinsic value of all living beings and the integrity of their natural home, along with a sense of the limits of the human role in the scheme of things.

This awareness, in turn, permeates Buddhism with its teachings of impermanence, causality, non-self or emptiness, equanimity, loving kindness and compassion, which , in turn, reflect the doctrine of "oneness" of all living beings in Deep Ecology and deep spirituality. (Amidon and Roberts, 1996). The Dhamma/Dharma (laws and teachings of Nature), or the orientation of Buddhism toward nature, has numerous principles which correlate with Deep Ecology. As a highly respected world religion or philosophy, it has a great potential for influencing people in their thought, values and behavior toward a Deep Ecological view of nature. However, little of this potential has been realized, because few monks, nuns or laypersons of the faith have yet been introduced to Deep Ecology per se.

The Deep Ecology platform was written by two ecophilosophers, Arne Naess and George Sessions to promote and encourage a sense of commonality, clarity, and consensus on the core principles of the philosophy, while still recognizing and allowing for differences among supporters of the movement. The platform consists in eight points:

1. The well-being and flourishing of human and nonhuman life on earth have value in themselves (synonyms: inherent worth, intrinsic value). These values are independent of the usefulness of the non- human world for human purposes.
2. Richness and diversity of life forms contribute to the realization of these values and are values in themselves.
3. Humans have no right to reduce this richness and diversity except to satisfy vital needs.
4. Present human interference with the nonhuman world is excessive, and the situation is rapidly worsening.

5. The flourishing of human life and cultures is compatible with a substantial decrease of the human population. The flourishing of nonhuman life requires such a decrease.
6. Policies must therefore be changed. The changes in policies affect basic economies, technological structures. The resulting state of affairs will be deeply different from the present.

The ideological change is mainly that of appreciating life quality (dwelling in situations of inherent worth) rather than adhering to an increasingly higher standard of living. There will be a profound awareness of the difference between big and great. Those who subscribe to the foregoing points have an obligation directly or indirectly to participate in the attempt to implement the necessary changes. The Deep Ecology movement is calling for radical social change as well as for a spiritual dimension to environmental concerns. They ask for deeper questions about the real causes, such as ignorance and greed, behind ecological crises. Deep Ecology recognizes Homo sapiens as a single species in the integrity of the eco-universe amongst countless other species of plants and animals in their interrelationships and mutual dependence. (Sessions, 1996)

This deep ecological awareness is basically spiritual in nature and recognizes that the well-being of other forms of life on earth have intrinsic value and inherent worth in themselves, regardless of what people think about their "uses." It recognizes that human beings are only one strand in the web of life and calls for a paradigm shift from anthropocentric to ecocentric. Deep Ecology and its spirituality calls for a new perspective on values that stem from a recognition of the "oneness" of all life. Elizabeth Roberts and Elias Amidon have set forth the principles of Deep Ecology Education as follows:

- Wherever possible, how we teach should be congruent with what we teach. The teacher should understand the relationship between those learning activities and content principles.
- Experiential learning is core to Deep Ecology education, including a balance of these components: experience,

reflection, comprehension, application, and relational work..

- It is important to establish safety, trust, and intentionality at the start of the work deeply and with full heart.
- Learning can and should be of the body as well as mental and emotional.
- Teaching is place based, promoting a contextual frame for learning.
- Mindfulness is the underlying practice in all Deep Ecology teaching with a goal of generating awareness itself.
- Faculty should acknowledge their own positions and sources of Motivation for their work.
- Teaching involves creating a learning community with give and take between facilitator and group.
- Deep Ecology teaching is enhanced by collaborative teamwork drawing on diverse faculty strengths.(Roberts and Amidon, 1996)

In Buddhism, there is the concept of non-self, or voidness, as contrasted with the Western emphasis on the self, the individual ego. However, the "Ecological Self" associated with Deep Ecology presents ways of perceiving selfhood based upon fluctuating impermanent processes in nature.

PRINCIPLES OF THE "ECOLOGICAL SELF"

- The universe can be seen as a communion of subjects, not a collection of objects or of fragmented parts and relationships.
- The human subject in all its complexity has co-evolved with the earth's story. It is part of a much bigger self-correcting and self- regulating system (including its primordial heritage from evolution and earlier species).
- Enlarging one's sense of identity with the larger systems erodes the false sense of a separate self in isolation.
- The ecological self is the relational self, engaged with and shaped by numerous complex and subtle relationships

with other humans, non-humans, landscapes, weather, and places.

- One's capacity to experience the Ecological Self is strongly determined by human perceptual limitations as well as one's social and personal history of consciousness.
- Ecological identity is shaped by place, social position, property, lineage of ideas and people (past and present), social values, and personal habits of action.
- Feelings of pain (grief, fear, rage) and joy for the world are natural and healthy, a sign of connection with the world; unblocking repressed feelings releases energy for ecological consciousness and constructive action.
- Human consciousness includes and depends upon the lives of others (human and non-human) and is grounded in the particularity of individual and group relationships.
- Ecological "self work" includes investigating the social self and how differences are psychologically and socially constructed. This involves acknowledging barriers of privilege, history, and culture between people (and other living beings) which prevent effective action. (Roberts and Amidon, 1996)

Buddhist monks, and nuns, along with scholars, join scientists and environmentalists in recognizing a close relationship and correlation between Dhamma and Deep Ecology. Dhamma and Deep Ecology both recognize that nothing can be done in isolation. There are always relationships and it is not possible to do one thing without affecting other things. This recognition is illustrated in James Lovelock's Gaia hypothesis which states: "The entire range of living matter on Earth, from whales to viruses, and from oaks to alga, could be regarded as constituting a single living entity, capable of manipulating the Earth's atmosphere to suit its overall needs and endowed with faculties and powers far beyond those of its constituent parts." (Badiner, 1990)

The earth is the only planet of nine orbiting the sun to support life. There are over 6 billion human beings, 1,667,000 billion wild animals, 4.4 billion domestic animals, 580,000 billion water creatures along with many more billions of insects, land plants, water plants, and bacteria. All of this life on earth lives within a thin layer called the biosphere which is a very complex and fragile web of interdependent life.(Morris, 1988) Alienated from the cosmos and imprisoned by narrow frames of reference, human beings do not know themselves as a species among other species nor as a dimension of an emergent universe or Dhamma. (Swimme, 1984). As Swimme notes, "Only by establishing ourselves within the unfolding cosmos (and its creative planet earth) as a whole can we begin to discover the meaning and significance of ordinary things." (Swimme, 1984) Thus, when one views a fish, for example, one is viewing a fellow living being that has evolved with ourselves millions of years ago.

It is this type of cosmic or universal view that can give rise to awareness and perspective associated with Buddhism and Deep Ecology. In years of psycho-physical work involving trans-species experience, Grof concluded, "In a yet unexplained way each human being contains the information about the entire universe or all of existence, has potential experiential access to all its parts, and in a sense is the whole cosmic network, as much as he or she is just an infinitesimal part of it, a separate and insignificant biological entity.(Macy, 1991)

In her lecture on "Thai Temple Architecture: The Universe in Miniature," Umemoto notes, "The Wat compound is by no means a haphazard collection of buildings. In its entirety, as well as its component parts, from its boundary walls to its stapes to the murals inside its halls of worship, it has rich symbolism, all geared toward a single purpose: to bring the worshiper in tune with the rhythm of the universe and ultimately to a state of enlightenment, outside of time and space, removed from matter and passions." (Umemoto, 1993)

The symbolic foundation of Thai religious architecture is based on Pali Buddhist scriptures that are derived from many different sources found on the Indian sub-continent (where Indian mountain temples imitated the creation of the universe and represented an attempt to bring man into harmony with the oneness of all things).Primarily, one set of concepts relates to the deep folk tradition concerned with ensuring the endless cycle of the earth mother; another set relates to the structure of time and the shape of the universe. All aim for oneness with the divine through a symbolic encouragement, or even reliving the act of creation, thereby ensuring that the universe will endure and prosper.(Umemoto,1993) As Albert Einstein wrote,

A human being is part of the whole called by us 'universe,' a part limited in time and space. He experiences himself, his thoughts and feelings, as something separated from the rest—a kind of optical delusion of his consciousness. This delusion is a kind of prison for us, restricting us to our personal desires and to affection for a few persons nearest us. Our task must be to free ourselves from this prison by widening our circle of compassion to embrace all living creatures and the whole of nature in its beauty. (Einstein, n.d.)

In the Buddhist view, human beings are a product of an impersonal universe and not a special creation. The universe was not created for human beings nor are human beings the highest form of intelligence. Nor does Buddhism recognize any essential difference between human beings and lower animals; the differences are considered to be qualitative rather than absolute. (Htoon, 1961). As Boonyanate notes, "Indeed, Buddhism does not deny differences between man and the rest of the universe. Nevertheless, it is important to note that these differences are not in kind but in degree. All things are the same in essence; all are conditioned by ever changing conditions." (Boonyanate, 1992)

Thus Boonyanate goes on, . . . It would not be unjust to say that Buddhist environmental philosophy does offer an alternative channel to coping with the environmental crisis we are now facing by dispelling the predominant assumptions traditionally based in Western thought. This is particularly relevant to Asia with the spreading to our side of the globe of the process of modernization and industrialization. Buddhism not only offers the possibility of a deliberate decision to accommodate nature in our moral realm in the level of expediency but it offers more: Without having to resort to mysticism, it offers the true and necessary unity of an environmental ethic and the wisdom of man. (Boonanate, 1992)

In noting that this environmental direction needs to come from nature or Dhamma, Bates states, "In defying nature, in destroying nature, in building an arrogantly selfish, man-centered, artificial world, I do not see how man can gain peace or freedom or joy.

I have faith in man's future, faith in the possibilities latent in the human experiment: but it is faith in man as a part of the nature . . . faith in man sharing life, not destroying it."(Farb, 1967) Much of the essence of Deep Ecology is to keep asking more searching questions about human life, society, and nature, particularly as they pertain to values. It involves the study of our place in the earth household and a search for a more objective and ecological consciousness and state of being through an active deep questioning and meditative process, and way of life.(Devall and Sessions, 1985)

Both Deep Ecology and Dhamma would profess an understanding and appreciation of the sacredness of the natural world and the appropriate role of human beings within it. Arne Naess indicates two norms of Deep Ecology as:

- Self Realization which involves spiritual growth or unfolding from isolated and narrow egos into an ecological self or organic wholeness which merges or identifies with all forms of life or nature, and
- Bicentric Equality, which is an intuition that all things have a right to live and reach their own individual forms of unfolding and self-realization within the above larger (a) Self Realization. Thus, we come to know that if we harm nature/living beings, we are harming ourselves, with the recognition that there are no boundaries and everything is interrelated.(Devall and Sessions, 1985) Much of this redirection correspond with Dhamma, particularly in the selfless and Oneness aspects. Deep Ecology, Dhamma, and deep spirituality (place in universe) can often be considered to be very similar in this regard.

Dhamma and Deep Ecology call for the protection of natural areas and biodiversity for the sake of nature and other living beings for their own intrinsic value and worth. The recognition of this intrinsic value and worth may well be bound up with the intrinsic value and worth of human beings as a species, including their humanity and spirituality. Recognition and protection of nature and biodiversity for its own sake requires new approaches and perspectives. Much of Dhamma and Deep Ecology simply calls for changing our values and ways of thinking about ourselves as well as the environment. This change can come about in many ways. An illustration of change in thinking occurred for Aldo Leopold when he was a young forester. After shooting a wolf and going to where the wolf was lying, he reflected:

We reached the old wolf in time to watch a fierce green fire dying in her eyes. I realized then, and have known ever since, that there was something new to me in those eyes—something known only to her and the mountain. I was young then, and full of trigger itch; I thought that fewer wolves meant more deer, that no wolves meant hunter's paradise. But after seeing the green fire die, I sensed that neither the wolf nor the mountain agreed with such a view."(Leopold, 1966). Leopold referred to this transforming experience as "thinking like a mountain," and it later become a slogan for Deep Ecology as well as the title of a popular book in this area by John Seed and others. Much of Dhamma understanding and wisdom involves thinking like a mountain or nature from an ecocentric rather than an anthropocentric viewpoint. This same kind of thinking requires one to look within as well as without under a Dhamma and ecological perspective, i.e., to look at oneself and at one's relationships like a mountain.

DHAMMA AND ECOLOGY: In the process of enlightenment, Buddha examined himself to discover the true nature of the physical and mental structure. He penetrated the subtlest level and found that the entire physical structure of the material world was composed of subatomic particles (pali-attha kalapa). He further discovered that each subatomic particle consisted of the four elements: earth, water, fire, and air and their subsidiary characteristics. He found these particles are the basic building blocks of matter and that they are themselves constantly arising and passing away. They do this with great rapidity, trillions of times within a second. Thus there is no solidity in the material world, which is nothing but combustion and vibrations. Through experimentation, modern scientists have confirmed the findings of Buddha, that the entire material universe is composed of subatomic particles which rapidly arise and fall away. (Goenka, 1987)

With the ecological self or true self arising and breaking out of the prison-self of separate ego, moral exhortation becomes more and more irrelevant, particularly under non-self and Deep Ecology. Thus Dhamma or nature helps us to overcome our alienation from the world and its living creatures and changes the way we experience selfhood through an ever-widening process of identification with other living beings and forms of creation. In this process, the individual self is not simply trying to protect something in nature. Rather, the experience of self is extended to what it is trying to protect through the power of caring based on deep concern and identity.(Macy, 1990) In describing this identifying process, Seed, Director of the Rainforest Information Center in Australia, notes, " I try to remember that its not me, John Seed, trying to protect the rainforest. Rather, I'm part of the rainforest protecting myself. I am that part of the rainforest recently emerged into human thinking . . . I found the illusion of separation to be very flimsy, and that there are just a few conceptual filters that prevent us from being reunited with the earth . . . Recognizing our connection with nature is very simple and accessible regardless of where we are living." John Seed describes the shift from ego-self to eco-self as a, "spiritual change," which generates a deep interconnectedness with all forms of life.(Seed, 1992)

Meadows states, "In a situation of uncertainty, the appropriate procedure is careful assessment and slow experimentation, followed by constant, truthful evaluation of results and willingness to change strategies. It is possible to complement rational analysis with nonrational or super rational analysis-with intuition, insight, deep familiarity, respect, compassion . . . Nature has its own value,regardless of its values to humans." (Meadows, 1989)

This approach would certainly involve applying the teachings of Buddhism/Dhamma to situations of uncertainty in nature. The principle of reciprocity would certainly apply to the concept of "Oneness." It is recognized that the day-to-day maintenance of our life support system in nature is dependent on the functional interaction of countless interdependent biotic and physiochemical factors, including the impermanence of things in constant change. De Silva notes, "Since the inherent value of life is a core value in Buddhist ethical codes, the notion of reciprocity and interdependence fits in with the Buddhist notion of a causal system. A living entity cannot isolate itself from this causal nexus, and has no essence of its own. Reciprocity also conveys the idea of mutual obligation between nature and humanity, and between people." (DeSilva, 1990)

In his last novel, Island, Aldous Huxley writes, "Never give children a chance of imagining that anything exists in isolation. Make it plain from the very first that all living is relationship . . . 'Do as you would be done by' applies to our dealings with all kinds of life in every part of the world. We shall be permitted to live on this planet only for as long as we treat all nature with compassion and intelligence. Elementary ecology leads straight to elementary Buddhism."(Huxley, 1962) Rather than random groupings, populations of organisms characteristic of a particular environment are organized into a community. The community includes all living organisms (plant, animal, microorganisms) interacting in that particular environment and living together in a reasonably orderly manner. This living system or community and the abiotic components of the environment, along with the ecological processes that take place such as energy flow and water cycle, make up an ecosystem which is the result of the complex interplay between biological, physical, and historical forces. (Revelle and Revelle, 1992). Generally, high biodiversity is correlated with ecosystem stability.

However, like everything else, the community or ecosystem is subject to impermanence or change as well as the laws of nature or Dhamma. Thus individuals within populations arise, exist, and die while populations of species change in numbers, distribution, etc. Nothing is permanent. A Buddhist monk, Phra Prasak, said that he could observe impermanence in a forest by observing young trees, middle aged trees, and dying or dead trees. He could also observe this concept through the young, middle aged, and dying leaves on a single tree. (Phra Prasak, 1993). Succession involves change or impermanence as well as causality. From an ecological viewpoint, succession involves an orderly sequence of change, with different plant and/or animal communities succeeding one another over a period of time in a given area.

Ecotones are borderlines and zones of tension and transition between communities. While many communities may blend gradually into each other, there may sometimes be abrupt borders between them. Sharp physical boundaries, for example, create sharp ecotones or boundaries. Such boundaries may occur, for example, where the underlying geological formations cause the mineral content of the soil to abruptly change. These boundaries often map out the distribution of certain plants and animals. However, ecotones are generally blurred boundaries where the interfacing and intermixing of some species of each community occurs. (Rickles, 1976)

Under changing conditions, ecotones are dynamic; like all of nature, they disintegrate. There are no stable or static things. There are only ever-moving and ever-changing processes.(DeSilva, 1992). Thus, ecotones can be considered a transition between two or more diverse communities such as grassland and forest. Besides containing many of the organisms of each of the overlapping communities, an ecotonal community also contains organisms which are characteristic of, and often restricted to the ecotone. The tendency for increased variety and density at community junctions or ecotones is known as the edge effect. (Odum, 1971)

By walking the ecotones, it is possible to see a large variety of birds which like to live and feed in these boundary areas. The habitat of an organism is the physical surroundings or place where it lives or where one would go to find that particular organism. An organism's habitat includes both living and as well as nonliving elements. The ecological niche includes not only the physical space occupied by organism, but also includes the functional role of the organism in the community and environment.(Odum, 1971).

Thus, the ecological niche of an organism depends not only upon where it lives, but also on what it does in its behavior, transforming energy, modifying its physical and biotic environment, and how it is constrained by other species, particularly in predator and prey roles, all of which are subject to constant change or impermanence through internal and external change. It could be said that the habitat is the organism's address and the niche is its profession or way of life, biologically speaking.(Odum, 1971)

Territory often involves individuals, pairs, or family groups of vertebrates, and the higher invertebrates which commonly restrict their activities to a home range. If an area is actively defended, it is called a territory. However, territoriality can involve any active mechanism that spaces individuals or groups apart from one another, so that plants and microorganisms along with animals may be included within the definition. Territoriality tends to regulate populations at a level below the saturation point. (Odum, 1971) Under Liebig's Law of the Minimum, an organism must have essential materials which are necessary for growth and reproduction if it is to occur and thrive in a given situation or habitat. These basic requirements naturally vary with the species and situation. The essential material available in amounts most closely needed will thus tend to become the limiting one.

An organism, consequently, can be considered no stronger than the weakest link in its ecological chain of requirements. (Odum, 1971). This limiting factor could be water, a nutrient, absence of prey, etc. Under the Buddhist law of causality, a lack of any one of these in a given place or situation would account for the absence of a species. The food chain is considered the transfer of food energy from the source in plants through a series of organisms with repeated eating and being eaten. With each transfer, a large proportion (approximately 80 to 90 percent) of the potential energy is lost. Consequently, the number of steps or links in a sequence is usually limited to four or five. The nearer the organism to the beginning of the chain or the shorter the food chain, the greater the available energy. Thus, food chains can be visualized as ecological pyramids. Food chains are not isolated sequences but are interconnected with each other. The interlocking pattern of food chains is considered to be a food web. (Odum, 1971)

Food chains, as the channels for the constant flow of energy through the community, operate as energy flows/budgets under the first and second laws of thermodynamics. Energy inflows balance outflows under the first law, while each energy transfer is accompanied by a dispersion of energy into unavailable heat under the second law. (Odum, 1971). Under biological magnification, organisms are united through food chains. Materials taken up by the prey can accumulate and become concentrated in their predators. Thus, passage of substances through several trophic levels in a community could result in concentrations hundreds of times those that were initially present in the environment. The greatly magnified indirect results of pesticides like DDT present a striking case of biological magnification. (National Research Council, 1986). The accumulation of dukkha and sankaras (unpleasant experiences) would offer some analogy to this process.

Many ecologists believe that predation and competition for space, food, and other resources are the two main forces that determine what species are found in particular communities. How abundant a species is in a community is often determined by how well it meets the challenge of predation. How well a species competes with other species present will often determine whether it will obtain enough resources to survive and reproduce. Under the principle of competitive exclusion, two organisms cannot live in the same habitat, occupy the same niche and use the same resources on an indefinite basis.

Eventually, the better competitor will eliminate the weaker species from the community. (Revelle and Revelle, 1992) There are complex linkages between species in ecosystems with the result that the effects of changes are often indirect in terms of competition, predation, and other interrelationships. Obvious and direct influences are sometimes not as important as indirect influences which are less obvious. Keystone species are those species which exert influences over other members of their ecological communities out of proportion to their abundance. Keystone species can have various roles and important linkages to various species in ecological communities. It is also recognized that each individual in a sexually reproducing population is unique. (National Research Council, 1986)

As Devall notes, "The Dharma teaches us that all is impermanent. All is changing. Change, in the form of evolution,has no direction, no finality. However, evolutionary change tends to develop greater diversity. Protection of biodiversity is another precept of an ecocentric Sangha." (Devall, 1990) In discussing these natural systems, Meadows notes four principles:

- Everything is connected to everything else;
- Systems are more than the sum of their parts; they are dominated by their inter-relationships and their purposes;
- Systems are organized into hierarchies, which means that everything is connected to everything else, but not equally strongly; and
- Natural systems are finely tuned and resilient. Diversity increases this resilience. In considering tropical forest ecosystems as natural systems, Meadows states: "[they] . . . are designed so that subsystems take care of most of their own needs and purposes yet simultaneously serve the needs of the larger aggregate system. This harmony between the subsystems and the total system creates tremendous stability, resilience, and efficiency. Every species in a rainforest maintains its own integrity yet contributes to the interlocking web that constitutes a productive ecosystem." (Meadows, 1989).

TROPICAL FORESTS

In the Asian and Pacific Region, tropical forests, particularly in their natural state, contribute many values to the lives of human and other beings. From a public participation and Buddhist perspective, it is important to know some of concepts and values necessary to keeping tropical forests in natural states. This information is particularly needed with the rapid destruction and degradation of tropical forests now occurring in Asia and the Pacific as well as other parts of the world.

According to the National Academy of Sciences, each year at least 50 million acres of rainforest (an area the size of Nevada in the United States) disappears forever. If the destruction of the tropical rainforests continues at its current rate of over 150 acres a minute, tropical forests will be gone before 2025-within the span of a single lifetime. (Rainforest Action Network, 1993).

GLOBAL FUTURE states, "the best projections indicated that unless governments, individually and collectively, take action, much of the world's tropical forests will be scattered and highly degraded remnants by the first quarter of the 21st century." (Council on Environmental Quality, 1981). Protected areas such as national parks and wildlife refuges may well be the only feasible and permanent way of saving some of the remaining natural tropical forests areas and their rich biological diversity. The Buddhist community, particularly Buddhist Forest Monasteries, have been strong proponents of protection of natural tropical forests.

Meetings, conferences, and other gatherings have been organized through Buddhist Monks to call attention to tropical forest destruction, much of which is operating on an illegal basis. Buddhist Monks actually "ordained" trees so that they would not be cut by illegal loggers, but even these desperate measures did not work in a number of occasions. Nevertheless, the Buddhist community, with its strong basis for a reverence for all forms of life, continues to press for forest protection through education and other measures.

As previously noted, forests and trees have played an important part in the life of Buddha and Buddhism. As the royal ruler in one of the Buddhist countries in Southeast Asia, Thailand, H.H. King Bhumibol Adulyadej, on his sixty-fifth birthday (December 5, 2537 or 1994) made the following pronouncement on forest protection" In order to make the forest flourish, it is not necessary to plant one more tree. What is more important is to let the trees that are there grow of themselves and not to interfere with them. Just to protect them and not harm them is enough. This royal statement was quoted in a brochure by an organization of farmers in Northern Thailand who, in combination with Buddhist monks, pledged to ordain thousands of trees and to create an awareness of forests and their needs for protection.

The ceremonies involved placing orange robes on trees as part of the ordination so that they might be regarded as ordained "monks." Tropical forests are moist and dry forests in the humid tropics where temperature and rainfall are high and the dry season is short. These closed (non-logged) and broad-leaved forests are a global resource. Located almost entirely in developing countries, where population is expected to double in the next 25 years, tropical forests are extremely important to all life everywhere on planet Earth.

Tropical forests are the richest and most diverse expression of life that has evolved on earth. Their continuous history spans more than 50 million years in some areas. Tropical forests approximate the primeval forest biomes from which they originally evolved and contain well over half of the world's estimated 10 to 100 million species of plants and animals. Tropical forests are complex and fragile ecosystems with webs of interlocking, interdependent relationships among diverse plant and animal species and their non-living environments. Irreversibly, tropical forests are literally disappearing within our lifetimes. Nearly half of the original areas of tropical forests have either been destroyed or degraded over the past 100 years. Major causes of tropical forest destruction are:

- Shifting cultivation which is responsible for nearly half of the total forests destroyed each year,
- Clearance for new settlements,
- Timber extraction for fuel, construction, and imports (Japan, South Korea, the United States, and Western Europe are major timber importers, and
- Clearance for cattle raising.

Many tropical forests are too complex and their species too diverse to regenerate themselves from this destruction or to be managed on a sustained yield basis. Thus, tropical forest destruction must be considered permanent and irreversible.

Worldwide recognition is growing that, in addition to the conservation efforts of the tropical countries, tropical forest destruction is an urgent global problem which requires international action and assistance. In addition, greater awareness of the values and concepts of tropical forests is required by the public, thoughtful leaders, including Buddhist monks, nuns, and lay-persons, and decision-makers. It is vital to address not only the destruction but the reasons why we should not destroy the oldest, richest, most complex, and most productive ecosystems on Planet Earth.

By maintaining intact tropical forests in as close to natural condition as possible, they can make immensely diverse, productive, and valuable contributions to all life on earth on a long-range basis. Present and future protected areas in or near national parks and refuges may well be the only feasible and permanent way of saving some of the remaining tropical forests and their rich biological diversity.

Because the loss of tropical forests is irreversible, so are the negative consequences which include:

- Loss of biodiversity with loss of not only individual life forms (approximately 250 species lost daily) but also alteration or annihilation of entire evolutionary processes with tropical forests containing 50-90% of all plant and animal species,
- Destruction of forest-based societies, with more than one thousand rainforest cultures existing in conflict with development strategies,
- Land degradation and soil erosion, with most nutrients contained in the vegetation rather than the soil, which turns into a desert after a short period without trees,
- Floods and droughts through deforestation, which diminishes the ability of soil to hold water (the Thai government banned rainforest logging after severe flooding and mudslides from deforestation killed approximately 200 villagers),
- Climatic disruption through deforestation with loss of rainfall and ecological services, and
- Increase of impoverishment and famine by ignoring the value of rainforest goods and services to local human populations. (World Rainforest Movement, (1991)

In listing some of the values of tropical forests, it is recognized that values are complex in both interpretation and influence, but still we must try (Note: Much of the following is summarized from the author's article, "Tropical Forest Values in Protected Areas," TIGER PAPERS [October-December, 1991]). Biological Diversity: Tropical forests are the most diverse and complex biomes on earth, from both an ecological and general biological perspective. From 50-90% of all species on earth live in tropical forests. Yet tropical forests cover only 6% of the planet's land surface.

The earth's tropical forests are estimated to contain most of the 10 to 100 million species of plants and animals (many are insects) in contrast to the 1.7 million which are now officially classified. But we are losing more than 200 species daily according to conservative scientific estimates. A typical four square mile area of any given tropical forest may contain up to 1,500 species of flowering plants, 750 species of trees, 125 species of mammals, 400 species of birds, 100 species of reptiles, 60 species of amphibians, and 150 species of butterflies. The number of individuals of each species per unit tends to be low, but the total number of species can be enormous. As the most complex and diverse ecosystem on Earth, tropical forests are rich webs of interlocking and fragile relationships among plant and animal species and among these species and their non- living environment. Most species in tropical forests are scattered and highly specialized, with very low population density. For example, only one tree species may be present in a sample area. Without adequate areas to sustain reproduction and vital ecological interrelationships, tropical forests are extremely susceptible to extinction.

Species Protection

The value of protecting known and unknown species of plants and animals is of rapidly growing importance. The intimate and complex linkages of tropical forest species to numerous others require more attention to habitat preservation than is necessary in temperate areas. Thus the protection of species and of their natural habitat are one and the same process. Each species is a unique original, just like a rare original painting—and for each, extinction is forever. While the good and potential good that tropical forest species provide is also justification enough for their protection, many believe that plants and animals have a right to exist and to carry on their struggle for survival for no higher value than for their own sake. Also, the better known or more spectacular species attract public support for the habitat that also contains less known or unknown species.

Agricultural/Industrial/Medical

These economic uses depend, directly and indirectly, on the biological diversity and genetic pool associated with the above. At present, human populations utilize only about 20 plants of the many thousands of plants known to be edible such as perennial corn of Mexico and the winged bean of tropical forest ecosystems of South East Asia. Tropical forests can provide a wide range of genetic materials for industry. More than 40% of the world's drugs, with a commercial value of more than $40 billion per year are obtained from wild plants or are synthesized from wild derivatives. Plant drugs from tropical forests are usually inexpensive as well as an accepted part of the culture of many Asian and Pacific countries. A recent item by Rainforest Action Network states: A tree in the Malaysian rainforest that promised some hope in the fight against AIDS has been cut down. Teams in the field are still looking for the tree whose latex-like sap could be the source of the compound. The first sample of the derivative Calanolide A was taken from the tree Calophyllum lanigerum and was highly effective against virus HIV-1.Soejarto heads plant-hunting teams funded by the National Cancer Institute. Scientists have been unable to find a similar one, according to plant researcher D.D. Soejarto of the University of Chicago who investigates plants in Southeast Asia in hopes of finding new medicines. (Rainforest Action Network, 1993)

Tropical Forest People

Approximately 200 million people live within or on the margins of tropical forests. Their tropical forest environments provide these populations with food (e.g., fruits, wild animals, nuts, fish, honey, etc.) and raw materials for fuel, wood, clothes, buildings, and medicine. Indigenous forest dwelling tribal people are distinguished by their special relationships with tropical forests; they are completely dependent upon natural tropical forests for their livelihood and welfare. Their cultures have evolved in harmony with this environment, and their identity and life styles are tied to living in tropical forests permanently.

Development in tropical forests brings pressures on traditional forest dwellers with disastrous results for their survival and culture.

Inevitably, native tribes fall prey to outside diseases, weapons, technology, alcohol, and drugs imported by outside cultures. Thus, entire tribal societies and their native knowledge and wisdom about their tropical forest environment are rapidly disappearing as their natural role in these ancient ecosystems is destroyed.

Scientific Research

In their natural or near natural states, tropical forests present the oldest, most diverse, and complex ecosystems for scientific research. Charles Darwin and Alexander von Humboldt are only two of many great scientists whose scientific contributions depended primarily on their tropical forest experiences. These forests offer insights into the ecological and evolutionary processes for basic and applied research. One tree species was even found to be pollinated by a mouse.

The fact is clear: tropical forests contain the answers to basic questions which have not even been asked yet. One noted tropical forest scientist, Gerardo Budowski, believes that the loss of tropical forests to the scientific community would be irreparable. He considers tropical forests to be "living laboratories" and "a factory and storehouse of genetic diversity" which contains "incredible variations in life forms, functions, behavior, and interrelationships of which we know very little at present . . . (where) new discoveries take place every day."

Watersheds

Tropical forests protect watersheds. In their natural or near-natural states, they retain water and release it gradually throughout the year. Tropical forest watersheds are thus able to maintain and restore reliable supplies of high quality water which benefits surrounding and downstream needs. More than 40 percent of farmers in developing countries live in villages which depend on the sponge-effects of tropical forests to absorb and slowly release water.

Soil Protection

Tropical forest soils are fragile, of poor quality, and unsuited for agriculture. Almost all the nutrients are found in living vegetation rather than in the soil. With deforestation, the thin layer of topsoil quickly washes away. The remaining soils rapidly deteriorate and lose their fertility, leaving hard-packed clay or sand that is limited to only one or two more poorly nourished crops or to very short-term grazing. Thus the very productive land of tropical forests becomes a virtual desert when its poor soil is exposed through deforestation. Maintenance of the Web of Life: Ecological interactions in tropical forests impact on life and conditions throughout the world. Destroying a link in these delicate interactions produces repercussions which can sometimes be observed, such as serious disturbances in bird migrations far into both the northern and southern hemispheres. Most repercussions, however, are difficult to predict. For example, the removal of tropical forest may result in increased insect, rodent, and other pest infestations in nearby agricultural and village areas where birds and other natural predators of these pests had depended on the now-damaged and destroyed forests for their survival.

Climatic

By their physical presence on the planet's continents, tropical forests make essential contributions to local, regional, and global climate. The influences of tropical forests on climate is another area that is not fully understood. It is recognized, however, that tropical forests do serve as moderating and maintenance influences for climatic stability. Rainforests generate local and global rainfall, receiving 50% of all the rain that falls on the land.

Spiritual

Human beings are innately spiritual creatures capable of, and drawn to, abstract thought. Although intangible, spiritual values and influences are clearly present and appreciated by most human beings who travel in tropical forests. The prolific diversity and enormous variety of innumerable life forms in tropical forests create a powerfully spiritual environment, endlessly different and surprising as the most mysterious of all natural worlds. This spiritual response obviously has significant impact on virtually all human beings, regardless of their spiritual, social, or cultural backgrounds.

Creativity

The art, writing, poetry, photography, and other creative endeavors of a country and culture draw upon its environment. Tropical forests provide a unique, mysterious, and natural environment of complex, changing beautiful mosaics with great potential for creativity, stimulation of the senses, and as a rich source of artistic inspiration. The wide diversity of tropical forest life forms and colors produces an esthetically rich landscape and myriad images which can inspire the natural human sense of wonder, and refresh the human connection with nature and innate human creativity.

Cultural

Tropical forests are intimately related to the cultures of tropical peoples through diverse influences on the entire range of knowledge, traditions, and values of the cultures. These tropical forest influences may range from concrete, economic uses such as firewood and fuel to such less tangible values as scenery and "atmosphere" in the lives and well-being of tropical people. Thus tropical cultures are very much a product of the unique interface between people and tropical forests.

Outdoor Recreation

National parks and reserves of selected areas of tropical forests can provide outdoor recreation for the general public. With the increased hours of leisure now available in many developing countries, people find time to experience the unique form of outdoor recreation available in tropical forests. Although outdoor recreation in tropical forests is in its early stages, visitations have increased significantly. Outdoor recreation in natural areas can draw on the rich diversity, superlative wonders, and unique scenery of natural tropical forests.

Ecotourism

The new concept of combining tourism and ecology/natural history in tropical forests holds a great deal of promise. Ecotourism or nature-oriented tourism is based on the use of natural areas, including scenery, topography, water features, plant life, and wildlife. A recent World Wildlife Fund study defined it as, "traveling to undisturbed natural areas to study or just to admire and enjoy the scenery and its wild plants and animals as well as exotic cultures. " Ecotourism often combines elements of scientific investigation, recreation, and adventure (real or synthetic).

Educational

Tropical forests can serve as living museums, inspiring classrooms to a variety of formal and informal activities. Developing naturalist interpretive programs about tropical forests for the general public may include self-guiding nature walks, naturalist conducted walks, natural history exhibits, slide programs, popular publications, and other activities.

New knowledge of the ecology and natural history of tropical forests will greatly contribute to and enhance the understanding, appreciation, and enjoyment of the public.

This type of knowledge also motivates and increases public support for conservation in general and for tropical forests in particular. Use of tropical forests for formal education is rapidly increasing in Asia and the Pacific in the form of field trips and studies at various levels, including the graduate level.

Future Generations

Concerns and responsibilities for tropical forests must extend to future as well as present generations because these threatened ecosystems are highly susceptible to irreversible removal or very serious and damaging reductions, resulting in loss of natural values and options for survival and quality of life.

The moral obligation to protect tropical forests for future generations of one species, Homo sapiens, must extend to future generations of all species, known and unknown. In short, the active ongoing protection of natural tropical forests for their own sake for the future is essential. Future generations of all forms of life require that tropical forests be protected in an intact and natural state.

Humankind needs tropical forests. But tropical forests could survive quite well—in fact, better—without human presence and impact. It is only within intact natural tropical forest environments that diverse and interdependent forest species can carry on their struggle for survival and evolution. In addition to any conservation measures to protect earth's tropical forests, efforts need to be increased to safeguard tropical forests for future generations of all life by establishing and maintaining national parks and reserves.

The values associated with tropical forests deserve understanding, appreciation, and emphasis, for in them we find deep values for the immediate present and for countless future generations of all life: the protection of natural tropical forests as a vital part of the earth's biosphere. We must be assured that generations yet to come benefit from tropical forests and share their dynamic values for the survival and quality of all life on earth.(Henning, 1991)

6 Dhamma/Deep Ecology Experiential Exercises

Reading Plato or listening to a lecture on T.S. Eliot doesn't educate the whole human being; like courses in physics or chemistry, it merely educates the symbol manipulator and leaves the rest of the living mind-body in its pristine state of ignorance and ineptitude. (Huxley, 1962) A variety of exercises and approaches lend themselves to reconnecting people with nature on an ecological, experiential basis. The best emphasize experience over intellectual knowledge. Some of these methods, exercises, and approaches are presented in this chapter.

The nature and mechanics of these exercises are as follows: Buddhism and Deep Ecology Trip Susan Offrer recalled her experience under the tutelage of renowned forest monk, Phra Prachak: It was called a Buddhism and Deep Ecology Trip. I knew we would be walking in Dong Yai forest for one week with Phra Prachak, the forest monk well-known for his conservation efforts and tree ordination ceremonies, but I didn't really understand what "deep ecology" meant. Thinking like a Mountain, a book by John Seed on "I am a leaf," he said. "We are all leaves. We share life needs and life processes. We become alive, grow. wither, and die. We are dependent on each other in one interconnected ecosystem." Asked how he managed to continue his struggle to save the forest with so much positive energy in the face of government pressure and military threats, he replied:

"Is that rock over there heavy? Not if you don't lift it. Remember that now in your life: if you don't lift it, it isn't heavy." At every rest along the trail Luang Phor shared spiritual philosophy and practical wisdom. He taught us we have a responsibility to promote social justice for all creation, not just humanity. We did not enter the forest alone. Villagers carrying enormous food packs, monks and nuns with food bowls and glots, and backpacks, illustrated our attachment to material comforts and convenience. We trudged through cassava fields into the forest, dense undergrowth, thorn and vines impeded every step, tangling our hair and raking our skin. Luang Phor Prachak disciplined us through walking meditation.

After meditation and chanting and hot drinks, we began our trek, around 10 a.m. for the day's lone meal. We walked several hours, pausing to mourn at huge, felled trees blocking our path. Two logging gangs we met reminded us these trees are lumber that support their families. Clearly, forest conservation is not a black-and-white issue.

Each night we camped amid dense jungle. No cleared, level campsites. Lots of nocturnal forest life joined us as we slept; we heard scamperings, hummings, and rustlings. Our drinking water dissipated quickly despite the numerous tanks the villagers carried for us. Water became a key concern. We found water in slow trickles, a muddy puddles, or in the dark soup of decaying leaves. Hot chocolate or sweet coffee disguised the taste and color of water we would not have wanted to bathe in before. Droppings at water's edge showed elephants bathed and drank there. So why couldn't we?

Our days were variegated by changes in terrain, talks by environmentalists in the group, and regular gatherings by candlelight among the trees. After the silent walking, we shared painful experiences of nature's destruction and joyful experiences of nature's wonder. Luang Phor Prachak told us of his struggle for this forest—protests, arrests, and ongoing conservation efforts.

In one of our rituals, we each imagined ourselves as one part of nature, and spoke out about its life and experiences. We heard the "voice" of leaf, hornbill, otter, air, eucalyptus, and water buffalo. Then, the eldest villager roared: "I AM AN ELEPHANT!" When he had finished his story, we knew further logging of this forest would be the death sentence for the elephants roaming there. Mid-trip, we scattered to split up and spend 24 hours alone, contemplating and observing the forest. Luang Phor Prachak coached us how to deal with fear in the darkness of the wild. Our solitude became a waking dream filled with the roar of elephants nearby, flashes of intense fear or an unseen animal lying down to sleep beside an umbrella tent. We gathered at our next noon meal, feeling a part of forest life, yearning to coexist without endangering nature, realizing that to do so would endanger ourselves. 101 We walked through kilometre after kilometre of eucalyptus plantation that had supplanted the rich diversity of the forest. Charged by our powerful experience, we separated after committing ourselves to concrete action to preserve the environment, in particular this forest in Buri Ram.

Each of us understood Deep Ecology in ways shaped by our personal belief systems. Though our experiences differed, we shared a spiritual philosophy of the environment. To me, Deep Ecology recognizes the sacredness of creation, our humble role in it, and our responsibility, now, to reverse the damage we have so carelessly done through neglect, over-consumption, and greed. It also emphasizes the interdependence of all beings and parts of nature, the need for us to identify with these parts, and join with them in their cry for survival. If we destroy them, we destroy the balance that guarantees our own survival. We are leaves. They neither possess, nor control, nor take more than they require. We must learn to be leaves."(Offrer, 1993)

A basic understanding of simple ecological concepts is essential. Some of these concepts were discussed in the previous chapter. Literature on the subject can be obtained at almost every library and there are now large numbers of paperbacks on ecology available. Elementary ideas and principles of ecology can be understood by anyone. Human relationships with nature should be based on an understanding of ecology principles. All living things, including human beings, are related and interdependent with one another in some manner.

What affects or influences one form of life will, directly or indirectly, affect others. Ecological concepts to be studied on walks include: habitats, food chains or pyramids, biodiversity, territoriality, succession, competition, ecotones, niches, biomes, adaptations and energy flows. With a little imagination, these concepts can be reduced to simple ideas. For example, biodiversity can be illustrated by simply counting the large number of species of plants, trees, insects and other life forms in a given area. Ecotones can be identified as boundary areas, for example, between forest and grassland communities.

In a tropical forest, competition for sunlight is a very important concept in tree and plant distribution. The tops of the tallest dominant trees make up the canopy layer which receives full sunlight. Thus it produces more food than does any other layer and many birds, animals, fungi, and insects live there. Shorter trees grow beneath the canopy and form the understory. These understory trees receive less sunlight than canopy trees and consequently produce less food. Some understory trees may eventually join the canopy layer. The shrub layer beneath the understory consists of many shrubs or woody plants that have more than one stem, while the herb layer beneath the shrub layer is made of soft-stemmed plants.(Camp, 1984)

HOW TO LEAD ECOLOGY WALKS

Begin with background reading on ecology. Otherwise, a group may be exposed to a random bunch of plant and animal names with little ecological understanding or insight. Ecology, the study of interrelationships between plants, animals, and their environment, provides a central focus for the walks. It also offers a means for illustrating the inter- dependencies of people Look for special survival strategies. Some plants have developed reflective blue cells to use the light of the forest's dim understory. Berry bushes offer birds fruit in exchange for spreading their seeds Berries contain a mild laxative that ensurses the seeds are deposited rather than digested. Owls hunt at night when most small mammals are active. The bright coloring of warblers ensurses the purity of their genetic line in a woods shared by a dozen closely related cousins.

The forest floor consists of the soil, small living organisms, and droppings. Almost all the nutrients of the forest are contained in the leaves associated with the forest floor layer. Some trees shed their leaves all at once, enabling them to grow a new crop while recycling the old crop at their feet. Some trees even kill others to feast on the falling leaves. Many species linger as shrubs or seeds in the dim light of the under story. A storm rages and a giant tree falls, tearing an opening in the canopy that permits sunlight to reach the forest floor. A race to claim the new opening ensues. The winner flourishes as a new monarch of the forest. Losers wither and wait.

In a tropical forest, the majority of life thrives in the canopy. Wildlife is often difficult to observe during the day. Most animals feed at night. Overnight trips present more opportunities for observing nocturnal wildlife. During the day, bird and insect life, including butterflies, add much to ecology walks. Every area offers something to illustrate ecology concepts. Ask someone familiar with ecology to take you for a short nature walk. Your guide will note several examples in a short time and distance.

You will be amazed at how much your understanding of the how's, why's, and wonders of the area and its life have increased. Too often, without ecological observation, we walk cut off from this rich and essential understanding. Planning ecology walks requires familiarity with the area and its life. A wealth of information and literature is usually available for most general localities through libraries, natural history museums and government agencies. A knowledge of some of the common names of the plants, birds, insects and other animals in the area can be learned from field guides before and during the walk or by a pre-trip with a local individual. The best field guides have pictures and simple identifications so that everyone can get involved in looking up the name of that "new" wild flower, tree, bird or animal.

Conducting the walk

With the emphasis on ecology, it is helpful to formulate and define the general objectives of the walk before departing. People usually see only what they are looking for. Objectives build a sound environmental attitude. These objectives should relate to the interdependence and interrelations of living things as well as the role and responsibility of people. If several walks are planned for one area, each walk might stress a particular or general aspect of life, e.g. water, insects, soil. Other aspects then can be related:

the relationship of water to plant life, the relationship of water to wildlife, and so forth.

It would be interesting, for example, to have a walk with the objective centering strictly upon the influences and history of people on a given area in terms of environmental quality. But objectives should not be rigid. Flexibility, fun, interest, and the "unexpected" should also be guiding principles in this experience.

It is perfectly proper to say, "I don't know," when necessary. An effort should, however, be made to find out. Attention should be directed to what the leader does know as well as leading the group in possible explanations. It is essential to keep one's objectives in mind throughout the walk in reference to:

(a) showing the interrelationship of different forms of life,

(b) stressing the interdependence of life,

(c) introducing ecological ideas, and

(d) pointing out the role and responsibilities of people on the basis of the above.

The names of plants and animals need not be overemphasized. One should not "lose sight of the forest for the trees."

Nevertheless learning exercises such as counting the different plant species to illustrate biological diversity, observing the canopy and other forest layers, or searching for obvious signs of competition and ecotones, can be very helpful in illustrating ecological ideas and relationships. A good learning situation should be created. A leader should be enthusiastic in helping other members of the group enjoy these natural wonders. Questions and humor should be encouraged. Informal conversation on the walk should be directed toward ecology and environmental responsibility, with special reference to involvement and participation. The leader should walk at the head of the group, keeping the members together at all times. When stopping to make explanations, eye contact with all members of the group is important.

The group should experience the various forms of life encountered through all senses, e.g., listening for sounds of wildlife, feeling soil texture, touching, tasting, and smelling plant and tree life as well as seeing. It is often interesting, particularly for the children, to tell a brief story about a plant or animal from the previous sources mentioned.

It is often meaningful, however, to have the members walk in silence for some time, preferably with a considerable space of about 100 meters between them. Continuous conversation and communication of any kind may sometimes result in "small talk" and distract from the natural experience and awareness in nature. Contemplation and reflection on nature through silent periods should be incorporated into the walk so that the participants can "absorb" the total experience.

After The Walk

At the conclusion of the ecology walk, the leader summarizes the group's observations and members share their experiences and ideas. Most facts and details are easily forgotten, but people will usually remember major ideas about ecology and their personal involvement.

AWARENESS EXERCISES IN NATURE

Exercises in nature should be simple, easy to explain and to carry out, while addressing adults and children alike. Long explanations and details may distract the general outlook and/ or inhibit the participants in their free expression and participation. Some of the following exercises could be applied to indoor as well as outdoor experiences. Awareness of the six sense-doors: The six sense-doors as described in the Buddhist teachings are: Ears, eyes, nose, tongue, body, and mind.

Close your eyes, close your nose with one hand and gently breathe through the mouth and listen. Try to put the whole consciousness into the sense of hearing. What are the sounds you encounter? Sounds near you or in the distance, sounds from the wind and animals such as birds and insects. Close your ears with your hands and open your eyes, note everything that your eyes encounter, the colors, shapes and forms, the light, the dark, the shadows and movements. Close your eyes again and see what your nose will experience. Take a few deep breaths and smell . . . Then breathe through your mouth and try to distinguish between different tastes of the air, the air that enters your body and the air that leaves your body when breathing out.

Walk around and touch the trees, leaves, berries, flowers, grass or water; whatever is there, touch it gently and examine the different surfaces of form. Let your mind wander for a while. What does the surrounding environment remind you of? Recall pictures from the past and see how they affect your present mind. or evaluates, observe that. Don't get involved with the thoughts or try to change them. Just observe them. We understand by doing. After fifteen or so minutes of observation, you may begin to notice the part of you that's observing.

Give yourself time in which you will not be disturbed. Decide for that time to do nothing but observe. Sit or lie comfortably. Be still and be.

The mind will present some good ideas to do something else. Do nothing with these ideas—simply observe them. Emotions will want something more exciting. Do not fulfill them. Observe them. The body will demand attention. Do not attend to it. Observe its demands. Notice how ideas, feelings, and body demands are impermanent and changing in form and intensity just as nature is always changing.

If you ache to change positions, do not. Just observe the desire to change positions. If you itch, do not scratch. Observe the itch. Your mind, body, and emotions may become agitated. Observe the agitation. You gain authority over them by doing nothing, by simply observing. You can extend sitting observation to moving or walking observation. As you move through nature, observe everything. Observe your reactions to everything.

Observation is a basic tool of awareness. The more you observe what you are normally unconscious of, the more conscious you become.(Roger and McWilliams, 1990). Thus, you will notice the small, dead leaf on the trail, the orange brown butterfly on the tree trunk, the different colors of green in tree leaves, the small bird flitting through a distant canopy, and other of nature's phenomena and impermanence by really observing and becoming aware and conscious of nature.

Looking for signs of impermanence

Find signs of impermanence in your present environment. Look for natural indications of dying or death such as dried leaves or fallen trees, dead insects, rotting fruit, etc. Also look for signs of "arising" such as buds, new young leaves, seedling trees, etc. And, finally, look for indications of "existing" with regular trees, flowers blooming, insects crawling, etc. It may be possible to find all of these signs of impermanence on the same tree.

Outside a natural area, observe artificial indications such as roads, electric overland cables, logging sites, dams, and other changes brought about by humankind. What impacts have these changes had on the land? Inside the natural area, observe signs or impacts of human beings such as trees that might have been illegally cut, littering, pithed or burned out trees. Discuss in the group how these different signs or indications of impermanence affect your emotions and thoughts.

Observing Nature

Observation of nature is a tool of acceptance. To observe is to think, feel, taste, smell, hear and see without attachment or judgment. Observe whatever information your senses offer.

Looking for the Elements

Acknowledge in your surrounding environment the different manifestations of the four basic elements with their corresponding qualities: earth (solidity), water (fluidity/coercion), fire (temperature), air (motion). Remember your birth—and then the time in your mother's womb. Now meditate on your history as it was told in the lives of your parents and grandparents—and all the great-great-grandparents. Consider how many grandparents have contributed to your genetic history. With your observer, pick out what characteristics you see in yourself. Choose one of your grandparents as a guide if you wish.

Speak to them. Going back 15 generations, about 400 years, your direct ancestors number about 32,000. Go back another 15 generations to the Middle Ages and your lineage expands to relate to the entire population of Asia, or Europe, if that's where your roots are. These people are survivors. They have come through plagues, wars, invasions, earthquakes, great floods and fires.

Now zoom back several thousand years to about 8000 B.C. at the beginning of agriculture and sedentary village and city life. Join your family as they learn to plant seeds, domesticate animals, and trade. Consider and regard the night sky through their eyes.

Continue your journey back through the thousands of years humanity lived peacefully as hunter-gatherers, and again consider the night sky and the powerful earth forces that shaped your dreams and the way you relate to the world.

Now go back to the dawn of our species when we were emerging as toolmaking, communicating, loving creatures. And even before when our history fades into the millions of years of evolution from single-celled life to complex, beautiful forms such as dinosaurs, giant tigers, and dolphins. I see a thing . . . This game can be carried out while walking or sitting while outdoors. One of the participants chooses one object in the surrounding environment and says: "I see a thing and it is. . . .(i.e. green, round, long, making a sound, etc.) Now the other participants can ask for more characteristics which are answered only with yes or no. The participants have to guess what the object is and the one who guesses can select the next object.

GUIDED MEDITATIONS TO TRACE OUR ECOLOGICAL/ HISTORICAL ROOTS

There is an "observer" in all of us. We will use this observer in this exercise to connect us to the universe and to "all of our relations," as the Native Americans expressed it, so that we can better experience and understand our ecological history and roots from a Deep Ecology perspective.

Close your eyes. Take ten deep breaths, mindfully breathing in and out. Keep your body relaxed and let your observer go back slowly through your personal history, not just your own actions and big events in your life, but also the story of your whole being, how your body has changed, how your character and personality have developed and evolved in your personal history. Observe your history, yesterday, last week, last year, back to your childhood.

And still go back even before life began on earth, when the atoms which compose our bodies were being transformed by the earth's physical processes. We were present at the birth of the earth as our sun and the solar system were formed from stardust as it exploded and whirled through the cosmos. We were present at the beginning when the cosmos was a point of energy responding to the "I Am" of the Creator. Rest here at the point of the beginning let the story find its source at the center of your being.

Now begin at the beginning and dream your history forward to the present. Remember, the stars and galaxies that formed the building blocks of your; body the supernova that gave birth to our sun and solar system; the earth that gathered stardust and processed it into living matter; the air, fire, water, and earth that transforms all things and are the basic elements for all things. Your story is shared by myriad animals, the two-legged ones that represent your species, the birds, the fishes, the creeping and crawling creatures, all living things that have been in your ecological and historical roots. Come back and slowly gather your ancestors, thanking them for their contribution to the unique manifestation of the cosmic story that is yourself. Place this history at the center of your being as a sacred treasure. Come back now to the present and those who are gathered around you. Become more aware of your breathing as you mindfully take ten deep breaths and then open your eyes. When you are ready, you can get up. (adapted from Kirsch, n.d.)

RITUALISTIC EXPERIENCES

The sacredness of the earth not only calls us to ecological consciousness, it calls us to perform rituals that honor that sacredness. Through such rituals we place ourselves within The earth community and, at the same time, bring to it the unique gift which we as humans have to offer, self-reflective celebration. The creation ritual is a response to the affection nature bestows on us. (Kirsch, 1988)

THE TEN-STEP EVOLUTION METHOD DEEP

1. Begin with yourself today. Examine the many non-self elements that have combined to make you what you are

today. Contemplate the many people, the places, and the events that have shaped your life and brought you here to this meditation tonight.

2. Go back to your birth, the day that convention says your life began. However, you were already a fully formed human infant at birth. You had existed in your mother's womb for seven to nine months before your birth. Go back to the moment that a sperm from your father entered an egg from your mother to create your unique genetic constitution, the information that makes you what you are today: your sex, your eye color, your height and weight, and many of your behaviors. Contemplate the conditions existing when you were conceived and when you were born. Consider the lives of your parents. Who were they? Where did they live? How did they live? What were their greatest joys? What were their greatest sorrows?

3. If we look a little deeper, we can see the egg and sperm that joined to create your genetic constitution had already existed for a long time before they joined together. We know from biology that the egg your mother contributed had already divide to determine which genes she would pass on to you while your mother was still a fetus inside her mother. Consider the time of the birth of your parents. Contemplate their parents, your four grandparents. Who were they? Where did they live? How did they live? What were their greatest joys? What were their greatest sorrows?

4. Continue looking deeper into your origins. Go back in time 1,000 years, approximately thirty to forty generations. One thousand years ago you had millions of ancestors. The genes present in every cell of your body tonight were then shared among those millions of ancestors; they were spread out around the world, in Europe, Asia, North America, Africa. Who were they? Where did they live? How did they live? What were their greatest joys? What were their greatest sorrows?

5. Go back to 100,000 years ago. You then had uncounted ancestors. They were humans physically similar to us today, but separated by evolutionary change over many

generations. Your many ancestors then lived in Africa, Europe, and Asia. Who were they? Where did they live? How did they live? What were their greatest joys? What were their greatest sorrows?

6. A million years ago. All your ancestors were in Africa. They were primitive humans who possessed the first awakenings of human awareness. Look out over the African savanna; you were there, in the form of your ancestors. Who were they? Where did they live? How did they live? What were their greatest joys? What were their greatest sorrows?
7. Ten million years ago, before the time of humans. Our ancestral stream has now been joined by the ancestors of our closest relatives: chimps, gorillas, and orangs. Our journey backwards through our ancestral stream has brought us back to a primitive ape in central Africa. It is more and more difficult to see ourselves in our distant ancestors, but continue. Who were they? Where did they live? How did they live? What were their greatest joys? What were their greatest sorrows?
8. One hundred million years ago. The world is a very different place. We would not even recognize the continents if we could look at the earth of 100,000,000 years ago from outer space. Dinosaurs were common in Montana and around the world at that time. Our ancestors were a small species of primitive mammal. They had hair, our five digits, and our breasts. We have now been joined by all living mammals in our journey in our ancestral stream. Who were they? Where did they live? How did they live? What were their greatest joys? What were their greatest sorrows?
9. One billion years ago. We have now been joined by all the living species that we recognize in our daily lives in our ancestral journey. We are the wolf, the bear, the whale, the salmon, the pine tree, the flowers on the altar. Our ancestors are simple one-cell organisms living in the warm waters of the primitive earth. Who were they? Where did they

> live? How did they live? What were their greatest joys? What were their greatest sorrows? 10. The last step in our journey: 3.8 billion years ago. There are no signs of living organisms here. The stream of ancestors that we have been following has ended in a series of complex chemical reactions in which non-living elements are becoming the simplest of possible living organisms. Our ancestors: Who were they? Where did they live? How did they live? What were their greatest joys? What were their greatest sorrows? (Allendorf, 1997)

When we want to understand something, we cannot just stand outside and observe it. We have to enter deeply into it and be one with it in order to really understand. If we want to understand a person, we have to feel his feelings, suffer his sufferings, and enjoy his joy. The word comprehend is made up of the Latin roots cum, which means with, and prehendere, which means to grasp it or to pick it up. To comprehend something means to pick it up and be one with it. There is no other way to understand something. In Buddhism, we call this kind of understanding "non-duality." Not two. (Thich Nhat Hanh, 1992)

THE COUNCIL OF ALL BEINGS

"The shaman speaks for wild animals, the spirits of plants, the spirits of mountains, of watersheds. He or she sings for them. They sing through her. . . . " (Snyder, 1977) The first Council of All Beings workshop occurred in March, 1985, just outside of Sydney, Australia. Forty people participated in this workshop, led by Buddhists John Seed, Joanna Macy and Pat Fleming.

Inspired by the writings of Arne Naess, Professor Emeritus of Philosophy at Oslo University, the three initiators had long tried to create an experience that would incorporate the inevitable feelings of sadness, regret, or remorse when facing the environmental crisis, with a deep ecological and spiritual connection with all life. The Council of All Beings was created to help people establish a sense of responsibility for the earth on the basis of understanding and compassion. Seed says: "It is a form which permits us to experience consciously both pain and the power of our interconnectedness with all life." (Seed, 1988)

Seed continues, In the Council of All Beings, we channel the energies released by despair and empowerment and other rituals into facilitating a profound change to deeply ecological awareness. In our experience, "affective education" learning from the heart and body, and the Council of All Beings is just one example-goes much deeper than the exchange of ideas because it is based on the premise that we already possess within us the knowledge we need, and what is necessary is to bring it to conscious awareness. The knowledge we require is embedded within us and needs to be awakened. In our mother's womb, our embryonic Rituals

One of the prices that modern civilization is presently paying is alienation from the wonders of nature and its laws. Civilization seems to go hand in hand with a continuous process of separating the individual from the whole. While aiming at promoting and satisfying people's personal desires, science isolates us from nature. Most research focuses upon exploitation of natural resources. Nature is judged by its usefulness in gaining power, wealth or fame. Little thought is given to how we might give back to nature. Many people express a deep feeling of loneliness and loss within, a kind of loss that cannot be satisfied with more materialistic gain. The high suicide rates and violence in developing and developed societies may be an indication of this loneliness and loss of universal identity.

The playful character of the following rituals and games, some of which are adaptations from native rites, have proven a powerful way of helping people to actually feel what otherwise would have been intellectual understanding only. The latter generally provides little to awaken people's awareness to their habitual separation from their environment.

Bodies recapitulate the evolution of cellular life on Earth. We can begin to feel the inner body-sense of amphibian, reptilian, and lower mammal because these earlier stages of our life are literally part of the ontogenetic development of our neurological system . . . if we wish to reunite with nature, the first requirement is that we have the intention to establish this contact. (Seed, 1988) such as a mountain, tree, fish, bear, endangered species, grass, lake, soil, rock, etc.

Evaluation of the experience and commitment to active personal care in some area of environmental protection.

The Council of All Beings, the way it is adapted here, is based on the book Thinking like a Mountain, which was written by the above initiators of the workshops. They have led and now lead workshops for a growing number of followers from all over the world where numerous Councils of All Beings have been established. Conducting a Council of All Beings can be a spontaneous outdoor or indoor activity or it can be planned and conducted in detail in advance. Educators who would like to organize such a council for the first time are advised to plan some time in advance. Information on council workshops can be obtained by contacting Dr. John Seed, Director, Rainforest Information Centre, P.O. Box 368, Lismore, New South Wales, 2480, Australia. Tel. 066-218505. Seed introduces: "In the Council of All Beings workshops, we participate in a series of processes that weave together three important themes: mourning, remembering and speaking from the perspective of other life-forms." (Seed, 1988)

The Councils are held in three phases:

1. Preliminary exercise of acknowledging negativity, emotions, mourning, despair; care and love for the environment and remembering the evolutionary roots of all human existence.
2. Council of Beings meeting, where all participants have the opportunity to speak out for a particular non- human being,

1. Acknowledging/Mourning/Remembering

Looking at the speed at which whole species on earth are disappearing raises a lot of sadness, rage, feelings of helplessness and weakness in many people. These feelings are often suppressed for "fear of experiencing the despair that such information provokes." (Seed, 1988).

The Council of All Beings aims at providing a safe surroundings in order for people to confront these feelings of despair, grief, anger or helplessness. Through finding ways of expressing and sharing their emotions, many people feel refreshed and reconfirmed in their care for the Earth and wish to participate in programs to solve global problems. Seed says: " Often after such experiences, people come together to form ongoing support groups or join existing groups to take action on peace and/or environmental issues."(Seed, 1988)

" The first step in despair work is to disabuse ourselves of the notion that grief for our world is morbid. To experience anguish and anxiety in the face of the perils that threaten us is a healthy reaction. Far from being crazy, this pain is a testimony to the unity of life, the deep interconnections that relate us to all beings." (Macy,1991) There might be some preliminary sharing of emotions, impressions, perceptions about nature before the actual council starts. They may consist of exercises like:

Sharing Sadness

The whole group sits together in a circle. Every participant has the chance to talk for a few minutes about a certain sad experience of nature's destruction. No comments are made by listening participants. The meaning of this exercise is to recognize those feelings, that some people have never allowed themselves to express, listening, and to becoming aware that others have similar feelings.

Sharing Joy

The group sits in a circle. Every participant can talk for a few minutes about joyful moments of interconnectedness with nature. No comments are made by those who listen.

Remembering

The group sits in a circle. Through guided of all life on earth. visualizing themselves as algae, then slowly climbing up the ladder of evolutionary development, the participants are led through existence as snails, worms, insects to fish, amphibians, mammals, apes to human beings. These exercises serve as an example and are unlimited in design or structure. Yet at this stage the participants should have enough emotional space for grief, anger or sadness to be expressed, as underlying these emotions they will discover their deep sense of caring: "One by one, people bring forward a stone or twig or flower and, laying it in the center, name what it represents for them— something disappearing from their lives, the meadow becoming a shopping mall, a paved-over creek, safe food . . . And in the ritual naming of these losses, we retrieve our capacity to care." (Macy, 1991)

2. Council of All Beings: Speaking for another Life Form Ritual

For the ritual of the Council, a quiet pleasant environment should be chosen, preferably in a forest, near a lake, or in the mountains. The evening hours by a campfire or in candlelight may help create an intimate atmosphere of mutual trust and openness.

To support imagination, a simple mask may be worn by the speaker. The participants can easily make them beforehand out of forest materials like leaves, twigs and dead tree bark or cardboard and colored paper with a stick to hold it in front of the face or a rubber band to fasten it around the head. The leader may begin the ritual through playing a drum, introducing and explaining the general structure. Trays with the four elements may be passed around the circle to remind the participants of the basic elements of which all life on earth consists: -soil or certain minerals representing 'solidity'.

- water representing 'fluidity'.
- a burning candle representing 'heat'.
- incense representing 'motion'.

The four directions may be addressed by the leader while the participants turn their bodies to the directions accordingly: East, South, West and North. The Council culminates in shedding of one's human dignity and speaking from the perspective of another life form. Before the Council meeting, one takes time alone to be chosen by a plant, animal, or landscape feature that one will represent at the Council.

Seed suggests, "Find a place that feels special to you and simply be there, still and waiting. Let another life form occur to you, one for whom you will speak at this afternoon's Council of All Beings. No need to try to make this happen. Just relax and let yourself be chosen by the life form that wishes to speak through you. It could be a form of plant or animal life, or an ecological feature like a piece of land or a body of water. Often the first that occurs to you is what is right for you at this gathering." (Seed, 1988). Spontaneous expression flows through the structure created for the ritual councils and creative suggestions for human action may emerge. Invocation of powers and knowledge of these other life forms also empowers us.

The participants then put on their masks (if appropriate) and following the circle everybody introduces the being they are going to speak out for:

"I am a mountain, I am speaking for all the peaks of the world."

"I am an elephant, I speak for all elephants in the jungles."

"I am a leaf, I speak for all leaves of the forests."

"I am a squirrel, I speak for all squirrels in the world."

Then, starting the circle again, the beings have the chance to tell their story.

For example:

"I am an elephant. I am a strong animal, I am tall and full of strength. I live with my herd in the jungle and we travel from water hole to water hole to drink and bathe to take the insects out of our skins. We have lived in this area for ages and no other being has ever encroached upon the lands we inhabit. But lately the forest is getting smaller and we often hear from our hiding places the chain saws and the screams of the old trees falling which grew from the bones of our ancestors. Streets have been cut through our habitat and we cannot reach water holes in the far distance when closer ones dried out. Our home is this shrinking forest, there is nowhere else we can go. . . . "

The group acknowledges: "We hear you, elephant." "I am a Redwood tree. I am as older than the history of Buddhism as the first council took place when I already spread my leaves.

Generations of humans and animals sought shelter in my shade and I exhaled my oxygen for Jesus Christ, Columbus, Napoleon, Martin Luther King and Marie Curie. I withstood storms and rains over the centuries, but I cannot withstand the machines people use to cut my trunk to make paper bags and chopsticks out of my wood. I ask myself what went wrong with the humans that they have so little reverence for our old age and for all we contribute to their well-being."

The group acknowledges: "We hear you, redwood tree." After some non-human beings have spoken, they turn back into human beings to listen to what the other non-human beings have to say. In similar fashion, everyone in the circle speaks out for a non-human being and then later listens as a human being for some time. The humans may sit in the center of the circle for their listening. The council may be continued by the humans addressing the non-human beings, expressing their impressions about what they had to listen to. For example, "We hear you, fellow beings. It has been very painful to hear, but we thank you for your honesty. We see what were destroying, we're in trouble and we're scared. What we've let loose upon the world has such momentum, we feel overwhelmed. Don't leave us alone—we need your help, and for your own survival too. Are there powers and strengths you can share with us in this hard time?"

Thus the humans may ask the non-human beings to share their strength with the humans in order to find ways to overcome the weaknesses, guilt, and shortcomings the humans felt. The nonhumans take up their masks again: "I, the eagle, offer you my far-seeing eyes to understand what effects your present actions may yield." "I, the weed, offer you our power as weeds-that of tenacity. We keep on growing wherever we are. This is what we share with you our persistence." "I, rainforest, offer you my powers in creating balance and harmony that enable many life-forms to live together. Out of this balance and symbiosis new, diverse life can spring. This I can offer you." (Seed, 1988)

Every non-human being who has offered its gift, joins the human beings again in the center of the circle. "While the opening of the ritual is preplanned, the nature of its ending can never be foreseen. How it concludes depends on the mood of the group and the dynamics unleashed."(Seed, 1988) Accordingly, the Council may end in silence or with chanting or singing. Later on, the group may wish to release the non-human beings that they had spoken for through burning the masks in a fire. As the participants, one by one, step to the center of the circle, they may thank the non-human being they had embodied while placing the mask on the pyre or in the fire.

BURNING RITUAL FOR HANG-UPS, SHORTCOMINGS, AND ECOLOGICAL DEFILEMENTS

As water is associated with purifying properties, fire is associated with the transformation from one aggregate to another. Fire is commonly used to address the spiritual world by all religions of the world. The Catholic church's burning of frankincense, Chinese ancestor-worshipers burning paper money for their deceased and, again, the burning of incense in Hinduism, Taoism, and Buddhism, as an offering to the spiritual world, are but a few examples. Most societies cremate their dead. In many parts of the world where strong seasonal changes occur in nature, ritualistic fires are lighted in spring as a symbol for the burning of the old year. There is something refreshing, invigorating, and transforming in watching a fire eating away the old, the outworn.

In the Burning of shortcomings and hang-ups ritual, this transforming property is addressed to convert the feelings of negativity, helplessness, depression, sadness, of one's own ignorance and exploitative behavior, into awareness, compassion and active care for the environment and all living beings. In short, it is a rite to remove one's egocentric attitudes and problems that interfere with one's environmental work and to change them to ecocentric attitudes and approaches through confession and the flames of purification.

For Buddhists the concepts and images of ignorance, defilements, or delusions might be evoked and burned. They can be replaced by awareness, ethical behavior, and wisdom for a better life and environmental work.

Again, the group of participants may sit in a circle around a fire. (It is interesting that American Indians always form circles during important ceremonies or rituals; a circle is believed to contain spirit and power and to be interconnected and non-ending.) If space or ground does not permit a fire, a large candle safely placed on a big plate or tray may serve the purpose. Every participant now takes out a sheet of paper and, in silence, all participants write down aspects of their character, patterns of behavior, negative feelings, short-comings and hang-ups that they would like to change in terms of their lives and in terms of their environmental work, i.e., things or problems that are interfering or reducing their effectiveness in life and environment. Each one may then individually read aloud what they have written and then burn the paper to ashes, committing themselves to work towards letting go defilement, hang-ups, and shortcomings and toward working on higher goals for themselves and the environment. However, if participants would like to keep the contents of their paper to themselves, they may burn it in silence.

This ritual may be followed by a silent meditation, a prayer, or some chanting. (see under MEDITATION AND PRAYER) "Then Jesus was led by the Spirit into the desert (wilderness)to be tempted by the devil."(Matthew: 4: 1)

Pipop Udomittipong writes of " . . .the method of teaching which is frequently used among followers of forest monasteries in Thailand. The very beginners in meditation are usually left alone in the forest, because in the darkness, one will realize how scared oneself is. Then this fear will cause them to firmly grasp to their consciousness which is a basic for meditation." (Udomittipong,1993).

Spiritual sojourns have been performed and promoted by most of the great spiritual teachers like Buddha and Jesus Christ. Monks and nuns in Tibet, China, India, and Thailand, as well as lay people all over the world, have chosen solitary sojourns in nature for their spiritual practices in the past and present. The following exercise is based on a traditional ritual called Vision Quest, which is performed by native American Indians. Fasting for four days in the wilderness, members of the tribe seek spiritual guidance or a "vision" from nature and its non-human inhabitants. An eagle, a bear, an insect or the wind may be the carrier of answers to questions these men may have. The answers are often interpreted later by medicine men or elders of the tribe. Through fasting and a continuous contemplative state of mind, powerful visions or dreams may also occur which are also interpreted by the medicine men or elders after returning to the village.

This kind of nature quest has been acknowledged as a powerful means of reintegration into and re-connection with nature and the natural environment. The idea has been modified by John Milton in his Vision Quest program to help those who feel disconnected from their source of life. Although the Native Americans as well as John Milton perform a number of preliminary exercises and rituals to deepen the experience for the participants, here only the solitary.

SPIRITUAL SOJOURN/VISION QUEST

Suzanna Head: "Then they enter the alone time, taking nothing but a blanket—no clothes, food or water. For up to four days they sit within a sacred space marked by a circle of stones, sometimes within a pit dug out of the Earth." (Head, 1990) "The Buddha taught three kinds of solitude of which the first, physical aloneness, is conducive to the second, the oneness of mind in jhaṇa when the hindrances have been suppressed. This 'solitude' in turn is helpful for the final aloneness of the mind which has no more assets (upadhi), another way of speaking about Arahantship" (enlightened state). (Khantipalo, 1977)

It is recommended that groups new to a natural environment start with a 24-hour solo. However, the time spent alone may be expanded. The appropriate equipment for the participants to take depends on the locality. Here some general recommendations:

- 1 blanket (or sleeping-bag)
- mosquito-net if necessary
- water
- vegetarian food (dried fruit, nuts, raisins etc.)
- tooth-brush (used only with water, no soap or tooth-paste)
- Band-Aids
- a whistle (to blow in case of danger)

- clothing as appropriate
- flashlight or candles
- a camp knife

A tent may be necessary in areas of frequent rain. In a forest or mountain area, the participants can choose their place for themselves in consultation with the advisor. However, there should be considerable space between participants so that they are definitely out of sight or sound of one another. There should be no communication between the participants for as long as the solo lasts. In dense forest 100 meters apart may be enough, whereas in open mountainous areas more space might be needed.

I chose a spot a thousand feet up a cliff near a large cave, whereas the others were down in the riparian area along the creek that flowed from the mountains. Theirs was a lush, mossy area, protected by large old trees. But since I felt the need to be up high where there was a lot of space and a vast view I sacrificed the presence of water. (Head, 1990) I wanted to go back to the stream where we had been before. Then I found a nice spot not too close to the stream, I did not want to get into trouble with elephants. (Offrer, 1993)

Before leaving the participants by themselves, some instructions may be given.

- not to try to contact their neighbors
- to use the whistle only in case of danger
- not to write or read during the sojourn
- to use meditation and prayer to connect with nature
- to eat moderately and use the water mindfully
- to practice awareness at all times

Strong feelings such as fear or anxiety may come to the surface since some of the participants may never have spent days and nights out in the wilderness on their own before. These feelings are natural fears of separation, of helplessness and of powerlessness. Fear is a very likely part of the experience. Many spiritual practitioners do solitary sojourns of this nature so they can face their fears which are brought out by the experience.

Luang Phor Prachak believed in the necessity of making us open enough to experience the forest with all of our selves. He made the connection between our inner selves and the outer environment, explaining that if we were calm inside we would be able to handle our fears of forest nights, indeed, all our fears. "If you have a tiger inside you, you will meet a tiger outside as well. First get rid of the tiger inside you," he said. "Then his serenity will help us perceive in new ways any threats from outside 'tigers', and if we do by chance discover a tiger near us, we will know better how to respond." (Offrer, 1993)

"The first step in dealing with feelings is to recognize each feeling as it arises. The agent that does this is mindfulness. In the case of fear, for example, you bring out your mindfulness, look at your fear and recognize it as fear. You know that fear springs from yourself and that mindfulness also springs from yourself. They are both in you, not fighting, but one taking care of the other." (Thich Nhat Hanh, 1992)

"I just sat there and all fear drifted away. At night an animal came to lay beside me. After a couple of minutes I realized that I wasn't on his menu. It was big and I could hear its breath. We just stayed together." (Irving, 1993)

The Buddhist concept of equanimous observation in meditation may be very helpful in addressing and dealing with sudden fears or feelings of insecurity. Often encountered fears tell about hidden emotions that come to the surface of the mind through the unusual confrontation with oneself. A woman who spent 24 hours in the forest alone on her first solitary sojourn said that she once was awakened in the middle of the night by an unidentified sound. She realized that she was more afraid that it was a man than an animal. She reflected that people were so irrational whereas animals just followed their instincts and hence she could feel safer with the latter.

Naturally the nights of darkness and sounds of unknown origin may give rise to anxiety. But the nights may also serve as a means of taking refuge in the protective forces of nature. On the Dong Yai Forest Buddhism and Deep Ecology solitary sojourns, the majority of participants reported seeing and hearing nocturnal animals such as cats and other small predators. Also, a small herd of elephants did pass through the general area where some sojourners were located. In tropical forests, much of wildlife activity occurs at night, so sojourns of this nature present excellent opportunities for wildlife observations besides spending the evening in a forest solitude.

"After counting twenty shooting stars, I surrendered to a sense of wonder." (Head, 1990)

"I was sitting in the forest. Looking at the green leaves, I was sorting through my personal life. Eventually I lit a candle." (Greene, 1993)

Many people express the transformation of their fear as a new overwhelming feeling of gratitude and interconnectedness with nature as a whole. Being encompassed by the natural surroundings without civilized means of protection, one replaces the notion of being an intruder or a separate entity within nature. There appears, instead, a deeply reassuring feeling of interbeing with the trees, the insects, the birds, the air, the water, the forest soil, the animals. One feels at home or "in habitat" in his or her sacred place and one cherishes this time and place as unique and spiritual as well as ecological.

"Perhaps it was the dawning of reverence, that poignant mixture of joy and sadness, longing and gratitude that arises when one glimpses the sacredness of the world. I found myself all that day making prayers and offerings to the place. Of the little food that I had left, I offered bits and pieces at small shrines I made on rocks in my favorite places, feeling that I had to give something back." (Head, 1990)

At the end of the sojourn, all participants may meet again in a circle, sharing their experiences, feelings, and encounters. Many people emphasize afterwards the inner harmony, oneness with nature, and peace they discovered behind their initial uneasiness. While doing walking meditation or just sitting on the forest ground, they become aware of how little power they really had as a human being in nature and how comforting it was to hand over to nature the burden of a separate self. Many participants express their appreciation towards the close relationship between meditation and nature experience that they had the chance to encounter. Here the connection between Buddhist practice and nature-consciousness becomes very obvious. Listening and Awareness of the Devas of the Place Exercise:

This exercise will help in providing insights and messages from the Devas (a Sanskrit term meaning angels, spiritual beings, free flowing energies, or energy fields of a place, i.e., the unseen spirit or soul of an area and its beings). The Deva could be the group soul of a species or landscape soul of a place as well as the individual soul of a spiritual being.

Although this exercise can obviously be done without a group, it will now be described as a group exercise which can also be used on an individual basis. Depending on the time available, this exercise can be accomplished in three to several hours. Ideally, the "wilder" the place, the better for this Deep Ecology exercise. Group members should be instructed to go forth alone in a wandering walk from a central location. They should all depart in different directions and avoid any close proximity to other individuals. It would be helpful to have a short meditation session before they depart to set the right mood for their wandering walk. As they depart, they should be instructed to keep their hearts and minds open and to listen to their intuitions, instincts, and imaginations. They should be further instructed not to have their own "agenda" or preconceived notions of what they are looking for and what Devas or spiritual beings might say or talk to them about. That is, they should avoid all anthropocentric projections.

By staying open to place, they will eventually wander to a place where they feel more attuned or "at home" with the surrounding areas. When they arrive at this location, they should ask permission of the Devas of the area if they can remain there for the purpose of communicating with them. In some cases, the Devas or spiritual beings of a given place at a given time may not wish to communicate with human beings and this should be respected by politely moving away while being constantly receptive to other locations in one's wandering walk. Usually, the response from the Devas or spiritual beings is positive, as based on one's intuition, instincts, or imagination. It is usually best to go by one's first impression or inner message in this matter. Then the individual should make herself or himself at home by sitting in a meditative position.

In this spiritual communication, it is best to first focus on:

(1) whatever you consider or understand to be your higher spiritual power and its unconditional love for you,

(2) this transmitted and unconditional love for yourself,

(3) the interrelationship of unconditional love and communication between you and the Deva or spiritual being so that your higher spiritual power, you, and the Devas become one. In this Oneness of Spirit, it is important to be attuned and attentative to any messages that the Deva(s) or spiritual beings of the selected location or area may wish to give to you at this time.

Communication with Devas is often a two way process with the individual asking questions of the Devas at times. But the key is to be attuned and to listen with an open heart and mind without preconceived agendas, notions, or projections. The messages from the Devas may naturally vary a great deal from the simple to the complex, from the Deva of a place (like a river), group of species (forest), individual living beings, stones, etc. (and may even include messages from unborn living beings about their futures). They may also vary in terms of their Deep Ecology or general messages as well as personal messages or advice to you.

Generally, the messages are helpful and, to a degree, philosophical and loving and a variety of things of this nature. Try to correlate and understand your feelings associated with the messages. Sometimes, it may be necessary to focus on one of these messages or themes so that it can become more meaningful for insight and application.

After you feel you have completed your "session" with the Deva(s)and/or when it is the group-designated time to meet, thank the Deva(s) and return to the central location for the group. You may wish to write down some of the major points from this experience. When all or some of the group members have returned, select a partner and sit facing each other. Each partner should share (or what they choose to share) of their personal experiences during the exercise and what messages that the Devas may have had for them. Often the personal messages or advice may be paramount, particularly if one is struggling with a particular issue or problem in his or her life (which often may interfere with one's Deep Ecology work). However, some Deep Ecology messages are often present in some form, directly or indirectly. Both partners might also expound on how the messages can be applied in their personal lives and in Deep Ecology understandings, activities and hopes.

Later, the group should meet as a whole and the two partners can share what they choose to share of their experience and discussion. It is often wise to summarize the messages received by the individuals of the group on a general basis for more understanding of how the process works and of what the collective messages of the Devas are. One should not be discouraged in this exercise process. Sometimes, few or no messages from the Deva(s) may come through at a given time and/or place; it is unwise to compare or contrast. The more times one does this overall activity, the more opportunities are presented and the better one gets at tuning into the Deva(s) of different places.

In the event of limited time, often the process can be completed by individuals in less than an hour or even a few minutes, so that a major message or insight can be obtained from the Deva(s) of a given place if all goes well. The key again is to open your heart and mind and to trust your first impressions or instincts. As an example of communicating with a group Deva or soul of Trees, Dorothy Maclean, from Findhorn, Scotland, made the following presentation on the "Essence of Nature" (transcript of (unpublished) paper presented at the Third Wilderness Congress, Oct. 1983, Edinburgh, Scotland):

We come in with a lordly sweep. We are not just the little trees that you see in your garden. We are denizens of magnificent species of great hills of the sun and the wind. We put up with being hedges, but always in our inner beings is the growing towards sun kissed places where we stand out in clustered grandeur. You feel in use an almost intolerable longing to be fully ourselves. We in the plant world have our pattern and destiny worked out through the ages, and we feel it quite wrong that we and others like us are not allowed to be because of man and his encroachment.

Trees are not so much doers of the world as Be-ers. We have our portion of the plan to fulfill. We have been nurtured for this very reason and now in this day and age many of us can only dream of the spaces where we can fulfill ourselves. The pattern is ever before us, out of reach, a dream that we are forever growing towards, but which seldom becomes reality. The planet needs the likes of us in our full maturity. We are not a mistake on the part of nature, we have our work to do.

Man is now becoming the controller of the world forests, but is beginning to realize that trees are needed. But he uses silly economic reasons for his selection with no awareness of the planet's needs. He should not cover acres with one quick growing species (Eucalyptus), which, although admittedly better that none, shows ignorance of the purpose of trees and their challenging of diverse forces. The world needs us on a large scale, perhaps if man were in tune with the infinite as we are and were pulling his weight the forces would be balanced. But at present the planet needs more than ever just what it is destroying—the forces that go through the stately trees.

Here are these facts of life and none to listen to them. We have rather dumped this on you (and I was feeling dumped on) though you feel at one with us, you feel unable to help. You are only looking at it from a limited view, we know that the very telling of this to you does help. That a truth once in human consciousness then percolates around and does its work, and we feel the better for communicating. Let us both believe that the almighty one knows all this better than both of us, and that something is being done.

Well, whenever I tuned into a tree, I got the variation of this same theme, and the need for trees on the surface of the earth, for example saying that they are the skin of the earth, and that if more than a third of the skin of any being is destroyed then that being perishes. Saying that they have a job to do in their maturity, just as child cannot do the work of an adult, so an immature tree cannot do the work of a mature tree, and I found that in forests, trees are most often cut down before they are mature, and allowed to develop their canopy.

So they had a job to do in the channeling of forces, which only they can do in their maturity. They said they had a special gift for humans in this day and age when we are so troubled and upset and chaotic that they give us mental stability. I know that when I go for a walk in the forest I emerge at peace again, and they even suggested that we build large forests beside our cities, so that trees can give that gift to us humans.

So every time I attuned to the trees, I got a variation of this same theme.

Another example of communicating with a tree Deva follows: "A Tree's Plea," by Daniel H. Henning (while a Fulbright Scholar studying tropical forests and protected areas in Thailand): The four park guards and I climbed a steep hillside in the tropical forest In Tublam National Park, Thailand. Suddenly, we came upon a magnificent tree-huge and noble. It would take three men to get their arms around it. I estimated it to be over 400 years old and 120 feet In height. There were just a few simple branches at the top of the huge trunk that seemed to reach into the heavens. And there were relatively few leaves on the branches. But the top of the tree was like an open hand reaching outward. It was powerful, gorgeous, and natural.

I put my hands on the trunk of the tree and felt captured by its energy. It was like holding another human being. It seemed so powerful, but calm, with a balanced and harmonious energy that was the essence of life itself. I felt the energy flow from the very womb of the earth to reach through the trunk and its open branches to embrace the sun and the sky. The energy seemed to be flowing both ways between God and the Earth with light and love. I held onto the tree and was spellbound. The park guards stood watching me as I pretended to be studying the tree scientifically. But I was experiencing one of God's creations. Then I heard (or thought I heard) an appeal emerging from the tree and its energy. It simply said, "Protect me."

Tropical forests are disappearing at approximately 100 acres a minute on a global basis. Many experts believe that tropical rainforest areas will be mostly deforested in Asia and elsewhere by the early 21st century and that they will not regenerate in similar form. National Parks and other protected areas provide a major way for keeping some remaining rainforests. But the protection must be internal as well as external. Tropical forests are fragile and complex ecosystems with diverse and abundant life. Poaching of logging and wildlife can create serious abuses and inroads into the ecosystem and national park integrity, particularly when dominant trees are removed.

When we finally started down the hillside, I felt a sense of tragedy, as if something was very wrong. We were going cross country down a steep slope. Then we came upon a magnificent tree, huge and beautiful like the other. But It was lying down. It had recently been cut down by log poachers. The tree was being cut by a hand saw into small beams to be carried out. The tree would bring about US$800 on the local market. It had been cut down in a watershed drainage area of a national park. The downed tree and the beams being taken from it gave a sad feeling, almost like a friend had died. I went over to the tree, touched and blessed it.

TREE TRANSITIONS FOR CHANGES

Buddhism and Deep Ecology-bring many changes to our lives which require us to be still, accept ourselves, have faith in the process, and to be open. We can call upon a tree as a symbol to help in our transition so that we can become more open to change. Select a tree which you are attracted to and which seems to call to you. Put your arms around the tree-hug it and merge with it as a living symbol for you in transition. Feel the energy vibrations of the tree. Trees are silent and magnificent providers for planet earth. They are wise, patient, balanced and centered. Humble yourself and ask for the gifts and identity of the tree.

The tree reaches deep into the earth with long roots pulling sustenance upward from exposed extremities. Reaching upward with outstretched arms, the tree pulls energy down from the heavens into branches and leaves. The tree is a great mediator upon the earth and serves each day between spirit and substance, between Mother Earth and Father Sky. The tree accepts your exhalation of carbon dioxide and transforms it back in life giving oxygen. In relationship with the tree, you are dependent on the tree for shelter, food, and air for your existence. The tree is vulnerable while being a silent server and peaceful observer of the ecosystem. The tree appreciates anything you might give and asks little of you.

In the endless cycle of life and death and the impermanence of rising and falling away, the tree moves as master without clinging. Standing erect as bridge between Mother Earth and Father Sky, the tree has profound wisdom and true humility (humility from humus or soil of the earth). The tree accepts the inevitable as well as the perfection in all of life and its diversity. The tree remains unchanged with the passing of the seasons. Thus you can look to the tree as your symbol of transition. For the tree is very much a part of the earth as it reaches toward the stars. The tree is grounded, but always growing and expanding while embodying peace, grace, and serenity. Though the winds of change may try to sway the tree with endless motion, the tree remains steadfast to a commitment to remain still and grounded. The tree is your teacher. Listen to the wisdom of the tree so that your life might be centered, nourished, grounded, balanced, and harmonious with all life.

Use an abandoned leaf as a symbol of those things in your life that are no longer necessary. Although once vital and essential, the life of the leaf has been used up and the tree lets go. Write on the dead leaf those things in your life that are ready to pass away—to let go of. Place these leaves upon a fire that will create a transition from substance to spirit. Any negativity will be transformed and then released in a more positive form.

On another leaf, write those things you wish to hold onto in your life—things you want to encourage and retain in your life. Tie these prayer leaves to a tree which will unite them with their creator or Great Spirit—just as your prayers unite you with all creation.

Choose a tree seed—a symbol of rebirth, continuation, and promise of growth and hope. Plant the seed in the earth along with your prayers. Know that what you ask with sincerity will be delivered. Know that the divine spirit inherent in all life will grant you your highest good so that your dreams, desires, and wishes will mature and grow strong and bear fruit as the seed that you have planted in Mother Earth. (Adapted from Dorian Beitz, "Receptivity to Change")

MEDITATION AND PRAYER

Prayer is the way we can remind ourselves of the whole thing, and also ask for any divine help which is allowed under "the rules of the game." And since we don't know what all the rules are, we have to use our best guesses about how to pray (or what to pray for), and we must accept on faith that every prayer is heard and answered in the best way, for our own good—even when it doesn't look like it to our limited vision. (Lazoff, 1992)

"Meditation is suitable for people of all ages, cultures, and times. It is a large field of study in theory and practice. The correct practice of meditation has tremendous psychological health and spiritual values." (Sri-Ruan Keawkungwal, 1989) Just like true meditation, prayer itself is not really a "method"; it's more a relationship to God (or to Self, life, the universe, however one wishes to want to say it). Praying as a spiritual practice is just like that: it's practice. After enough practice, and as we get more mature, prayer just starts happening all day long-again, just like meditation. (Lazoff, 1992) "When sitting, care should be taken to be at once relaxed yet holding the body erect. There should be no strain but neither should the head droop nor the lumbar regions sag. The body should feel poised and balanced upright." (Khantipalo, 1992)

"Meditation is to look deeply into things and to see how we can change ourselves and how we can transform our situation. To transform our situation is also to transform our minds. To transform our minds is also to transform our situation, because the situation is mind, and mind is situation. Awakening is important." (Thich Nhat Hanh, 1992)

Buddhism offers a clearly defined system of ethics, a guide to ecological living, right here, right now. Meditation is its primary tool for raising ecological consciousness. In meditation, awareness of our environment deepens and our identity expands to include the multitude of circumstances and conditions that come together to form an existence. Curiosity and respect for the beauty and power of nature is enhanced, revealing an innate spirituality. Resensitized to our feelings and immersed in awareness, we may find ways to avoid irreversible damage and ultimate self-destruction. (Bandiner, 1990)

Guided Tree Meditation

Take off your shoes. Close your eyes and slowly and attentively take ten deep breaths. Slowly move your attention down to your feet . . . Feel how they touch the ground, connecting your body with the Earth. Now feel your feet as they slowly turn into the roots of a tree. Follow your roots on their way into the soil and humus layer, twisting and turning their way into the Earth and along the humus layer of the soil.

Your roots give you stability. You are a tree. You will spend all your life on this one spot where you feel that your roots embrace the Earth. They hold your body erect but yet flexible under strong winds and storms.

Now examine your roots more closely with their root branches and rootlets and pores, where water and nutrients from the soil and its humus layer pass through into little root canals leading up into your body . . . Water flows around your roots and with your attention you now start following it up from the smallest tiny fibers into bigger rootlets, into the flowing stream of life that slowly vibrates up your trunk.

As the planet's juices of nutrients and nourishment flow through your body, you are aware that you are a part of this planet. Slowly spread your arms, naturally, comfortably and open your hands like leaves to the sun. You are a fully grown tree now. Your trunk is strong, it has grown over years of taking in the nutrients and water of the soil and humus layer and returning them back through fallen leaves.

In the tropical forest that you are in, almost all the nutrients are contained in the leaves on the ground and in the trees. Feel the energy vibrating in the myriad lush green leaves. As the water reaches each cell, it floods the leaves with nutrition. A. Sitting and walking with mindfulness of breathing:

Meditation in a natural environment can be practiced while sitting, standing, lying down, or walking. The most commonly used are sitting and walking. -Sitting meditation in mindfulness of breathing: Sit in any comfortable posture, preferably with crossed legs in full or half lotus. Keep your back straight. Close your eyes and watch your breath as it comes in and goes out. Try not to fight thoughts, but also not to hold onto them. Let thoughts pass like clouds in the sky. There is no time limitation, but for beginners 15 to 30 minutes might be enough.

Walking Meditation

Select a small trail or clearing in the forest. Determine two turning points at a distance of about 15 steps apart. Walk slowly and attentively. Feel the ground underneath your feet. Try to be aware of the process of walking, without the notion of I or me who is walking, i.e, walking without a walker.

When touched by the rays and energy of the sun, the little green laboratories in your leaves (chloroplasts) produce sugar—pure energy. This is one of nature's miracles, photosynthesis, taking place within your leaves.

Your leaves have tiny openings, like pores, oozing out life giving oxygen for all breathing beings on Earth after taking in carbon dioxide from them. Your breath is your way of interbeing with the walking beings who inhabit the Earth. They are breathing out the carbon dioxide that you need for your act of transformation it into oxygen. Together with all life on Earth you are breathing in and breathing out, breathing in and breathing out, breathing in and breathing out.

Now turn your attention to your arms. If they feel tired you may lower them slowly, but do not lose the feeling of being drawn towards the light . . . Your arms are your branches . . . You are fully aware that you were placed here to fulfill your destiny as a tree. The elements you consist of are in constant communication with the elements of your surroundings. You feel the warmth of the sun's power.

Without the sun nothing on Earth would grow—heat. You feel the water flowing through the outer layer of your trunk and the vessels of your leaves like rivers and brooks on the Earth—fluidity. The whole world is nurtured through this element—fluidity.

You feel the lightness of your breath, going in, going out—motion. You are contributing to the winds, exchange of breath—motion. Breathing in and breathing out. Life is a miracle of interchanging elements through impermanence. Some of your leaves slowly die. They fall to the forest floor and humus layer. The nutrients in the fallen leaves eventually return to water and nutrients in the forest soil.

Yet, new leaves grow on your branches. The cycle of rebirth is illustrated in your leaves with new leaves arising, regular leaves existing, and old leaves dying and returning to the earth to carry on the processes of impermanence. Now lend your attention to the surface of your trunk. You have many guests in the folds of your bark. Welcome your guests: the little spiders, beetles, ants, caterpillars and butterflies. Your guests are part of the food chain of the forests and when they die they give back their nutrients to the soil and water. Cycle of rebirth . . .arising, existing, and dying. Your leaves and branches provide shelter for squirrels, birds, and other living things.

You are part of the whole ecology. Through the process of birth, decay, death and rebirth you are a true representative of the law of nature, the universe, the Dhamma/nature law of arising, existing, and passing away, or impermanence. Your reality is not within yourself; rather, it is in interrelationship—the totality of nature or Dhamma. A oneness and interconnectedness with all living and non-living things is reality in nature and Dhamma. Feel this oneness, feel this interconnectedness as aggregates in process. You are in the cycle of rebirth or change, arising, existing, and dying, arising, existing, and dying. Breathing in and breathing out, Breathing in and breathing out.

You are a living, spiritual bridge between Mother Earth and Father Sky. As you slowly change back from the solid structure of a tree trunk to the softer human form, you are aware that as a human being you consist of the same elements as the tree: heat, fluidity, solidity and motion . . . And as you fill your legs, your torso, your arms and hands with your consciousness, you also become aware of how gifted you are to be able to move your body. Nature has given you the greatest blessings of thought, motion and compassion so that you can be aware of life in other beings like trees. Realizing these gifts fills one with deep joy and gratitude towards nature and its trees. Trees are part of the life-giving energy and part of us. Their breath of life is our breath of life. Through breathing, the trees and we inter-are. Thus, harming a tree is harming oneself . . . How can we protect trees more?

May all beings share the joy of care and compassion toward all.

May all beings be able to carry out their own struggle for survival, undisturbed and without disturbing others. May all beings, visible or invisible, far or near, dwelling in motion or still, be well and happy.

Metta Meditation

May I be free from all destructive and exploitative behavior towards nature, of which I am not only a part but dependent upon. May I be free from all the egocenteredness, the greed and craving for more than I need.

Ecological Meditation

I recognize that within my mind there is a dark room of separation from universal love, where I cannot see the light.

This room is where my ignorance originates, where my suffering gains its form and where hatred and ill-will raise their ugly heads. I recognize that it is I, my selfishness, my ego-centeredness which separates me from Dhamma law, that does not neglect anyone. I recognize that all suffering starts where the light of Dhamma cannot reach. I recognize that this creation has been exploited and destroyed by mankind. I seek from the universe the help for the world to be healed. I am an instrument for peace, of love, of care, of light, so that I may allow a brightness into the dark corners of my mind and that of others. I am an instrument of wisdom, that will enable me to become a caring keeper of Mother Earth. Where there is injury, may I bring a healing power. where there is despair, may I bring the spirit of hope; May I be free from all ill-will, animosity and resentment toward those who do not conform with my understanding.

May I understand that all life occurs under the same law of causality and condition and that all beings inter-are within this law. May I develop the wisdom of understanding this law of inter-relatedness in nature and through my compassionate understanding, may I develop peace and harmony, goodwill and compassion towards all beings, not only humans, but all non-human beings as well. May all beings share this peace and harmony with nature.

May all beings share this joy and gratitude for having the chance to experience the wise organism we call Earth. May all beings be free from negativity, unhappiness, and suffering where there is hatred, may I bring the spirit of love; where there is poverty, hunger and thirst, may I bring the spirit of sharing; where there is guilt, may I bring the spirit of forgiveness; where there is waste and exploitation, may I bring the spirit of loving care; where there is separation, may I bring the spirit of inter-being.

May I rather seek to understand more than criticize and judge, that I may rather seek to serve than to be served. May I not turn away my head in the face of injustice but try to reconcile and equalize. While carrying out my mission, may I always be aware that the power-rest in the Dhamma are mine, but yours, which shines through me in oneness. With wise reflection I eat this food Not for play, nor for intoxication Not for fattening, nor for beautification Only to maintain this body- To stay alive and healthy To support the spiritual life. Thus I let go of unpleasant feelings And do not stir up new ones Thereby the process of life goes on Blameless, at ease, and in peace. A fundamental aspect of meditative and spiritual life is a mindful and wise use of the necessities of life-clothing, food, shelter, and medicine. Of these, the Lord Buddha gave special emphasis on food and to the practice of moderation in eating.

This food reflection is not a prayer of grace. A wise reflection is a means of working toward right understanding and right intention, the first links of the middle way. We begin by considering what food is not for-some silly, frivolous, and dangerous reasons for eating: games, entertainment, culinary, competition, sensual indulgence, and vain shaping of the body. Then we consider what food is for: to maintain physical health for the Brahma Cariya—the highest most exalted spiritual life.

To let go of unpleasant feelings or to get rid of them, refers to the mental dissatisfaction or disliking that we know as hunger. To not cause new ones to arise means not to cause new Dukkha (problems or troubles), feeling bloated, cramped, lazy, sleepy-by overeating or eating too quickly or ravenously. Thus when practiced wisely, eating helps to clean up old Dukkha without causing any new Dukkha. In this way, life continues with fewer difficulties, in purity and peace and in physical/spiritual health. Buddhist Spiritual Food Reflection from Thailand The following food reflection was found at Suan Mokkh Buddhist Forest Monastery at Chaiya, Thailand. Now deceased Ajahn Buddhadassa tranlated this food reflection from Pali, the original language of Buddhism in India,, into Thai and Ajahn Santikaro and Ajahn Dhammabalo translated it from Thai to English.

PUBLIC PARTICIPATION

Forests are not saved by governmental enlightenment. Keeping streams pristine has never been the aim of giant corporations bent on making profit. No environmental protection measure was ever successful without public pressure. Conservation begins at the grass roots. If the people clamor to save or restore a habitat, they might succeed. If they are silent, the natural treasure is lost. should be Deep Ecology. Not only deep but universal, because there is pollution in our consciousness. Television, for instance, is a form of pollution for us and our children. Television sows the seeds of violence and anxiety in our children and pollutes our consciousness, just as we destroy our environment by chemicals, tree cutting, and polluting the water.

We need to protect the ecology of the mind, or this kind of violence and recklessness will continue to spill over into many other areas of life. (Thich Nhat Hanh, 1991). Elizabeth Roberts writes, . . . to engage the silence in every moment leads to a true ecological activism. It asks a deep slowing down, achieving more by doing less. Meditation and mindfulness give character to our actions.

They prevent us from being too driven in the pursuit of success. Since they show that no action is final, they keep us from taking ourselves too seriously . . . While our environmental actions may be turned aside from their purpose or taken over by the milieu in which they occur, our practice cannot be taken over. It attains its goals because it is its goal. It brings an end to living in front of things and a beginning to truly living with them. (Roberts, 1990)

SOCIALLY ENGAGED BUDDHISM

A human being, like a tiger, tree or ant, is part of the environment. Like ants, we do our most constructive or destructive work collectively. But, unlike the instincts in an ant colony, humanity's social consciousness can be changed. We find this truth illustrated in isolated colonies of the human animal, in societies that live in harmony with nature, in cultures that consider earth their mother rather than a rival to be conquered.

Socially engaged Buddhism is a vehicle for change. To save this planet, we must first change the social consciousness of the earth's most destructive creature. In his "Ecology of the Mind" meditation, Thich Nhat Hanh states, We need harmony, we need peace. Peace is based on respect for life, the spirit of reverence for life. Not only do we have to respect the lives of human beings, but we have to respect the lives of animals, vegetables, and minerals . . . Ecology In the spirit of Dhamma practice, there is meaning in socially engaged work within an organization. Olendski states, "One very true and sincere manifestation of Dhamma is a fundamental and uncompromising regard for the preservation of life and a recurring impulse toward simplification and purification in both oneself and in a organization." (Olendski, 1990).

International Buddhist organizations have been (relatively) recently formed to engage in more societal and environmental "outside" work. For example, during the Vietnam war, the Tiep Hien Order or Order of Interbeing was created by Thich Nhat Hanh. The order recommends that Buddhism be taken outside of the meditation hall into daily life and society. It addresses social justice, peace, and ecological issues.

By directing people to focus on their interconnection with other beings, Thich Nhat Hanh is asking people to act in collaboration and mutuality with others in the dynamic unfolding of the greater truths which nurture peace, justice, and ecological balance so that they can experience true development of the continuity between the inner and outer world. (Sivaraksa, 1990).

In 1978, the Buddhist Peace Fellowship was formed. It is an international Buddhist organization that promotes awareness of the need for ecological balance in our economic and social development. The Buddhist Peace Fellowship offers Buddhists a way to take their practice into the world of political and social action. The mandate includes raising peace and ecology concerns among Buddhists. It also includes bringing the Buddhist perspective to contemporary peace and ecology movements. (Sivaraksa, 1990)

In February 1989, the International Network of Engaged Buddhists (INEB with headquarters in Bangkok) was formed to link concerned organizations and individuals. The network emphasizes non-violence and self-transformation through insight meditation, to address problems on both the social and spiritual levels. It has the following objectives:

- Promoting understanding and cooperation among Buddhist countries, different Buddhist sects, and socially conscious Buddhist groups.
- Facilitating and carrying out solutions to the many problems facing our communities, societies, and the world. (Two priority areas for INEB are environmental issues and women discrimination issues).
- Articulating the perspective of Engaged Buddhism regarding these problems and training Buddhist activists accordingly.

- Serving as a clearing house of information on existing Engaged Buddhist groups.
- Cooperating with activists from other spiritual traditions. (INEB, 1993)

The orientation of these and similar organizations and efforts in socially engaged Buddhism and environmental affairs (as well as other societal areas) reflect the changing needs and conditions of modern society.

Schalk notes, "Socially engaged Buddhism, which has cultivated diaconical work and social questions is of course an adequate answer to the demands of a new developing functionally differentiated society, which demands from the religious sector border transgressing achievements." (Schalk, 1990) Sivaraksa concurs, "We cannot retreat from the problems and needs of others or our society. We can and must extinguish greed, hate, and delusion by combining spiritual practice and action. We must transform ourselves and our societies if we are to survive." (Sivaraksa, 1993).

Many Buddhists may not accept the interplay between Buddhist practice and activism. Although Buddhists may accept that every being has a purposeful existence and that everything is interdependent, it is difficult for some to accept that one has a responsibility for all that occurs. At the same time, many leading Buddhist writers have recently encouraged Buddhist participation in social and political activities as an extension of spiritual practice. There is a need for some to remain in the temple while others attend to those injured by arrows at the gate. However, when critical destruction of other living beings presents itself, it is difficult to turn away from an opportunity to alleviate suffering and death. (Deike, 1990)

Maha Goshananda, the leading monk in the Cambodian Peace Movement, observes, "We Buddhists must find the courage to leave our temples and enter the temples of human experience, temples that are filled with suffering. This will be a slow transformation, for many people throughout Asia have been trained to rely on the traditional monkhood, but we monks must answer the increasingly loud cries of suffering. We only need to remember that our temple is with us always. We are our temple." (Goshananda, 1992)

Along this line, Kotler argues, To think that we can practice Buddhism independently, in an isolated cell, is to fail to grasp the Buddha's teaching of non-self meditation practice helps us to learn to act with composure. Equanimity ensures us that we are able to sustain the duress of witnessing such extreme suffering. But meditation is not an end in itself. It is a practice which can help us live more peacefully, and share our peace with others I have come to discover that the phrase, 'engaged Buddhism,' is redundant.

We know that an awakened life is possible and our chanting 'May all being be happy' is not just a sacred litany, but our daily responsibility. The Four Noble Truths and the Eightfold Path are no other than a call to know ourselves and to engage in the world in the most enlightened way we can. (Kotler, 1990)

In this sense, Buddhist forest monasteries and temples need to be more open to the world so that they can become the true carriers of the message of Dhamma, a message of engagement and active care. This means being more aware and responsive to people and environmental situations outside as well as inside by providing more access to the monasteries and temples for the purpose of environmental education and public participation activities aside from traditional and meditation practices.

Although the Sangha was originally considered a community for priests and nuns, it was later expanded to include all, including laypeople, who practiced the Buddhist Way in mindfulness and harmony. The Sangha can serve as a bridge for participation between the public, government, private enterprise, and interested parties involved with the environment in a variety of ways.

This is particularly true for situations involving villagers and forests where experienced and respected Sanghas are familiar with local problems and the possible alternatives to solving them. The basic objective of Buddhism and the Sangha, the extinguishing of suffering for all beings, can become a strong motive for public participation of all parties in a given conflict.

Thus the Sangha can serve as a basis for environmental education and public participation based upon the teaching of Dhamma with its love of nature. Phra Debvi notes, "Buddhism teaches that in order to make people love nature they have to be happy with nature. If people are happy with nature, then they will love nature automatically. Therefore we do not need to 'teach' them to love nature. In the Buddhist way of self development, people do not feel forced at all." (Debvedi, 1993)

A love of nature for its own sake will automatically inspire public participation efforts to protect nature. Much of this love can come from extending one's ecological identity to a oneness with nature through the Sangha and practice of Dhamma. Through this liberation, compassion, selfishness, greed, and egoism are removed so that mindfulness, awareness, loving kindness, and wisdom emerge for a true merging with nature. By really recognizing one is a part of nature, one then wants to participate in protecting nature out of love rather than from the "shoulds" of morals and ethics, i.e., a free and flowing love of nature for its own sake without attachments or ego.

GENERAL

Public participation must be based on integrity and truth, both personally and professionally. The Buddha warns against lying and has created a precept to avoid this problem. When one lies, one distorts or muddles one's perception of reality as well as the perceptions/realities of others. Consequently, it is not possible to make good decisions based on false and untrue perceptions and assumptions of the real problems or issues involved. The end result can then accentuate or increase the problem issues by poor and misguided decisions which actually do more harm than good, let alone provide effective and long term solutions.

This is particularly true in the environmental field where governments and industries may sometimes not deal with the full truth of environmental issues while providing the public with only distorted or partial information that may make the public participation ineffective and/or a farce. In the same vein, manipulations, which are a form of lying, may try to get the public and other sources to do what the vested interests want while providing selected and biased information that does not reveal the true picture for a given environmental problem or issue. With the resulting distorted perceptions for the parties involved, it becomes very difficult to address the environmental realities of the problems or issues on a causal or effective basis.

Thus lying and its manipulative forms may become a kind of ignorance (the Buddha observed that ignorance and greed with attachments are causes of suffering) which results in the actual ignoring of environmental problems and issues.

These special interests cloud and distort the issues so that some members of the public may actually assume that "things are being done" in many cases. Yet the STATE OF THE WORLD, 1992, finds that not a single serious environmental trend has been reversed over the years, including the thinning of the ozone layer, 200 plant and animal species condemned to extinction every day, global warming, 17 million hectares of forests vanishing every year, the world population growing at over 92 million annually with 88 million of this total being added to the developing world, over 150 acres of tropical forest destroyed every minute (or half the size of Germany each year). According to studies associated with UN/ ESCAP, approximately 10,000 vertebrates which include birds, amphibians, etc. are destroyed with each square mile of rainforest that is destroyed.

Until ignorance, with its lying and manipulations, are removed, these trends will continue to become extremely grave and call for more complex responses and changes, especially effective and strong public participation. Much of the public may recognize the overall environmental picture as very tragic with denial. Thus there is the need to acknowledge denial and to ask these questions:

- When you consider the world being left to your children, how do you feel?
- What happens when you try to share your feelings with other people?
- How can you help others to overcome their denial of these problems?

In this sense, people need to open their hearts to these questions (much of Buddhism calls for thinking with the heart rather than the mind) and recognize their feelings of grief and helplessness so that they can make the best choices. Based on a "web chart model," it is possible to identify various causes behind environmental issues such as water pollution and erosion due to the destruction of watersheds, the effects of industrial and agricultural pollution, etc.

These problems can be further traced to spiritual corruptions such as greed, ignorance, selfishness and indifference as recognized both by Buddhism and Deep Ecology. It is these deeper causes that must be addressed in public participation, yet they seldom are. Thus Buddhism and Deep Ecology both call for spiritual answers such as loving kindness, compassion, and equanimity as well as recognizing the living forms of land.

There is an interconnectedness and correlation between social and economic structures and their effects upon spiritual problems such as greed and ignorance. These effects are nowhere more clear than in the exploitation of the Southern, or developing countries, by the Northern industrialized nations. But this generalization becomes complicated as newly industrial countries such as Thailand emerge to join the exploitation of other countries. The important consideration here for public participation, however, is to get at the basic causative forces and values in social and economic structures behind the initial developmental proposals which may threaten the environment and its living beings. In this sense, Deep Ecology of the last twenty-some years gets at the causes and asks deeper questions in a deeper dialogue.

The old reform environmentalists of the US and elsewhere from the early 1900's to the present did not challenge the basic assumptions of the system. It simply is not working, and the educational system has also failed. The social, economic, and political systems are at fault in asking merely, "How much is enough?" without really addressing the consequences of this posture. Thus, Deep Ecology brings out the spiritual side of the above. It creates a deeper dialogue for real public participation to address the basic values and causes for change.

The above posture also requires a change of perspective toward science and "experts" for effective public participation. It requires that we put on our "Deep Ecology Glasses" to see things correctly, particularly interrelationships and causes. Too often, the public is intimidated or manipulated by science and its spokesmen for governments and industries. The old science is reductionist and separate, with fixed forms based on control, competition, and assumptions not connected, simple to complex. The new science recognizes life as a flow of energy in what outwardly might be called fixed forms. It recognizes that everything is connected and interrelated to everything else, e.g. co-dependent origination with no hierarchy of simple to complex. Everything is related to everything else and everything is changing. Through using a web chart model, it is possible to identify these energy flows, interrelationships, causes, and basic values behind various environmental problems and developments relative to public participation without being deluded or rebuffed by the old science and "experts."

A major point here is that effective public participation, through Deep Ecology, needs to transcend the old science and establishment experts who tend to intimidate or manipulate the real issues. (Some of the above points on "new" science were gleaned from the Advanced Deep Ecology Workshop with Elias Amidon and Elizabeth Roberts on Dec. 8-17, 1996 at Children's Village School, Kanchanaburi, Thailand). Professor Arne Naess, in his paper on "Experts and Deep Ecology" warns people about the role of "experts" in public participation and environmental/developmental concerns. He notes that private and governmental policies and programs are basically justified by referring only to what hired "experts" say in their official reports. The experts are asked certain carefully selected questions and only these questions are answered in publications by the agency. (Naess, 1984)

Further, officials who pay the experts choose those who will give them answers best suited to justify the policies they wish, or have decided to carry out. This is further complicated by governments having private industries carry out their own environmental assessments and/or impact statements and hence be their own "experts" for the official environmental report to the governments, which, in turn, are also used as official documents for public participation. (Naess, 1984)

Thus Professor Naess says, "On the whole, argumentation must be one-sided and shallow, because the questions are of that character. The aim of government seems to be to justify their economic growth policy, a policy with vast, largely unknown, social and ecological consequences. Because of the kind of questions put and the one-sided choice of experts, the public tend to think that experts on the whole favor the policies their governments and other big institutions and organizations adopt." He recommends that the public seek out experts who are in sympathy with Deep Ecology as well as take a skeptical approach toward experts of government and industry, i.e, to apply Deep Ecology to their public participation efforts. (Naess, 1984)

CASE STUDY

Dhamma-yatra Around Songkhla Lake

"Si Nuan, Si Nuan." These were the most commonly heard words in our recent three week circumambulation of Siam's largest lake. Si Nuan literally means "soft tawny tan color" and is the name of the dog that adopted us from day one. She originally came along with the temple boys from Wat Talae Noi that we pressed into carrying our lead banner on day one. After the boys escaped at the end of the day, Si Nuan displayed a more intrepid ecological spirit and stayed even through the organizers' evaluation sessions at the end. Her name was introduced to thousands of villagers around the lake and the "fans" who followed the progress of the walk through various call-in radio programs. So it was that people who had never seen her before called out her name as she wandered and wagged among our straggling crew of monks, lay folks, students, foreigners, and for the last week a single nun.

The Songkhla Lake Dhamma Walk was conceived and planned by national and local members of Phra Sekhiyadhamma with help from Southern NGOs, village leaders and some government officials. Phra Sekhiyadhamma is a small but growing network of grassroots monks struggling to integrate our study and practice of Buddha- Dhamma with responsibility for the communities, culture, and society we see crumbling around us. Modernity brings many wonders but we ponder why so much is destroyed in exchange.

Further, we ask why the poor ordinary majority of the people seem to pay the most for and benefit the least from the wonders of "spinning according to the world" (the literal meaning of lokanuiwat, the most common Thai translation for globalization), while having little or no say in the decision making. We believe that Buddha-Dhamma is relevant to all forms of suffering, including these. We believe that Sangha is more than yellow-robed shavelings chanting for meals and ought to be a "Sangha of the People" fully engaged in solving their communal, ecological, and economic problems (dukkha). (It is still too controversial to suggest that monks might have a role in solving political problems, although senior monks have been meddling for centuries and local monks are allowed to broker villagers' votes in so-called "elections.") We dedicate ourselves to "the Dhamma for training ourselves" (the literal meaning of sekhiyadhamma) that enables us to effectively serve the Triple Gem and all beings within the present realities and structures of dukkha.

Our network organized the walk to test the value and effectiveness of peace walks as a form of moral persuasion within Thai Buddhist & Muslim cultures. Our first goal was to help bring attention to the dilemma of the lake, Siam's largest and uniquely complex and prolific ecosystem. In doing so, we wanted to establish a middle way between protest marches and apathetic silence. Some of us see ever more violent clashes over natural resources in Siam's future and hope that monks, nuns, and other Buddhist leaders can help mediate just and peaceful resolutions.

A second goal was to help build up the peoples' network around the lake in order to give them a greater voice in working out policies and projects. We see a natural role for monks as facilitators of such a network and wanted to encourage such participation from local monks. A few were already involved in their own areas but not yet effectively cooperating with other monks, village leaders, and NGO workers in other parts of the lake. Lastly, we wanted to identify local monks who would be willing to join us in our engaged Buddhist work, both around the lake and on national issues.

We were moderately successful in these goals. We stirred up publicity for the lake and the voices of the people living close to it (see below). We were accepted and praised by some senior monks, while no serious criticisms arose.

We were blessed with the presence, sharing, and advice of Samdech Mahaghosananda from Cambodia. A precedent has been set. And the strands of a Songkhla Lake Sekhiyadhamma that is able to work with the peoples' and NGO's networks are being woven together. The progress may not yet be large but it is nonetheless significant. New ground has been tilled. It was our first large-scale activity. Finally, we proved that such walks are possible here and that they have potential for popularity.

THE ISSUES

We generally presented ourselves to the people living around the lake as concerned "outsiders" who wanted to learn more about what the residents themselves thought than to offer our own analysis and solutions. We wanted to strengthen the voice of the lake's people, especially the poor and marginalized.

Here, we must be forthright about a certain bias for the poor community members, while trying to avoid being against the developers, land speculators, factory owners, middle-class suburbanites, and others who are slowly buying off, tempting away, and pushing out the locals.

The latter group already has a voice, plenty of influence, and significant political-economic power. We are not against them and are delighted to have some of them with us. (Most of the lay walkers were from middle-class urban lifestyles.) Yet it is crucial to create a space in which the ignored members of society the intimidated and downtrodden silent majority are encouraged to speak. Only then can there be true dialog and democracy on the issues facing us all (even farang like myself).

The issues we heard, then, from representatives of the people were many. I will summarize the main five.

(1) No fish to eat. The amount and diversity of fish and shrimp have deteriorated grievously, especially within the last 3 to 5 years. Many species have disappeared, including delicious ones. We heard stories of bow fish used to jump into people's boats, there were so many! People blamed the problem on over-fishing (by themselves and others); use of intensive fishing technologies, such as drag nets, electric shock and poison; fishing during the spawning seasons; and the deterioration of the water (see below). Manmade disruptions in the normal circulation of sea, rain, and brackish water through various channels between the sea and lake have interfered with the migrations of the fish fry that swam in the once interchanging currents. Destructions of mangroves and other spawning grounds due to "development" and prawn farms has cut the bottom out from under efforts of the marine life to reproduce.

(2) Bad water, and there isn't as much water as there used to be. Depending on your perspective, the water is either much more shallow than before, the bottom is silting up, or the whole system is drier. Further, the remaining water is dirty and unable to cleans itself naturally. Erosion due to deforestation on the mountains has to the North and East, the conversion of wetlands to rice fields, and the building of roads has led to dramatic levels of siltation. The pollution from towns, factories, agricultural chemicals, and tiger prawn farms has poisoned the water in many places. In some places, bathers end up with skin rashes where not long ago the water was potable.

(3) Theft of water. Increasingly, water is taken up for urban and industrial uses resulting in less drainage into the lake. Had Yai, in particular, is the primary excuse for a dam that most of the lake people do not want. This is on top of the use of lake water for irrigation some parts of the lake and tiger prawn farms in others.

(4) Loss of land: With the spread of Had Yai and other large southern towns, increasing land is covered with concrete subdivisions. Wetlands are turned into "Songhia Lagunas" for the middle class (while former residents are denied entry or even passage through these new "villages").

(5) Breakdown of community. With the loss of traditional livelihoods, the siphoning off of the young into towns, relocation of homes to the new roads, domination of former village leaders ("headmen") by government, and the deterioration of the Wats, the lake's communities have little strength left to hold them together.

Too often, the unifying factor is the lack of opportunities elsewhere. This is a tragic dilemma for a society to impose on its people, to deprive them of old joys, bonds, and strengths while denying them new ones. Seeing this convinced many of us that ecological problems are inevitably cultural and moral problems with profound cultural and moral consequences. In addition, let me add a couple observations of my own. I was shocked to find that the area we passed through at the beginning of the walk , the northwest shore of the upper lake, which had been converted from rich and diverse flood forests into rice fields, was as poor as areas in Siam's Isaan. Isaan, the Northeast, with poor soils, a harsher climate, and more patient, docile, happygo- lucky inhabitants is the poorest part of the country, while the South is much richer in resources and incomes. What was such poverty doing here?

The common denominator was rice! Farmers have been taught to deplete their soils and invest in chemicals. If they only kept books they would realize that there is no way they can make a profit on the rice crop. Thus, poverty by policy. There is not yet a strong enough coalition of peoples' leaders to arrive at the people's consensus needed to save the lake and its human resources. In fact, we often heard villagers in one area blaming their difficulties on their peers in another part of the lake. We suspect this is encouraged by some government agents.

We tried to be a channel through which villagers could begin to hear each other and begged them to visit their counterparts around the lake. Thus, in identifying the main issues of the people, and in a more detailed analysis to be published in Thai, we are hoping to work towards such a consensus in order that the people themselves will have a determining role in the activities undertaken to preserve the lake's ecosystem and cultural systems.

The basis for such a comprehensive approach is:

1. Dialogue among village and religious leaders from all around the lake.
2. Collective analysis of the problems and their causes.
3. Freedom from domination by the government, politicians, and business interests (although they must be brought into the process eventually).
4. And a solidarity plan of action determined by the people themselves, supported by NGO's and the government, with the moral guidance of engaged religious leaders. Such an approach will not happen easily. The people have been effectively brainwashed against such action.

There is always the danger that such walks will be seen merely as a "protest walk" and rejected. A walk led by monks would come under much criticism for overtly protesting, especially when many of us were from outside the area. Fortunately, we were able to establish a "middle way" of walking. Our role was to listen to the people rather than tell them what was going on and what to do. We avoided taking sides (although individual walkers often had their points of view).

With monks in the lead, a number of Buddhist customs and traditions came into play. Some were unexpected, even troublesome. At times, we didn't know what to do with the flood of food and the expectation of a sermon delayed our setting out until the sun was full up in the sky, that is, blazing hot in the middle of the hot, dry season. On the other hand, lots of people came out to see us, motivated by saddha, and raised our spirits.

We were warned to avoid the word "environment" by Ven PA Payuddho, Siam's leading scholar-monk and an advisor to Phra Sekhiyadhamma. He feels that the word, betraying its Western origins, separates human beings from the rest of Nature. In Buddhism, we ought to speak of Nature or ecology inclusive of everything, especially ourselves.

People kept giving us water bottled in throw-away plastic. We had not taken precautions to avoid this and similar ecologically destructive habits.

Those who came out to the Wats and joined us on the roads were primarily the old. This partly reflects the reality of village Buddhism; it is trapped in a time no longer relevant to the young. It also reflects the economic reality where young people are collected in pickup trucks to work in fish & prawn packing factories. We must be very creative in reaching out to all members of the community.

Many of the old people were delighted to see us walking. In their youth, everyone walked daily. A ten km trip to the market was ordinary. Now, the young need motor-scooters to get anywhere. It was much harder to get the young to join us for a stroll to the next village than the old folks.

As a minority of the community around the lake are Muslim, we hoped to involve them in the walk, too. With some exceptions, we were not very successful in this. The exceptions give us hope that we will do better next year. Especially as the monks (Phra Sekhiyadhamma) will share more of the organizing with local groups. Perhaps a few Muslim leaders will join us in reflections about the walk.

There has been little experience of monks and NGO's working together beyond the personal level. This was the first time we knew of that a group of monks worked with NGO's to plan a large-scale activity. A lot of learning and unlearning was required. Different working cultures, turf battles, prejudices about each other, communication styles, and the like only got in the way, but in the end, we found that we can work together in the spirit of Dhamma. Sometimes the monks were able to help the NGO workers to let go of an attachment, sometimes it was the other way around.

We were let down by some senior monks and our own Abbot (the chief organizer lives with me here at Dawn Kiam) who tried to talk us out of the walk. Paradoxically, one of them, a nationally respected preacher, has frequently praised Gandhi over the years, but in typical monkish fashion divorces Gandhi's actions from his words. Beautiful ideals are OK, but please don't stir up any trouble by putting them into serious practice. Yes, friends, Thai Buddhism is dying of hypocrisy masquerading as "objective Dhamma teaching." Still, there is a growing movement trying to breathe life back into the not-quite-corpse.

Walking together gave many opportunities for making friends, sharing hardships & joys, learning, and growing in Dhamma. These opportunities can be nurtured with good group process, which must be adequately prepared in advance. When we were able to include time for inter-personal work within the group, the results were satisfying and conflicts dissolved. The many friendships forged and strengthened are an important sign of the walk's value.

BUDDHIST REVIVAL

At heart, Phra Sekhiyadhamma is working for a revival of Thai Buddhism. We fear that the current hierarchy, used by politicians and bedazzled by the wealthy, is leading Thai Buddhism down the tubes. Along the walk, we saw pathetic signs of decay. Wats cluttered with garbage left over from festivals. The festivals put on by businessmen, not community members, who make big profits off of the gambling and drinking (and give the Wat a percentage). Monks hanging out all day with cigarettes drooping from bored lips and eyes gazing blankly. The Wat's crockery tossed into back rooms with no respect for the donors. Many Wats with just one octogenarian monk unable to look after the place or to communicate with people less than half his age (they lived in different worlds, eras).

Yet all was not hopeless and doomed. There were well kept Wats and on-the-ball monks here and there. The people came out in mass at Wat after Wat to greet and feed us. Seeds of faith remain, but must be watered with Dhamma teachings and cultivated with community development. Thus, we see grassroots engaged Buddhism as one way to salvage what is alive in the tradition and adjust to the future. It is a crucial element in any reversal of the cultural decay that is taking the Thainess ("Siamness") out of Thailand. The basic responsibilities of study, meditation, and service must be rejuvenated and encouraged in all monks, especially the young, and often aimless, ones. Then they will be able to find their way in partnership with the people. Although we did not find many nuns, they, too, must be supported to grow into a meaningful role within the temples and communities. this reason, Phra Sekhiyadhamma and its friends will remain mindfully vigilant.

Lastly, it is clear that the presence of foreigners—American, Bangladeshi, Chakma, Australian, Haitian, Canadian—helped to spark interest among local residents and to spread the word to other countries. Thus, we invite you all to join us next year. Perhaps you could walk with us for a week or two of Dhammayatra II, then join the Cambodians for part of Dhammayatra VI.

And Si Nuan, our mascot, will probably be there, too. She has been adopted by Phramaha Jaroen Dejadhammo, the leading activist monk at the south end of the lake and is being pampered, or prepared for next year. She was a bit ragged at the end, too, but her tail kept wagging and she joined all the meetings. (Santikara, 1996)

NEXT YEAR

Throughout the walk, villagers asked if we would be back next year. My reply was always, "It depends on whether local groups care enough to do the organizing." At the closing, the walkers themselves overwhelmingly wished for another walk next year. Some even wanted two: a second around the Lake and another elsewhere in Siam (tragically, there is plenty of ecological & cultural destruction going on in this "Tiger Cub"). Southern NGO's have agreed to help organize it, so plans are already underway for next year (mid-April through mid-May). Only four years behind our Khmer friends, Dhammayatra is now set to be enshrined as a legitimate form of social statement in Siam. With popularity, however, will come the danger that the Dhamma is watered down or filtered out by interest groups.

APPROACHES TO PUBLIC PARTICIPATION

The Deep Ecology movement can often be considered a response and resistance to the excesses of the exploitative use and destruction of nature through human domination. As a visionary movement, it encourages community building, bioregional approaches, culture of place, and public participation activism.

Ecological resistance actions can be considered creative public participation to protect biological and cultural diversity as well as to draw attention to agents, institutions, and their impacting activities which threaten this diversity. Deep Ecology activists are committed to creating sustainable alternatives based on the integrity of ecosystems and a joyous vision of healthy and natural interrelationships.

The Deep Ecology movement strives to transform biologically and socially destructive world views and behavior of modern civilization into life supporting activities on a holistic and value basis for spiritual, intellectual, psychological, and social arenas. The Deep Ecology movement draws on insights and liberation factors of other ecological resistance movements, including ecofeminism, anti-nuclear, social justice, peace, and animal rights movements. (Roberts and Amidon, 1996)

The belief that we are all part of all living things kindles an awareness that destruction of any part of the environment is a personal injury. Destruction of the Amazon rain forest wounds the stock broker living in New York. Pollution of a river in Ohio diminishes the life of a monk in the mountains of Tibet. Extinction of a species in Africa alters the life of a baby born today in Charles City, Iowa.

Public participation in environmental assessments, planning, and decision-making has become increasingly important in recent years. Up to now, public participation in conservation decisions has been rare and inadequate. Consequently, the decisions being made may not reflect sufficiently the experience, values and wishes of the people affected, and the benefits of the program or project may be fewer than expected. Lack of awareness of the benefits of conservation and of its relevance to everyday concerns prevents the public from seeing the urgent need to achieve conservation objectives. Ultimately, ecosystems and species are destroyed because people do not see that it is in their interests not to destroy them.

Participation tends to build public confidence and improve the public's understanding of management objectives. It provides additional data for planners and policy makers. Public participation is particularly important in rural development, for without the active involvement of the people—including identification by them of the problems that most need tackling and how to deal with them—little can be achieved.

Effective planning and implementation require specific information of the sort only local people can provide efficiently. . . . people usually cooperate more willingly in decisions in which they have participated. Integration of activities and services created under government auspices are those identified as more important and valuable. "The judgment of the people affected by development programmes is essential for the evaluation of such programmes." (IUCN, 1980)

To be successful, a country's environmental management effort must enjoy a high level of public support. This is particularly true of initiatives which affect the rural and urban poor. The importance of programs for forest protection, sanitation, family planning, pesticide management, and the like must be understood by citizens if long-term success is to be realized.

Many developing countries may use mass media to generate popular support for environmental management programs. In many areas, however, it may be fair to say that the most important stimulus to public support has been the public's direct experience of the consequences of inadequate environmental management. Ultimately the behavior of entire societies towards the biosphere must be transformed if the achievement of conservation objectives is to be assured. A new ecological ethic, embracing plants and animals as well as people, is required for human societies to live in harmony with the natural world on which they depend for survival and well-being. "The long-term task of responsible societies is to foster or reinforce attitudes (values) and behavior compatible with this new ethic." (IUCN, 1980) Until people understand why they should safeguard the environment, they usually will not do so.

Some overall objectives for public participation should include:

(1) to promote public involvement in planning and actions, with emphasis on the non-technical aspects.

(2) to keep the public informed about significant issues, problems, and changes in programs, associated values and alternatives.

(3) to make sure that government and personnel understand public concerns and values and that they are responsive to them, including public identification of issues and alternatives.

(4) to demonstrate that the government and agencies consult with affected segments of the public and takes public viewpoints and values into consideration when decisions are made.

(5) to foster public involvement in identifying problems, laying out and exploring alternatives, and setting forth a preferred alternative.

(6) to foster a spirit of mutual trust, support and openness between government and the public through contacts for public participation.

Formal Public Hearings: Formal hearings produce official hearing records of all information presented by all individuals, groups, and organizations. Although public hearings comply with legal requirements, they tend to involve high costs for recording, slow down the decision-making processes, and often intimidate the general public. Thus, public hearings are often employed because they are officially required.

Public Meetings: Open public meetings permit participation by all interested people. They may involve panel discussions and public forums. The former provide expert testimony and information to the public on complicated issues in a number of professional areas. A panel of experts can provide the public with all information pertinent to a plan or decision. A public forum is organized so members of the public can present their viewpoints, critiques and proposals to other people and to the agency itself. The stage for public forums should be set with a brief presentation of facts upon which the decision can be based. A group of alternative solutions with or without their pros and cons may be introduced. Clear guidelines, time limits, and "rules" should be given to those making presentation so that all have adequate time and orientations. All participants should be free to ask questions and make their views known.

Guided Workshops: These provide an opportunity for public discussion, debate and clarification of issues, proposed actions, and consequences of actions. If values, self-interests, and arguments are expressed, it is possible to correct rumors, create mitigating elements, and provide information. Public opinion is seldom organized or consistent over time and guided workshops The following represents a random list of some techniques available for public participation, as adapted and summarized from the U.S. Forest Service, A Guide to Public Involvement in Decision Making and the National Part Service, Public Involvement in Planning.

A guided workshop is characterized by two activities: facilitation of commentary and recording of ideas. Facilitation is a method of verbal communication intended to clarify messages by reducing distracting effects. It serves to check the accuracy of what is being heard. Recording is the creation of a written record of the points which are being made. This is usually done with a large notation pad completed in full view of the people in attendance. The joint efforts of facilitating and recording are to maintain a focus on the topic issues and to avoid ambiguity.

Informal Small Group Meetings: These can be invitational meetings with interested individuals or groups. A series of meetings may be necessary to cover the variety of groups as well as to keep the attendance small enough for informality and thorough discussion. The subject matter covered and the format of the meetings should stick to the basic issues. Informal meetings are productive if they are used early in the decision-making process, especially when personnel are gathering information and developing alternatives. This technique permits concerned people to participate and to have a meaningful input at a time when informed points of view are most helpful.

Advisory Committees: An advisory committee (board or commission) is a standing body formally established to advise or make recommendations. The background knowledge and the understanding of policies and programs of a committee allows it to provide sound advice. It should represent a wide range of groups and interests. Advisory committees can be very effective as a sounding board for proposals and as an indicator of public attitudes and interests. However, the selection of members may introduce bias so that the membership may not represent the entire range of the public interests. Regularly scheduled meetings of advisory committees can provide a continued forum for disseminating information, clarifying issues, obtaining advice, and gaining support.

Ad Hoc Committees: An ad hoc committee is a temporary committee to address specific issues and recommend solutions. When an issue is resolved or recommendations completed, the committee is dissolved. Committee recommendations can be by majority, consensus, or expression of individual points of view. Selection of membership should be oriented toward fair representation from sources and views that reflect general public opinion.

Working Groups: A working group consists of a manageable number (usually under twelve) of motivated members of the general public who want to be involved in the long term management and planning of an agency or governmental area. The group has autonomy and no formal relationships with the agency. Ideally, the working group will have a spectrum of viewpoints associated with the diversity of its membership. The working group is usually served by a resource person from the agency or organization. This individual basically supplies information. The agency assigns tasks to the working group and indicates that their inputs will be considered in decision-making. After various meetings, the working group presents its consensus recommendations in the form of written responses to the tasks after studying and discussing the issues and working out their own intergroup compromises.

Key Contacts: Advice obtained from key knowledgeable individuals about public issues provides counsel worthwhile to the decision-making process. Key contacts include people who are opinion leaders within the local community or region such as elected or appointed officials, media representatives, active members of organized groups, businessmen, and respected citizens.

Too close a relationship with a few selected individuals should be avoided so that opportunities for the broad solicitation of public points of view are not overlooked.

The emphasis should be on gathering their opinions and values about issues, ideas, etc., while not asking them to support any position. Strengths of key contacts are: (a) input and valuable insights can be obtained from informed, influential people who can often indicate important aspects of public opinion; (b) key people can inform others about issues and stimulate input; (c) the involvement of key people can contribute to public understanding and acceptance of decisions; (d) input can be obtained personally, and in depth and detail; and (e) they are sounding boards for ideas, issues, or approaches before they are finalized.

Letter Requests for Comments: Letters can be very effective when the individuals contacted have the necessary knowledge of the issues. Letters should address the broad interests and not be limited to the local area. Letters may be used with other methods to provide a public feeling of involvement to assure good decisionmaking. For example, fact sheets on development and/or management alternatives can be included in the letters. Follow-up on letter contacts and responses is essential.

Show Me Trips: Field trips early in the planning stage are very effective in involving the public and assuring an understanding of the issue(s). Show-me trips set the stage for quality and meaningful participation. Interplay among participant help clarify the issues and identify possible consequences. Show-me trips require detailed preparation, and trial runs are advisable.

Personnel Contacts with Public: Many organizational personnel routinely contact the public in carrying out their jobs and through community activities.

For example, personnel serving on local and regional committees have excellent opportunities to influence planning on regional or community projects, and to acquire information on current attitudes and interests of local and regional people by listening to their comments. Personnel need to be thoroughly informed so they can be a valuable bridge to greater understanding.

Standard Information Techniques: Standard information techniques include:

(a) the type of audience to be reached,

(b) the length of time available to prepare materials,

(c) the amount of detail expected to be covered, and

(d) the scope of the audience to be reached.

Several different information techniques can be used to fit the situation, such as visual aids, pamphlets, flyers and feature articles. The multiplying factor of newspapers, TV, radio and magazines will greatly expand the scope and impact of any message. Press releases, for example, can invite comments to assure that anyone may provide input into the decision making process. The news media may require background facts with which to inform the public, or may print a statement for which additional information can be obtained by writing the agency. Individual responses to press releases provide opportunities for input and follow-up.

The above techniques can be adapted and used in environmental education sessions dealing with public participation and related training areas. Role playing, with the participants acting out roles of group leaders or officials, can enhance understanding and increase skills of many of the techniques, including switching roles. Demonstrations of selected techniques using local people and situations can also be valuable. Case studies and audio-visual materials may be used to illustrate the above techniques.

Environmental education can provide a basic orientation for public participation activities and techniques, particularly with emphasis on values and Deep Ecology. A government agency generally may try to maximize public values within the limits of its policy, values, and management. The values of a given agency will seldom be represented by any single segment of public input. However, a value approach would permit greater responsiveness to public values. Following a public participation program or time period, agency personnel must interpret public responses so that their decision making can use it effectively. They should review all oral and written inputs. Informational categories can be developed to provide personnel and interested parties to evaluate the public input.

Categories might include the following: Who is replying to the issue or proposal under consideration? Is it the general public, developmental organizations, conservation organizations, key people, or others? What are they saying? Do they agree or disagree with the matter at hand or are their opinions (values) coupled with no important qualifications? Skimming letters and other written responses is helpful in determining the numbers and categories that may be needed.

Why are they saying what they do? Understanding the motivation (values) that underlie a person's stand may prove useful to the administrator. It may provide insight as to the gaps in public knowledge and understanding of management goals and conservation. Thus, it may also suggest directions for public environmental education programs of the agency. Where are the responses coming from? The geographical location of the letter writer can demonstrate the spatial extent of public concern. This, in turn, can provide personnel with some notion of how local versus non-local residents perceive and understand the problem at hand. Analyzing responses may also indicate where positive or adverse responses are coming from. For example, the majority of support for a development proposal may come from a local industry.

The evaluation and interpretation of public input is an art rather than a science. It can be qualified and objectively analyzed only in parts. Then the decision-maker must evaluate it qualitatively on an "art" basis. This is basically value interpretation and analysis to seek the overall "truth" and honesty in a creative manner. Thus, a value approach permits the identification and analysis of public inputs in terms of value considerations for decision-making.

Training in communications is very important. Communication "gaps" create vagueness and uncertainties which negatively affect public participation and increases the conflict between values and issues. These problems are difficult to resolve. It is essential to identify and surface, at the earliest stage of public review, the difficult problems and thorny issues that have the greatest potential for causing public concern and reaction. By urging the public to have the fullest and (earliest) possible involvement and input in developing alternative solutions, it is possible to build open lines of communication and trust for effective public participation.

But much depends upon what is our hearts and minds as noted by a statement by Phra Prachak, a Buddhist Forest Monk who lead us on a Deep Ecology walk in Dong Yai National Forest, Thailand, in December of 1994: Many of us have heard the Buddha's teachings and understand them here, in our minds—but not in our hearts. It's the same with the environment. We hear of its importance. We know that it is a home for the animals and trees, which also give us fresh, cool water. But the problem's in our talking as if there is a difference between the environment and ourselves.

Meditation, the process of self-examination, teaches us the natural law of impermanence. It teaches us about the inter-relatedness of all things. And when we truly see and understand this in our hearts, we see the forest as something more than something which needs to be protected or something useful.

The forest is life itself. It is us and we are it. When we destroy or harm the forest, we are doing the same thing to ourselves. And without the forest, it will not be possible for us to fully understand our proper place in the world. We simply will not survive. (Prachak, 1994)

A DOVE IN THE FOREST (OLD JATAKA TALE)

A long time ago, there was a thick forest. Trees were fresh and deep. The air was crystal clear; it was sending the echoes of birds singing a beautiful melody, enchanting comfortable life there. The sky was so blue and open. The forest was full of grace, hope and peace. In this forest, there were thousands and thousands of creatures living together as one in harmony with nature. One day, a dove flew over the forest to look for food for its babies. When she returned, the dove saw a big fire rising up in the forest! All the living creatures, including birds, animals, plants, and flowers were trying to escape, desperately crying for help in this terrible disaster.

The dove was astonished to see this happening, yet had no time to think. She immediately flew off to a lake far away. When the dove arrived at the lake, she jumped into the water and had its body completely soaked. The dove flew up again and hurried into the burning forest. Flying back to where the fire was blazing briskly, the dove shook its body and dropped a few portions of water. Then she took off to a long flight to get to the lake again. In this way, the dove made many trips between the lake and the forest. The Heaven above, upon watching what was happening in the forest on the earth, asked the dove, "Do you think that you, of humble body, can stop the fire with those few shakes of water?"

The dove answered, "The fire must be stopped as soon as possible. There are children. There are my fellows. And there is the very forest who nurtures all of our lives. Everything is caught is a big fire now. I have something to do. I will continue making trips this way, until I die." Eventually, the earnest wish and the prayer of this one little dove was taken to the Heaven. a heavy rain was brought to the forest and the fire ceased. The forest returned to a peaceful, beautiful place which it once was.

ENVIRONMENTALLY RELEVANT PRINCIPLES OF BUDDHISM

The philosophical principles of Buddhism and feminism overlap and complement each other in a number of areas, mutually supporting an interdependent, systems-oriented view of the environment. There are also several areas in which one of these is underdeveloped in its traditions, practices, or teachings and is enhanced or influenced by exposure to the other. I outline here six areas of confluence, with some comments on differences that are not yet fully addressed.

Experiential Knowing

In contrast to much of Western philosophy and theology, Buddhism begins with the truth of personal experience. Experiential knowing in relationship to spiritual development is valued over textual, abstract, or other sources of knowing, which are distant from the individual (see Suzuld 1949, 267-313). The early canons of Buddha's teachings repeatedly urged the practitioner to thoroughly study his or her own experience and mental conditioning in order to break through the limitations of the falsely constructed self. The Buddha insisted his followers not take his authority as a final say on any matter, but rather sincerely investigate the teachings for themselves. Meditation practices aim to quiet and stabilize the mind so it is capable of observing thoughts, sensations, and actions in great detail.

One's own mind and experience are the places in which one learns to recognize the universal nature of suffering (the first of the Four Noble Truths in Buddhism). Experiential knowing is based on embodied mindfulness practices that develop awareness of need and greed, the suffering of pleasure and pain, and the impermanent nature of things. The content for this teaming is always one's own life. One's spiritual challenge is to investigate in depth the accumulated patterns of response to physical, social, mental, and psychological stimuli in order to liberate the practitioner from the suffering of unconsciousness. By shining the light of awareness on the nature of one's own conditioned reality, one finds the freedom to act effectively and skilfully, grounded in thorough self-knowledge. This experiential knowing or study of self in body, speech, and mind lies at the heart of all traditions of Buddhist teachings. Dogen Zenji, ninth-century Japanese Zen Master, expressed this:

> To study the buddha way is to study the self.
>
> To study the self is to forget the self.
>
> To forget the self is to be actualized by myriad things. (Tanahashi 1985, 70)

Feminism is equally clear on the importance of experiential knowing as a foundation for social action and personal insight. The feminist movement in the United States, as well as in other countries, has consistently emphasized that women speak their own truths with their own voices. Feminists have encouraged women to reclaim the stories of their lives and speak what they know from direct experience. The personal is recognized as the political, for it is a genuine place of truth telling. This has meant speaking out about the painful suffering of sexual and environmental abuse, articulating the power of women's emotions, and hearing the realities of women's bodies and environmental health concerns.

In feminist religious studies in Buddhist and other traditions, women struggle with the discontinuity between personal experience and patriarchal tradition, looking for new language, forms, and community that match women's religious experience (see Plaskow and Christ 1989). Feminists have validated the important realm of subjective knowing, acknowledging the inner experience of self that places the knower in an interior as well as exterior context (Belenky et al. 1986). Subjective knowing in women has been consistently denigrated by Western patriarchal cultures as self-centered, romantic, and distorted by emotionality. The scientific inquiry method, which insists on the necessity of an objective perspective, is the extreme opposite of subjective or interior knowing.

It depends completely on the assumption that the actor can be separate from the object of one's actions (see Harding 1986). This overlooks the critical discipline of subjective knowing that reveals the inner structure and conditioning of the individual mind. It is this built-in conditioning that limits accuracy and objectivity in perception. Integrated, experiential knowing, which includes both object of knowing and the knower herself, is necessary for understanding the compleidties of the envirorinaental crisis.

For many women, the experience of knowing in relation to the natural world develops the mind-body's response to other beings and to lunar and seasonal cycles, informed by kinesthetic and sensory awareness. Body rhythms and responses to the earth have long been celebrated in earth-based spiritual traditions such as the Goddess cultures, not necessarily only by women. Among Buddhist cultures, the Japanese and others have cultivated an emotional and aesthetic attitude toward the natural world that represents intimate and pre-reflective encounter with the environment. In the Japanese view, nature is seen as the realm of "spontaneous becoming" a meeting ground for the dynamic unfolding of person, tree, rock, and bird (Tellenbach and Kimura 1989, 155).

The embodied knowing of child and mother can be a model for intimate relations with the earth (Levitt 1990). The child in the womb knows only mother as earth; it is surrounded by, sustained by, and conditioned by the mother as context. Likewise, the earth is body to the woman, completely informing, conditioning, and nourishing her life. This metaphor does not imply that women have preferred access to these truths (the "essentialist" position in feminist philosophy). Rather, embodied knowing for any person is a direct link to experience of relationship with the earth. The earth itself can be seen as Buddha's body, supporting all lives, being the Great Life.

Embodied knowing is a source of confidence for embodied spirituality and environmental political action. The Buddhist and feminist emphasis on direct experience of the environment is informed by the body as mind, rather than body and mind as separate. Through knowing based on experience, one becomes grounded in actual reality rather than in one's ideas of reality. Through this grounding, the practitioner gains a legitimate voice with which to speak personally and specifically of environmental relationships and how they are ignored, sabotaged, or otherwise denied.

Examining the Conditioned Mind

Central to Buddhist philosophy and meditation method is the practice of discriminating wisdom. This is the detailed study of how things work-both in external and internal realities and in the interaction and co-creation of the two. The purpose is to break through delusions that generate and perpetuate a sense of an independent and separately existing self. The discriminating mind can expose rationalized actions and mental cultural-emotional habits that perceive beings as separate objects rather than as members of a web of relationships. In the context of the environment, there are at least three prevalent patterns of thought that block relational perception (Kaza 1989). One common thought habit is stereotyping of animals and ecosystems by describing them in oversimplified terms.

People tend to lump the few characteristics they know of an organism or plant community into a generic representative that does not accurately reflect reality. For example, the generic whale is playful, altruistic, intelligent, large, and gentle -each characteristic fitting one species or another, but not existing anywhere in this combination in a real whale. Emotional responses to plant communities also lead to undifferentiated labelling. Deserts are viewed as wastelands, and all forests are seen as cool, dark places, despite the many differences in topography, climate, plant and animal inhabitants, and human history.

A second form of objectification is projection, in which the mind projects internalized ideas onto favored and unfavored elements of the environment. By reducing the reality of a forest to someone's idea of a forest, the community becomes objectified-seen as object with a convenient name and simplified description. "Cute" or "nice" animals, such as deer, rabbits, and songbirds, elicit more sympathetic responses than "mean" animals, such as coyotes, spiders, and bats (Keflert 1989).

Likewise, good land is land that can be farmed or developed; bad land is what is too steep, dry, or impenetrable to be subdued. A third prevalent thought habit is dualistic thinking, in which one object or idea is placed in opposition to another, often with the implication that one has power or superiority over the other. Self-other opposition forms the mental basis for anthropocentric relationships with plants and animals, as well as prejudice and racism. We-they conflicts, expressed in views of the environment as enemy, share the same mental polarizing structure as mind-body, creator-created, nature-culture dualisms (see Keen 1986).

The mind separates and distances one side of the polarity from the other, rather than seeing the opposites as complementary and inclusive, each arising in the context of the other. Feminism has exposed a particular aspect of conditioned thinking generally overlooked in Buddhism: the influence of gender identity and cultural habits of objectifying women. Many writers have described in depth the suffering that has resulted from oppressive dualistic thinking, projection, and stereotyping of women. Ecofeminist philosopher Karen Warren suggests three features of oppressive conceptual frameworks that apply both to treatment of women and the environment (Warren 1990).

The first, value-hierarchical thinking, refers to placing value or giving preference to what is seen as being of higher status, as opposed to considering all things equally. The second, value dualism, points to the typically Western pattern of viewing opposites as exclusive, and then assigning moral superiority to one-half of the dualism, i.e., male-female, day-night, temperate-tropical, vertebrate-invertebrate. The third feature is the theme of domination, the argument that justifies subordination of one opposite by the other.

To uphold this logic requires considerable mental and social cooperation with oppressive cultural conditioning. One can see this logic at work in rationalizing intolerable conditions for laboratory and factory-farm animals (Kheel 1989).The same dominating, objectifying mind that uses women for sex objects also justifies the use of land for strip-mining and forests for clear-cutting. Those with international power promote development projects for less industrialized nations that contribute not only to environmental degradation, but also to the oppression and further impoverishment of women (Shiva 1988).

In highly industrialized nations, women are subjected to aggressive domination by powerful market advertising that manipulates their desires for consumer products. Both Buddhism and feminism provide critical tools for examining deeply the roots of antirelational concepts that support envirommental destruction. Both insist on thorough review of all aspects of the conditioned mind that perpetuate mental and physical patterns of domination. However, because Buddhism has been transmitted almost entirely through patriarchal cultures, its investigation of gender conditioning is underdeveloped. This weakens the Buddhist argument for ecological interdependence, because it misses the critical link between patterns of oppression of women and the environment. The feminist Buddhist position includes the connection, observing the nature of mind in women and men that sustains a separate self, capable of dominating humans and environment.

THE TRUTH OF INTERRELATEDNESS

The fundamental law in Buddhism is the Law of Dependent Co-Arising: that all events and beings are interdependent and interrelated. The universe is described as a mutually causal web of relationship, each action and individual contributing to the nature of many others (Kalupahana 1987, 26). The Pali word for this law, Paticca-samuppada, explains the truth in its literal meaning. Paticca means "grounded on or on account of'; sam is "together," and uppada means "arising." Thus the whole phrase can be translated "the being-on-account-of-arising-together." Or in the text, This being, that becomes; from the arising of this, that arises; this not being, that becomes not; from the ceasing of this, that ceases.

An linage for this cosmology is the Jewel Net of Indra, from the Mahayana Buddhist tradition (Cook 1989, 213-30). The multidimensional net stretches through all space and time, connecting an infinite number of jewels in the universe. Each jewel is infinitely multifaceted and reflects every other jewel in the net. There is nothing outside the Net and nothing which does not reverberate its presence throughout the web of relationships.

This law is one of the most obvious connections between Buddhism and the environment. As ecologists point out in example after example, ecological systems are connected through water, air, and such pathways. Impacts of chemical pesticides on agricultural lands carry to adjacent wetlands; industrial carbon emissions affect global atmospheric climate patterns. Interdependence and interrelationship are central starting points for ecological research of food webs, nutrient cycles, and forest succession. Indra's Net, however, contains more than the ecological sum of biosphere, atmosphere, and lithosphere.

The Buddhist principle of interdependence includes human thought, perception, and values, and their impacts on the ecological-evolutionary conversation. This critical difference is what makes it possible and necessary for people in the Net to act ethically out of regard for the other beings in the Net. In the context of human relationship, feminist ethicist Mary Grey describes the metaphysic of connectedness as "revelatory paradigm" and "moral imperative." She suggests the ethics of care and responsibility naturally develop from a person's experience "trying to be faithful to relation or connection" (Grey 1991, 13).

A number of feminist ethicists and writers point to mutuality and solidarity as key values for the feminist movement (see Farley 1986; Daly 1989). These values spring from the need for sister bonding as a source of strength in facing the internalized pain of the victim of sexism and in organizing for institutional and social change. Full mutuality or interdependence is not possible for one dominated by the absolutizing, individualist "I."

Thus to experience the richness of full mutuality, one must transcend or break through the limitations of the thought habit of individualism reinforced as the dominant ideology in the Western world. For the woman who has suffered physical, economic, psychological, or spiritual oppression, freedom from the rigidity of the fixed "I"/self and release into the web of relationships means the choice of many more nourishing options for growth and development.

Because this maturation occurs in a shared context with others also suffering isolation, the feminist experience of interrelatedness is a process of mutual becoming, born out of mutual vulnerability. 'Me joy and satisfaction of this experience may then be a foundation for "passionate caring for the entirety of the relational nexus" (Grey 1991, 13). A woman who uncovers her own capacity for mutuality can then (and often does) extend her efforts and empathy to the many other women in different cultures and places who also suffer from lack of freedom of choice.

For both Buddhism and feminism, the core truth of interrelationship or mutual becoming is central to individual liberation or freedom from false reification of an independent "I." Feminist Buddhists who understand this path of liberation can be extremely effective and compassionate participants in the struggle for environmental consciousness. Acting from deep-rooted experience in the freedom to choose options other than oppression, they can work creatively and skilfully to open up environmental conversations that have been frozen by loss of relationality.

Emotional Energy as Source of Healing

The Buddhist practice of investigating conditioned body, speech, and mind includes detailed observation of the nature of emotions. In the Sutra on the Four Establishments of Mindfulness, for example, the meditator is instructed to practice awareness of pleasant, painful, and neutral feelings as they arise in the mind and body. In Thich Nhat Hanh's modern-day commentary on this Sutra, he suggests exercises for identifying and acknowledging feelings and seeing the physical, physiological, or psychological roots of particular feelings (Nhat Hanh 1990b). By becoming fully familiar with the nature of anger, grief, fear, desire, denial, or the blocking of these feelings, a practitioner gains confidence in living through the sweep of emotional responses that naturally arise from moment to moment.

The first step of healing from the suffering of difficult emotions is to recognize and fully claim the rich information and energy response of the body/ mind. In the investigation and mindfulness practice itself, energy is released and becomes available for healing through attention and understanding. Rather than suppressing deep emotions, Buddhist practice can help a person develop the capacity to consciously use this energy to relieve suffering.

Much of the response to the current envirommental crisis is an emotional response, fined with grief, fear, and anger at the loss and destruction of plants, animals, forests, and watersheds. The depth of response may be so overwhelming that people become immobilized and unable to act. Buddhist practices to validate and move through these waves of emotion can be extremely helpful in freeing up energy to take action on behalf of the environment (see Nhat Hanh 1990a; Macy 1983, 158-61). Western feminists also recognize the importance of emotional response in the process of awakening to oppression. Most Western white women have been conditioned not to express anger overtly.

Strong displays of empassioned emotion have been marginalized and viewed as unacceptable by the ruling patriarchy and its male model of "cool" and reserved emotions. Anger at sexual and environmental abuse qualifies as an "outlaw emotion," invalidated by those who wish to avoid hearing other experiences (Jaggar 1985). Feminists, however, are well aware that powerful social and gender conditioning can only be overthrown by a strong surge of energy and desire for change. Anger is very effective in marshalling the energy necessary to dismantle the structure that perpetrates violence against women and the environment.

If one begins with the fundamental truth of one's own experience, recognising that perception and conception are intimately related, it becomes necessary to know how we feel in order to act morally. As feminist theologian Beverly Harrison asserts, "The failure to live deeply in 'our bodies, ourselves' destroys the possibility for moral relations between us" (Harrison 1985, 13).

For Harrison, anger is a "feeling, showing that all is not well in our relation to others or the world around us" (Harrison 1985, 14). Powerful emotion is a sip of resistance to the unsatisfactory moral quality of our social and environmental relationships. This signal is the wake-up call to look more deeply into the situation at hand.

Harrison argues that the power to respond is the power to create a world of moral relations. This is the work of spiritual and religious practice, the transformative work that can serve to slow environmental destruction and heal the wounded biosphere. The combination of Buddhist mindfulness practice and feminist moral response is a powerful antidote to widespread despair and depression over the possibility of nuclear annihilation, environmental catastrophe, or out-of-control corporate greed.

This practice does not remove the threats or mitigate the devastating consequences of irresponsible actions, but it does help to generate the tremendous energy needed to address the complexities of the global environmental situation (see Macy 1983). Anger, despair, or other strong emotions alone are not enough to stop environmental tragedy, because they cause polarization and defensive reactions that block communication. Environmental activists already have a history and bad name in some circles for misusing emotions in the service of battle strategy. Habitual unexamined anger can harden into ideology that further erodes opportunities for working together. By cultivating a deeper, more fully informed emotional response, one cultivates greater possibilities for healing transformation of relationships between human beings and the environment.

Relational Ethics

Buddhist ethics are grounded in the truth and experience of the Law of Dependent Co-Arising. Sila, or guidelines for moral action, are central to Buddhist practice in all traditions. The Three Pure Precepts are vows to refrain from actions that ignore interdependence, to make an effort to act out of understanding of interrelationship, and to serve all beings in the interdepending web. The five (Theravada) prescriptive precepts to not kill, not lie, not steal, not abuse sexuality or intoxicants spring from a fundamental recognition of relationship. One aims to act as respectfully and inclusively as possible toward plant, animal, and human companions. In the Mahayana traditions, the model of enlightenment is the Bodhisattva who gains awakening in order to serve all beings.

This is in contrast to the 'Meravadan goal of achieving liberation to be freed from the cycle of endless suffering and rebirths in a human body. Buddhist or other religious beliefs that place emphasis on Otherworldliness, or some version of escaping from the drudgery of this world, are not helpful for responding to the escalating deterioration of the environment. Forests can only be replanted here on this earth by those who live here, not those who have ended the world. The Bodhisattva model encourages the practices of compassion for all others as a means of accomplishing a profound sense of interrelatedness. One can specifically cultivate "eco-bodhicitta" or the mind of enlightenment that serves all relations of the environment (Ross 1991).

The experience of compassion for others' suffering is what allows us to feel the connections with disturbed ecosystems and threatened species, distressing as they may be. Sensitivity and moral concern for the health of human relationships can extend as well to plants, animals, forests, clouds, stones, and sacred places. Buddhist relational ethics are based on knowing that one cannot act without affecting other living beings, that it is impossible to live outside the web of interconnectedness. The beautiful Jewel

Net of Indra is sustained and enhanced by the quality of moral intention and commitment to the many facets of the Net. To act from this sense of relatedness is deeply empowering, setting an ethical example for others to consider.

Compassion in Western culture, in contrast, is frequently associated with pity and powerlessness and relegated to the domain of women!s nurturing (Klein 1986). In examining Western psychological values, feminist researchers have challenged the traditional stages of moral and psychological development based on male socialization, as described by Kohlberg (Kohlberg 1981). In this model, moral maturity develops through increasing allegiance to universal rules or principles of justice and individual rights. Carol Gilligan's work, in contrast, suggests that women's moral development in the West is based on maturing responsiveness to relationships and consideration of others in moral choices (Gilligan 1982).

Kohlberg's male model reinforces an environmental ethic oriented to rights and justice; GUfigan's altemative model supports an environmental ethic of care and responsibility. Relational ethics as described by both Buddhist teachings and feminist writers might also be called contextual ethics. A contextual ethic, as I use the term reflects both the diversity of human voices in a given place and time (Warren 1990, 139), and the specific environmental relationships in which the human dilemma is embedded (Cheney 1987). Built into this approach to ethics is the rejection of any single authoritative ethical voice or posited human nature that exists independent of historical context. Abstract individualism is seen as ungrounded and relatively unhelpful in addressing the tensions of a specific environmental conflict. Environmental moral dilemmas occur in a web of relationships.

Each situation has a unique history, based on very particular causes and conditions. A contextual ethic represents a shift from emphasis on rights, rules, and predetermined principles to a conception of ethics grounded in specific relationships. Environmental actions based entirely on rules as moral guidelines inevitably leave out some aspect of the situation that is not included in the legal framework. Rules generalize; relationships are intricate and complex.

A relational ethic calls for compassion for all the relationships involved in the situation parent-child, tree-animal, bird-human, soil-rock. Relationships are not something outside of who we are; they, in fact, define who we are to a large extent as moral agents in a social and historical context As Warren argues, "Relationships of humans to the nonhuman environment are, in part, constitutive of what it is to be human" (Warren 1990, 143). Relational morality is not simple; it is extremely difficult to make sound environmental decisions when relatively little is known about ecological relationships. The stakes are often very high when the consequences of human actions mean the loss of millions of plant and animal lives. Trade-offs in tropical environments, for example, are almost a matter of triage today.

The practices of compassion and contextual reflection generate a deep appreciation of biological and cultural complexity and of the long-standing ties between humans and all other members of the biotic community. I believe this is an essential foundation for critically needed re-evaluation of what we are doing on the planet and what is ethically acceptable and life-sustaining.

The Role of Community

All Buddhist traditions venerate the three Jewels-the Buddha, Dharma, and Sangha. In environmental terms, the Buddha can be interpreted as all beings who teach, or the teacher within, or the Buddha as environmental teacher. To see all beings as teachers means one can learn from wolf, redwood, buffalo, river, and mountain (see Dogen Zenji 1985, 97-127).

To see the Buddha as teacher within means one learns from one's own experience with the environment. The Buddha as environmental teacher is the one who points to the truth of interdependence and co-dependent arising of all life forms. Dharma is the truth of the teachings in their many forms, perceptions, and experiences. Each plant and animal, as well as human, is an embodiment of evolutionary truth, a testimony to thousands of years of living more or less successfully in conversation with the environment. Each experience of connection with members of the environmental web is a taste of the deep truth of the nature of reality as mutually causal and interdependent.

The Third Jewel, the Sangha, is traditionally described in Buddhist literature as the monastic community, or those who practice within a retreat setting. Rules for sangha behavior are extensive, numbering over 300 in some traditions, with specific rules for nuns, often in subordinate relationship to monks. For most American Buddhists, some of these rules are inappropriate because of cultural differences, but even more, they are not specific to lay or non-monastic practice, which is the prevalent form of practice in the United States.

Deep ecologist BM Devall proposes the concept of "eco-sangha," in which people practice with aH the members of their bioregion or watershed area and consciously identify with and include the environment as community (Devall 1990). One then sits in meditation not only with others in the human community, but also with the surrounding biota, maples, jays, warblers, and wildflowers. Feminist Buddhist Rita Gross suggests that sangha is the "indispensable matrix of spiritual existence" necessary for human liberation (Gross 1991, 73).

She critiques the historical tendency in Buddhism to emphasize the lonely path to freedom, suggesting that too much aloneness is not a good thing, for it is not, in itself, instructive in how to get along with others. Her feminist reconceptualization of sangha rests on the values of community, nurturing, communication, and relationships, traditionally cared for by women in many cultures. With no theistic ultimate Other in Buddhism to provide guaranteed relationship to the person experiencing isolation, there is no alternative but to provide relationship for one another. She suggests, "It is necessary to create the social, communal, and compassionate matrix of a society in which friendship and relationship are taken as categories of utmost spiritual importance" (Gross 1991, 78).

A feminist interpretation of sangha validates and deepens the key feminist political and psychological values of solidarity and mutuality. Companionship and shared activities, including dialogue on environmental ethics, are then central to spiritual development and need to be cultivated as primary virtues. Women's friendships and love for each other and the mutual growth process may be threatening and confusing to some, because they challenge traditional ethics based in individualism. I believe that the friendship-sangha model is a helpful and appropriate basis for refinding and redefining our human relationships with plants, animals, and ecological communities. It is both enjoyable and sustainable, and can serve as a significant counterpoint to the recent history of industrialized attack and plunder.

A FEW POSSIBLE LIMITATIONS

These six areas of philosophical similarity or complementarity between Buddhism and feminism offer a solid foundation for a Buddhist feminist approach to environmental issues. I believe the environmental ethics generated from such a position recommend restraint in human activities that cause destruction and loss of habitats, species, and ecosystems, with the aim of reducing suffering for many forms of life. However, for effective evaluation of these two approaches, it is necessary to keep in mind the historical traditions of each source philosophy. There are several potential weaknesses of traditional Buddhism that may serve either to limit Buddhist involvement with the environment or, through dialogue and activity, may actually help define the evolutionary edge of American Buddhism.

Egocentrism as Central Concept

Buddhist philosophy and religious practice emphasize breaking through the limited perspective and conditioning of the small self or human ego, in order to experience the boundless interrelated nature of reality. The route to liberation assumes an over-valuation of self or ego, which distorts perception and perpetuates self-centeredness. This fundamental approach may not be as applicable for marginalized groups of people, including women. Teachings that point to the falsely constructed separate ego may be received as disconnected from the actual lived experience of oppression, or as a paternalistic strategy for pacification or assimilation.

For women and others experiencing social messages that continually devalue the self, the Buddhist emphasis on egolessness may only serve to further erode the not yet fully formed and validated person. Practices that suppress the ego may be misinterpreted as a denial of personhood which can be used as a method of subjugation and denigration of marginalized groups. Feminism has taken a strong position on self-advocacy as a key principle in fighting abusive patterns of social conditioning, whether in marriage, work, or health matters. Self-advocacy is critical to women speaking up for their rights, their existence, and more humane standards of behavior.

The marginalized or oppressed woman is encouraged to find her voice, her dreams, her capabilities, her inner strength. This is essential spiritual work, the challenge of distinguishing the true self from the many layers of social and gender patterns that deny the self. This critique of Buddhism is relevant to environmental work in at least two respects. One, in the realm of ecofeminist spirituality, there may be a tendency to overemphasize the subjective experience of environment as universal, in the enthusiasm for a women's nature-based religious practice. However, this may more accurately reflect the need to simply establish the existence and validity of women's personhood, long overlooked by many religions, including Buddhism. I suggest that Buddhist feminists seeking ecological spirituality examine the teachings in depth to recognize healthy aspects of self-development as well as the blocks to egolessness.

Second, recognition of the full "personhood" or intrinsic existence of plants, animals, mountains, and rivers depends on one's capacity to fully recognize one , s own personhood. For the Buddhist woman student, personhood may be displaced by the brilliant experience of boundarylessness before the self is fully developed. This then diminishes the person's capacity to deeply reflect and stand in solidarity with the fun existence of any particular environmental other.

Calling up the image of Indra's Net, this suggests that the reflective power of each jewel within the Net directly enhances the beauty and perception of all the other jewels. It is the quality of this reflection and existence that then guides our choice of envirommental actions; an ethic of restraint expressing respect and appreciation for the beauty of the other members of the web is not possible if one does not first fiffly and deeply appreciate the self.

Power Relations Analysis

The social conditions of power, status, and privilege critically affect environmental decisions, law and treaty melting, and natural resource negotiation. Social aspects of Buddhist religions are riddled with power relations, as much as any other organized religion. The social glue of power roles determines the nature of attitudes and actions of those in power and those not in power. While Buddhist philosophy clearly includes the relevant tools for examining the nature of power relations and the abuse of power, this area of inquiry is not a central emphasis in American practice today.

Gender power relations, in particular, are not generally addressed, most likely because Buddhist philosophy and practice forms have come through patriarchal cultures with primarily male teachers and leaders. In many schools of Buddhism, there is a strong emphasis on practice relationships with an authoritative teacher. This can be a relationship of respect, but it can also be a relationship of abuse, where power and status are used to gain sexual access to women students."

Issues of power relations have been raised by American feminist Buddhists trying to correct for Asian cultural influence in the historical development of Buddhism (see Boucher 1985; Gross 1986; Karabinus 1987). This inquiry into gender conditioning is not widespread and not necessarily well-received by American Buddhist centers or teachers. By broadening the field of inquiry to areas of hidden gender assumptions, feminists challenge the status of many of the governance and religious forms transferred to America from Asian patriarchal cultures. Those who hold religious or administrative power reinforced by Western male favoritism are generally not inclined to examine the language, behavior, and psychology of gender conditioning, despite feminist research showing the powerful capacity of gender conditioning to influence all other forms of conditioning.

This weakness in Buddhist philosophy as it has arrived in the Western world could have significant detrimental effects on the evolution of a Buddhist environmental ethic. The truth of interdependence, acknowledging the intrinsic value of each member of the web, is just a starting point for investigating the nature of specific relationships. The environmental crisis is driven by the complexities of power distribution, giving preference and status to some governments, some corporate ventures, some ecosystems, some species, some cultures over others.

An effective Buddhist environmental ethic is strengthened by the dimension of power analysis presented by feminist theorists. Political, economic, and personal power can serve the environment, if illuminated by awareness and social consciousness of the logic of domination. Without this awareness, the critical role of power can be overlooked by the Buddhist practitioner focusing on the beauty and miracle of interdependence.

Social Ethics and Engaged Practice

Buddhist ethics traditionally emphasize behavior guidelines and liberation for the individual, rather than structural change of social systems. The current literature on Buddhism and social change is somewhat limited in covering the history of commitment to social issues. In contrast, Christian ethics trace their origin to the earnest stories of Jesus' suffering and compassion, developing principles of social justice as central to Christian religious practice. In some cases, Asian Buddhist cultures reinforce the acceptance of reality to the extreme of passivity. This can make it very difficult for Buddhist religious or social leaders to advocate social change. Feminism is fundamentally based in a need, desire, and strong motivation for social change. This drive for change might be seen as incompatible with Buddhism, presenting possible difficulty in merging these two approaches.

The urgency and passion behind the feminist agenda may seem unmeditative to practicing Buddhists; the passive acceptance of Buddhist religious culture may seem unmotivated or apathetic to committed feminists. Yet each has something to gain from the other, particularly in developing a strong movement for environmental justice and a new code of environmental ethics. Social environmental ethics are more than the sum of individual ethical practices regarding the environment. They are the ethics necessary for dealing with the whole systemic pattern of environmental destruction, which has a force and momentum of its own. A religious practice that only advocates individual improvement in environmental actions (such as recycling, vegetarianism, or birth control) does not go far enough in investigating the roots of socialized environmental destruction.

The development of a social ethic to address the scale of environmental systemic disorder requires a motivation to work with the system as a whole and to uphold standards for the system as well as for the individual. In this task, the commitment of feminism may be a useful catalyst for inspiring Buddhist dialogue and activity necessary to affect the environmental situation at any long-term meaningfull level.

Buddhism and Our Environmental Obligation

Within our society, there are certain innate concepts that every individual is equipped with. Virtues, morals, or the concept of "right and wrong" are just a few examples of such ideals. To help make humanity a more positive atmosphere, there are a few models one should strive to accomplish in their everyday life. These include but are not limited to: compassion towards all individuals whom are less fortunate, non-violence towards any and all living and non-living things, and a natural want or need to help sustain the environment we live in.

The most critical of these ideals would be our responsibility to help reverse the immense damage already being done to our ecosystem in the forms of global warming, ozone layer depletion, deforestation, and a reduction in biodiversity, to name just a few. By incorporating the Buddhist philosophy, one can fulfill an environmental obligation towards bettering our "eco-crisis."

Sustainability, on the other hand, is an ideal that societies everywhere seem to slowly be adapting to. In definition, sustainability is the ability to provide a healthy, fulfilling and just life for all living beings on earth, now and for generations to come, all the while enhancing the health of ecosystems and the capability of other species to survive in their natural environments. Within the Buddhist philosophy, the Middle Way is followed to promote detachment and moderation in one's life. The Middle Way "avoids extremes of denial and overindulgence and produces a 'rationed life,' unlike in consumerist societies where maximum satisfaction of needs, wants, and desires occurs" (Sponsel 148).

Pertaining to Buddhism and the environment, though, there is a more direct path to supporting environmentalism. Buddhism encourages individuals to "limit their resource consumption to the optimal satisfaction of the four basic needs of food, clothing, shelter, and medicine" (Sponsel 147). The biggest growing issue about our society's environmental crisis, in my opinion, is the immense amount of over-consumption that occurs. Individuals have come to naturally consume large amounts of resources that are unnecessary. Buddhism, and rightly so, advocates a form of living that contains so much simplicity that could humbly save our environment in more senses than one.

Moving forward to other concepts of Buddhism and our environmental obligation, the principle of compassion is one that is in dire need of important attention. In relation to the Buddha, it is said that his choice of sharing his insight about the cause of and the path to end suffering after his own enlightenment occurred was an act of true universal compassion. Compassion is one of those virtues that, I believe, is open to numerous personal interpretations. Pertaining to the environment, though, compassion consists of being empathetic and showing concern to all forms of life whether it be humans, animals, insects, or nature.

Compassion thus refers to an unselfish, detached emotion with gives an individual a sense of urgency in wanting to help others. From the perspective of a Buddhist, helping others to provide a cessation to suffering by stopping the process of rebirth is the ultimate goal. According to one source on the origin of Bodhisattva, or a being whose aim is to achieve Buddha-hood, started when traditional Buddhist monks began to stray away from Buddhist ideals of love and altruism.

In order to steer the monks back on the right path, a sort of Bodhisattva doctrine was put into place with compassionate action as its motive. This new Bodhisattva doctrine required the selflessness of compassion as its ideal in order to direct the Buddhist monks back to the proper teachings and the goal of "saving all creatures" (Walsh-Frank 5). Living compassionately towards all living creatures, and nature as well, applies to all individuals whether they aspire to become a Buddhist or not. However, the concept of compassion towards all creatures, both living and non-living, is another Buddhist principle that advocates the said non-violent ecology.

One of the most influential and essential principles of incorporating Buddhism into environmentalism is the notion of non-violence. Within the eightfold path, the fourth imperative of "right" action represents abstinence from taking lives, or "ahimsa," and from stealing. A few conditions arise from this point of view that have transformed "ahimsa" in Buddhism to a more modern tone. Practicing Buddhists support "suitable" forms of killing and stealing. In the case of a poor man stealing to feed him starving family or a Buddhist exterminating pests who are destroying their crops, these actions are exempted from being considered wrong (Living Buddhism 18-30). Therefore, non-violence takes on many different forms in discussions pertaining to its depth, but holds true to one simplistic notion. With regards to the environment, all living and non-living beings should be respected as well as preserved.

Although not all individuals will be eager to wholly convert to Buddhism as a philosophical lifestyle change, I do concur that some of the Buddhist tendencies of awareness and simplicity can drive our environment to be capable of correcting its downfalls. Most importantly, the four basic needs of food, shelter, clothing, and medicine are aspects in which all individuals must strive to incorporate into their everyday lives.

While there are some principles of a Buddhist environmental ethic that move our ecosystem on the right path to salvation, there are still some included that I personally do not believe would be successful applications to the majority. The sustainability, responsibility, compassion, and harmony that encompass the Buddhist philosophy fully promote a better situation for our environment.

7 Environmental Ethics in Mahayana Buddhism

In today's world we face a range of environmental problems, such as global warming, ozone layer depletion, deforestation, and a reduction in biodiversity. The problems caused by a reduction in biodiversity are regarded as some of the greatest challenges facing humanity today. This is because a reduction in biodiversity affects our ecosystem, which in return also affects the life of human beings.

Based on a consideration of the consequences of biodiversity reduction, a proposal for accepting the right to life of all living things has been made in recent years.1 In this paper, I appeal to upholding the dignity of human life, and regard loss of life as of gravest consequence. It is for that reason that in the field of medical science, bioethics entails investigating what affects the life of human beings. In Buddhism, human life and other forms of life are regarded as being of the same matter. Therefore, since they are always related to living things, Buddhism regards environmental problems as essentially an issue of ethics.

The ultimate purpose of the practice of Buddhism is to attain Buddhahood, which in modern terms means to become as ideal a human being as that of a Buddha. Representative practices in Buddhism are the six kinds of practices by which a bodhisattva attains Buddhahood (paramitah). The six kinds of practices consist of giving donations (dana-paramita), keeping the precepts (sla-paramita), being forbearing (kanti-paramita), being assiduous (vrya-paramita), practicing meditation (dhyana-paramita), and cultivating wisdom (prajna-paramita). These six virtuous practices are required to become an ideal human being. It is thought that living with wisdom and upholding the precepts are especially appropriate as ethical norms.

In other words, the practice of Buddhism for solving environmental problems is in direct accord with the intention of Buddhism in that it results in removing pain from all sentient beings. This means that developing ethical norms and plans of action based on Buddhist practices not only leads to solving environmental problems but also simultaneously fulfills the purpose of Buddhism. In this paper, I will discuss environmental problems related to living things, and examine how an ethical norm that accords with Buddhism could be created.

Environmental Problems Related to Living Things

As I have discussed in a previous paper, there are various environmental problems related to living things. In this section, I would like to discuss some typical environmental problems as they relate to living things, as well as examine how they concern the question of human nature or ethics.

PROBLEMS OF DEFORESTATION AND COMMERCIALIZATION OF WILDLIFE

Deforestation and commercialization of wildlife have become a profitable business. Deforestation, however, destroys not only forests but also reduces bio-intensity5 and biodiversity, which means a reduction in the amount, as well as variation of, living things that, in turn, causes havoc on whole ecosystems. The cutting down of tropical rain forests is particularly detrimental to wildlife and other living things. The livelihood of local people, however, often depends on clearing forest areas using slash-and-burn farming techniques to make way for agricultural production, or harvesting trees for energy or export material. Commercialization of wildlife, either exported as food, pets, or fur, or usually further aggravated by over-hunting and deforestation, also reduces wildlife in some cases, to the point of extinction.

On the more positive side, even forest and wildlife can be recovered if given sufficient time and proper habitat. An often cited example of this is the whale. Although at the point of extinction due mainly to overfishing by Japan and other countries, the whale population has improved due to the prohibition of commercial whaling and the creation of protected areas. Likewise, environmental problems are caused by the speed at which forests are felled, wildlife killed, and ecosystems destroyed, all which exceeded the reproduction capacity. As the above example illustrates, we can observe that given a reduction in the speed at which destruction takes place, living things can be recovered with the regenerative power of nature.

It is important to also consider problems such as deforestation and the commercialization of wildlife at the level of human nature, or ethics. It is clear that deforestation and commercialization of wildlife result in destroying and taking/killing living things. Decreasing the amount and kinds of living things, as well as their habitat means nothing less than pillaging such life from the ecosystem.

Such behavior originates from certain violent and cruel aspects of human nature. This makes solving such problems fundamentally an ethical issue. This action is particularly relevant to developing countries where poverty plays an important factor in environmental destruction. Deforestation and commercialization of wildlife are often the only activities that support local people's lives and economy. Thus the problem becomes much more complex than to be solved simply by unilaterally denying local people the right to cut down trees or engage in commercialization of wildlife.

Moreover, it is important to consider the desires of people in developed nations as one of the causes of environmental destruction. Living things provide people of developed nations with wealth, as well as an improved lifestyle, exemplied by enriched economies, food sources, and leisure activities. Another reason for environmental destruction is the poverty of developing countries. In the above discussion I have attempted to show that there are three oppositional, although highly interdependent interests: wealth and lifestyle of people in developed countries; the livelihood of disadvantaged people in developing countries; and the survival of ecosystems and living things. One can not simply be given priority over another, which makes it a question of ethics.

PROBLEMS OF LAND DEVELOPMENT AND THE USE OF CHEMICALS

Land development, transgenic crops, and chemical pollution can also be seriously harmful to living things and ecosystems. The development of farmland, cities, dams, recreational facilities, land reclamation etc. seems obvious examples of activities that impose various environmental hazards. Ecosystems and the habitats of living things are destroyed as a result of such developments, which, in turn, impacts biodiversity and bio-intensity. The reduction in biodiversity and bio-intensity in developed countries has mainly been attributed to such developments as mentioned above. Transgenic crops are another technology that has also caused a reduction in biodiversity and a transformation of ecosystems.

Through a recombination of genes, transgenic crops at first glance appear beneficial to human beings as they have built-in protection against noxious insects, cold or dry weather, and specific agricultural chemicals. However, a closer look reveals rather frightening drawbacks. As transgenic crops introduce extraneous genes into the ecosystem, they create the potential for destroying or seriously changing the structure of ecosystems and mechanisms of evolution. There are also problems with chemical pollution, including heavy metals, agricultural chemicals, food additives, as well as endocrine disrupters. These problems are rooted in two main activities: extraction of naturally occuring materials such as heavy metals, and the synthesizing of artificial compounds by using, oil and chlorine, for example.

In general, living things throughout history have acquired the capacity to cope with various chemicals. However, as new chemicals are released into the biosphere, living things have had difficulty in adaptation. Many artificial chemicals tend to turn toxic when accumulated in the human or animal body. One clear example is agricultural chemicals, which are designed to kill insects that damage crops. Insects are killed by extraneous chemicals that destroy the mechanism of living. However, because all living things are fundamentally functioning by the same principle, agricultural bioaccumulate and become detrimental all living things. Endocrine disrupters have been shown to affect reproduction through lower sperm count, as well as ontogeny seen through higher risk of deformity.

As pointed out in *Silent Spring* by Rachel Carson, *Our Stolen Future* by Thea Colborn, and *The Feminization of Nature* by Deborah Cadbury, this problem is qualitatively different from past environmental problems. Although past environmental problems were a threat to the survival of individual lives, they did not function as endocrine disruptors do in acting against posterity. Now how do the above mentioned problems relate to human nature or ethics?

In addition to the problems associated with deforestation and commercialization of wildlife, the fundamental cause is associated with violence and pillaging, which indicates that there is a problem in human nature or ethics. This is clearly seen when developments violently destroy nature, where wildlife habitat is reconstructed and pillaged to suit the desire for comfort and profit. Furthermore, if human beings are incapable of considering or predicting how certain developments would affect an ecosystem, it becomes either a question of arrogance or ignorance.

If we do not feel a sense of responsibility for our actions on the ecosystems, it then becomes an issue of irresponsibility. We are deceiving ourselves if we fail to consider the consequences of certain developments and instead only emphasize advantages such as convenience and safety. Naturally, these developments are carried out to profit human beings by making life more comfortable and safer. From this we can conclude that profit and desire are usually intertwined.

If we also remain indifferent to the adverse effects of chemicals on our ecosystems, the problem then becomes an issue of arrogance. However, if we are unable to predict the influence of the use of chemicals on our ecosystems, it then becomes a question of ignorance. Moreover, since agricultural chemicals were made with the aim of killing living things, there is an aspect of cruelty to be found in human nature that must be considered. The desire for profit, however, tends to overrule this ethical dilemma and encourage the development of chemical compounds such as agricultural chemicals and food additives. Such new developments aim to increase profits for producers by manufacturing attractive, easy-to-preserve, and cheap food items as well as increase the purchasing power of consumers.

The desire of consumers for cheap and attractive food further sustains this process. But the synergistic effect of producers and consumers stimulating each other's desires is tends to increase in food and environments polluted by artificial chemicals. Such developments have also brought many disadvantages, such as general health hazards, destruction of ecosystems, and impediments to reproduction capacity in forms of lower sperm count and sterility which are detrimental to the posterity of living things. Considering these problems we can draw up two opposing interests: profits and disadvantages for human beings and disadvantages for ecosystems or living things. In the end, the problem is an ethical one.

PROBLEMS WITH ECO-PROTECTION MANAGEMENT

The killing of wildlife in order to protect the ecosystem has been a controversial. For example, measures have then been taken to reduce the number of animals that have been shown to breed abnormally, such as the Japanese monkey or the Japanese serow. These measures were taken to combat the increase of Japanese monkeys, which had caused a food shortage, resulting in their descending on a village, injuring people and damaging agricultural products. Moreover, the Japanese serow eats the bark and young leaf buds of newly-planted trees, thereby having a damaging effect on forestry.

In recent years the numbers of captured and exterminated monkeys have reached several thousand per year, becoming a hotly debated issue. The issue goes straight to questioning the violent and cruel aspect of human nature. This question deals with the dilemma of whether it is morally justifiable to solve the problem by taking the lives of these animals in order to reduce their number. On the other hand, a reduction in numbers carries certain benefits for human beings as well as for the ecosystem; fewer monkeys prevent harm being inflicted on people and economic losses, and regenerate the ecosystem.

Thus on the one hand, the beneficial outcome of exterminating animals for human beings and the ecosystem, and on the other, the obvious detrimental effect this has on the animals themselves.

THE PROBLEM OF ANIMALS USED FOR FOOD AND EXPERIMENTS

Although this is not an issue directly related to environmental problems, the fact that human beings consume living things, as in the case of medical research, give rise to certain ethical dilemmas. A large number of animals serve as food for human beings. The annual number of mammals used as meat for human consumption, mainly pigs, cows, sheep, and goats, is about 4 billion. Moreover, in 1989 11 billion chickens were consumed in the world. In Japan alone, the number of chickens consumed is now (in 2001) at 0.7 billion per year. In addition, it is estimated that as many animals as 200 million animals each year end up being used for experiments. In the United States alone for examples, there are an estimated 70 million rats per year are used in experiments.

However, animals used for food contribute to the survival of human beings, just as they contribute to the development of medicine that improves our health. To find a substitute for using animals in this way is appear to be impossible. Therefore, how we justify the taking of animal life needs to be treated as an ethical problem; there is a dilemma in using animals for the benefit of human beings but at the expense of the animals killed.

Biological Conservation and Buddhist Thought

Before examining the Buddhist view on problems of biological conservation, I will describe some fundamental concepts in Buddhism.

WISDOM

The attainment of wisdom (prajna-paramita) is part of the six kinds of practices by which a bodhisattva attains enlightenment (sat paramitah). This concept originally referred to the attainment of *absolute* wisdom (prajna-paramita). Here, I would like to examine the idea of wisdom in relation to two fundamental Buddhist concepts as a way to solve environmental problems. They are "dependent origination" (prat\tyasamutpada) and "the middle way." The doctrine of dependent origination teaches that an entity does not exist and generate independently. Instead it is characterized by its fundamental interdependence and interconnectedness to all phenomena.

This concept of fundamental interdependence and interconnectedness of all phenomena indicates a relation of space (ontology) and a relation of time (formation). The ecological environment of today is included in the relation of space and relation of time. This means that all living things on earth are related including the circulation of organic or inorganic matter.

Moreover, the time means not only movement between one generation and the next, i.e. a living thing is produced from its parents, but also indicates a historical relationship, such as the process of evolution over time. The transmigration of life as explained by Buddhism means rebirth of life. However, since in Buddhism the transmigration of life is based on the concept of non-self, it does not refer to the transmigration of life with a permanent entity. Broadly speaking, the transmigration of life exists in relation to time based on the concept of dependent origination. The second concept is the wisdom of the middle way. Akira Hirakawa has quoted "the metaphor of a koto" propounded by Shakyamuni, to describe in an easily comprehendible manner the principle of the wisdom of the middle way as "the middle way of pleasure-andpain." According to Hirakawa, "the metaphor of a koto" declares that the strength of a bowstring for a koto is most useful when it is neither too loose nor too firm.

"The middle way of pleasure-and-pain" describes the method of practice of Shakyamuni. Although Shakyamuni carried out austerities for six years together with five Buddhist monks, he was unable to attain spiritual enlightenment. After this long attempt, he realized the futility of trying to attain enlightenment through punishing himself. Indeed, after receiving rice gruel with milk from a woman named Sujata he recovered from his physical ordeals, and did in fact attain enlightenment.

The 'pain' of the penance principle indicates that although perhaps useful for developing strength of mind it does not lead to attaining absolute wisdom, or spiritual enlightenment. Instead, the 'pleasure' of hedonism shows that absolute wisdom can be acquired without taking recourse to punishing oneself. Therefore, the concept of the middle way of pleasure-and-pain denies a deterministic stand towards either hedonism or austerity.

That is, while accepting the value of both principles, the middle way demands harmony between the two and does not accept an inclination to either side. What I have been attempting to discuss in this section is how two fundamental principles in Buddhism, the wisdom of dependent origination and the wisdom of the middle way, offer us an ethical framework that can be used to arrive at a solution for environmental problems. Moreover, understanding the workings of these two concepts will work as a driving force for wanting to keep the Buddhist precepts, which will be discussed later on in this article.

THE VALUE OF LIFE

The problem of biological conservation necessarily entails a consideration of how we rank the value of living things. To examine what Buddhism has to say about the value of life, in this section I will use the following example from the Brahma-carya chapter of the Nirvana Sutra which propounds that killing living things constitutes a crime. "There are three degrees of killings: the lower, middle, and upper degrees. The lower degree constitutes the killing of any humble being, from an ant to any of the various kinds of animals. But the killing of any being that a bodhisattva has chosen to be born as [to help other living beings] is excluded. As a result of a killing of the lower degree, one will fall into the realms of hell, animals, and hungry spirits, and will suffer all the pains appropriate to a killing of the lower degree.

Why should this be? Because even animals and other humble beings possess the roots of goodness, insignificant though those roots may be. That is why a person who kills such a being must suffer full retribution for his offense. Killing any person from an ordinary mortal to an anagamin (Anagon in Japanese) constitutes what is termed the middle degree. As a consequence of such an act of killing, one fall into the realms of hell, hungry spirits, and animals, and will suffer all the pains appropriate to a killing of the middle degree. The upper degree of killing refers to the killing of a parent, an arhat (Arakan in Japanese), a pratyekabuddha (Byakushi-butsu in Japanese), or a bodhisattva who has reached the stage of non-retrogression. For such a crime one will fall into the great Av\chi (Av\ci) hell (Abijigoku in Japanese)."

This passage clearly expresses a hierarchy in the value of different life forms. For sure, Buddhism, especially Mahayana Buddhism of China or Japan asserts that all living things including animals and plants deserve respect since they possess the state of Buddhahood.

On the other hand, the above passage points out that the seriousness of killing is hierarchical, namely in the descending order of killing parents, arhats, pratyekabuddhas, and bodhisattvas being the worst crime one can commit, killing ordinary mortals and anagamins the second worst, and the killing of animals the less heavy crime of the three. This hierarchy in the seriousness of killing also depicts how Buddhism ranks the value of different life forms.

Therefore, although in principle all lives are regarded as equal in Buddhism, the value of human life is regarded is higher than that of other living things. I believe this means that although Buddhism is based on the spirit of egalitarianism priority is still given to human life.

KEEPING THE PRECEPTS

Keeping the precepts in the six kinds of practices by which bodhisattvas are able to attain enlightenment specifically means keeping "the five precepts" (for laymen and lay-women) or "the ten good precepts." The five precepts consist of the precepts of "not killing living things," "not stealing," "not committing adultery," "not telling lies," and "not drinking intoxicants." On the other hand, the ten good precepts are categorized into precepts that refer to good deeds, good words, and good thoughts. Good deeds, or bodily acts, are "not killing living things," "not stealing" and "not committing adultery."

Good words, or verbal acts, are "not telling lies," "not engaging in idle talk," "not uttering harsh words," and "not uttering words which cause enmity between two or more persons." And finally good thoughts refer to "not being greedy," "not being angry," and "not having wrong views." For the sake of establishing an ethical norm for solving present environmental problems, I consider the concept of keeping precepts an important contribution to that project.

Since Yoichi Kawada has already discussed "the ten major precepts" and "the forty eight light precepts" in the Brahma-net Sutra from the point of view of the role of Buddhist precepts in solving environmental and peace problems I will not go into further details here. Instead, I will examine the significance of two particular precepts, namely, the precepts of "not killing living things" and "not stealing" in the Brahma-net Sutra as they relate directly to the challenges facing biological conservation today.

THE PRECEPT OF "NOT KILLING LIVING THINGS"

The "First Major Precept on Killing" of the Brahma-net Sutra propounds: "A disciple of the Buddha shall not kill himself, encourage others to kill, kill by expedient means, praise killing, rejoice at witnessing killing, or kill through incantation or deviant mantras. He must not cre-ate the causes, conditions, methods, or karma of killing, and shall not intentionally kill any living creature. As a Buddha's disciple, he ought to nurture a mind of compassion and filial piety, always devising expedient means to rescue and protect all beings. If instead, he fails to restrain himself and kills sentient beings without mercy he commits a Parajika (major) offense."

This precept forbids the killing of any living thing, and further adds that although killing itself is an offense; the state of mind of the person at the time of the killing, i.e. whether a person kills intentionally or for no apparent reason, determines the graveness of the offense. Therefore, it is an offense to kill a living thing, but it is a major offense if "he fails to restrain himself and kills sentient beings without mercy," or out of pleasure. This ethical standard of Buddhism described in the precept of "not killing living things" can be used as the basis for solving problems or dilemmas related to the killing of living things.

The Precept of "Not Stealing"

The "Second Major Precept on Stealing" of the Brahma-net Sutra states: "A disciple of the Buddha must not himself steal or encourage others to steal, steal by expedient means, steal by means of incantation or deviant mantras. He should not create the causes, conditions, methods, or karma of stealing.

No valuables or possessions, even those belonging to ghosts and spirits or thieves and robbers, be they as small as a needle or blade of grass, should be intentionally stolen. As a Buddha's disciple, he ought to have a mind of mercy, compassion, and filial piety—always helping people earn merits and achieve happiness. If instead, he steals the possessions of others, he commits a Parajika offense."

This precept also forbids stealing especially when it is done intentionally (without reason). Since the standard of judgment is based on the life-state of a bodhisattva, which is to help people earn merits and achieve happiness, stealing is regarded as of gravest consequence (a Parajka offense). In today's world it is necessary to interpret this precept more widely and consider it an offense to not only steal from other human beings but also from nature, or the ecosystem.

The Meaning of Keeping Precepts

In considering environmental problems, it is helpful to examine the characteristics of Buddhist precepts, that is, the meaning and the role of keeping such precepts. Many of the precepts, such as the ten major precepts, and the forty eight light percepts of the Brahma-net Sutra, regulate the behavior of human beings. However, as described above, there are also many precepts to which the conditions of "without reason," or "intentionally" for example are attached. This means that precepts in Buddhism are not absolute.

Does that mean that any justification is acceptable? For example, in the tenth light precept "on storing weapons" (I will discuss this later) the statement "he must not even avenge the death of his parents" appears. This sentence clearly states that killing in retaliation is unacceptable even if it is for the sake of revenging one's parents' murder. This means that retaliation is not recognized as sufficient justification for killing.

Then, what kind of justification is acceptable? If we kill living things in order to support our own survival it is in fact justifiable. (How we decide on what we need to survive is of course something we must consider very carefully.

It is not my intention, however, to delve into that question here.) Eating a living thing, however, is still equivalent to stealing the body from such a living thing. But since this is the minimum requirements for supporting human life, the condition of "without reason" attached to the precepts of "not killing" and "not stealing" need not apply here.

Reasons for killing living things, which are contrary to Buddhist wisdom, are also prohibited. That is, human behavior which destroys relations in ecosystems, is also considered an offense since it runs counter to the concept of dependent origination, i.e. disrupting ecological and historical relations, and thereby undermines our own survival. In modern society, some precepts may be more relevant than others. However, regarding to environmental problems, what is the relevancy of keeping precepts in the first place? I suggest that the significance of keeping precepts is relevant in that it develops:

(1) An understanding that wanting to achieve a particular end does not necessarily justify the means. We should judge what is permissible according to Buddhist thought,
(2) The ability to put a halt to the continuation of reckless behavior that is controlled by our desires, and
(3) The awareness of the need to control our actions.

Biological Conservation and Ethics of Mahayana Buddhism

In the following sections, I offer a few guidelines found in Mahayana Buddhism that are useful when considering the basis for biological conservation. These guidelines are pertinent to deforestation and over-hunt-ing, ecosystems protection, use of agricultural chemicals, and the use of animals for food and experiments.

ETHICS FOR DEFORESTATION AND OVER-HUNTING

First, I will consider the problem of deforestation, and its impact on wildlife, which is, for example, further reduced by over-hunting and commercialization. As stated earlier, there are certain problems with destroying species and pillaging living things from the ecosystem. From a Buddhist frame of reference, these acts constitute breaking the notkilling- living-things precept, as well as the not-stealing precept.

An understanding of the concept of dependent origination makes the destruction of life, capture, or pillaging of living things a problem to be taken seriously. As described above, we should forbid such behavior in principle because it means, first, that we destroy the relation between each living thing, and second, that we destroy its future potential for being born again. Especially causing the extinction of a species should be absolutely forbidden according to the Buddhist canon because it destroys its future potential for reproduction.

Apart from the seriousness of species extinction, we must also give consideration to how the capture of wildlife and felling of forests are a means of support for local people. This corresponds to having a justifiable "reason" as discussed from the passage of "intentionally (without reason)."

Moreover, according to the ethics of the middle way, the destruction and capturing of living things will be acceptable as long as the generative power of an ecosystem is not destroyed. I think that the ethics of the middle way neither denies the survival of local people, nor affirms the destruction of an ecosystem, as long as securing the benefits for local people does not mean destroying the generative power of an ecosystem. However, in order to secure the protection of ecosystems it is important to have a system of surveillance and proper management put in place.

It is also necessary to consider that living things support the accumulation of wealth and general well-being of people in developed countries. There is no denial in Buddhism of comfort and wealth. Instead what Buddhism refutes is making desires for comfort and profit the basis of one's life. Surely desires are needed to motivate human beings to make effort towards achieving something. But it is when a life-style is caught up in overindulgence that Buddhism sees life as being excessively governed by desires.

Therefore, excessive or unnecessary destruction and capturing of living things is considered to correspond to the offense "he fails to restrain himself and kills sentient beings without mercy" described in the precept on "not killing living things." Moreover, if developed countries exploit local peoples for the sake of obtaining wealth, this would correspond to the offense described as "rejoice at witness killing" also expounded in the percept on "not killing living things." Therefore, when a consumer pursues a comfortable or profitable life, self-control that prevents him or her from becoming 'greedy' is a must. This should be the basis of a Buddhist ethical norm.

ETHICS FOR ECO-PROTECTION MANAGEMENT

Here, I would like to examine the problem of killing animals by ecoprotection management. The extermination or capture of monkeys and serows in Japan is a common problem, as was described earlier. In this case, from the viewpoint of dependent origination it is considered 'allowed' because it is done to protect the ecosystem and done so without cutting off ecological and historical relations.

This is because the ecosystem itself may be destroyed if no intervention takes place. However, it is undoubtedly more desirable to develop a method which does not kill living things, a method that avoids committing the offense of "killing" in the first place. This view is also prominent in the concept of "Land Ethics" advocated by Aldo Leopold who points out the appropriateness of maintaining the beauty and stability of the totality of a community of living things.

ETHICS FOR USING CHEMICALS

I now turn to the question of how we should view the use of chemicals, such as agricultural chemicals. The answer is to be found in the tenth light percept "on storing deadly weapons" of the Brahma-net Sutra. It says: "A disciple of the Buddha should not store weapons such as knives, clubs, bows, arrows, spears, axes or any other weapons, nor may he keep nets, traps or any such devices used in destroying life. As a disciple of the Buddha, he must not even avenge the death of his parents— let alone kill sentient beings! He should not store any weapons or devices that can be used to kill sentient beings. If he deliberately does so, he commits a secondary offense."

This precept admonishes against the possession of tools used for killing living things. According to this precept, we should make it a principle not to produce artificial chemicals aimed at killing living things such as is the purpose of agricultural chemicals.

Furthermore, as the production of artificial chemicals is considered to be the cause of change in reproduction such as endocrine disruptors, and destroys the potential for continued reproduction, i.e. destroys the historical relationship described in the concept of dependent origination, it should be forbidden. Still, although the tenth light precept, as well as the first or second precept cited above, forbids possession of tools used for killing living things, it also stresses *without reason* ("deliberately").

For example, if, like the present day, it is difficult to secure the harvest of crops and to supply enough food without agricultural chemicals, its use could be justified. However, I believe we should develop alternative methods to increase the yield of crops to agricultural chemicals. I have discussed this in a previous paper from the standpoint of the consciousness-only doctrine.

What can we then conclude from the above discussion on killing living things by using agricultural chemicals from the viewpoint of dependent origination? Certainly it is evil to kill a living thing using agricultural chemicals. At the same time, however, it increases food production and supposedly the supply to many people who would otherwise starve. In Buddhism, all living things are respect worthy because they are endowed with Buddha Nature.

However, when the value of human life is compared with that of other living things, human beings are given priority. Therefore, as a matter of course, priority should be given to supplying food to human beings, and people suffering from starvation.

However, it goes without saying that if we can develop a way to supply enough food without using agricultural chemicals, such methods should be used. Taking into account the influence on human health or on other living things of residual agricultural chemicals, we should naturally move in the direction of discontinuing this technology. Transgenic crops may appear to meet such expectations. However, if the genetic code of an ecosystem is disturbed, such transgenic crops would need to be reconsidered.

In the case of food additives, technology that does not use preservation agents, such as dried or frozen technology where the microbe is suppressed rather than destroyed is considered more desirable. That is because from the Buddhist standpoint of "not killing living things" technology that does not kill, in this case, microbe is considered to be more ethically sound. Such a standpoint is derived from the concept of the wisdom of the middle way. Making full use of the wisdom of the middle way and the wisdom of dependent origination is also considered to correspond to the ethics of the middle way in Buddhism.

ETHICS FOR USING ANIMALS FOR FOOD AND EXPERIMENTS

Finally, I would like to examine the ethics for eating livestock and conducting experiments on animals. Although these issues are seemingly not directly related to environmental problems as described above, they are important issues related to our daily life. It is difficult to separate such issues from environmental problems because they are directly related to how we treat living things.

The "third light precept on eating meat" of the Brahma-net Sutra states: "A disciple of the Buddha must not deliberately eat meat. He should not eat the flesh of any sentient being. The meat-eater forfeits the seed of Great Compassion, severs the seed of the Buddha Nature and causes [animals and transcendental] beings to avoid him. Those who do so are guilty of countless offenses. Therefore, Bodhisattvas should not eat the flesh of any sentient beings whatsoever. If instead, he deliberately eats meat, he commits a secondary offense."

The above precept forbids the eating of all meat. The reason is that "the meat-eater forfeits the seed of Great Compassion, severs the seed of the Buddha Nature." Moreover, the "twentieth light precept on failure to liberate sentient beings" of the Brahmanet Sutra states: "A disciple of the Buddha should have a mind of compassion and cultivate the practice of liberating sentient beings.

He must reflect thus: throughout the eons of time, all male sentient beings have been my father, all female sentient beings my mother. I was born of them. Therefore, the sentient beings in the six worlds are all my parents.

If I now slaughter them, I would be slaughtering my parents, as well as eating flesh that was once my own. This is so because all elements, earth, water, fire and air—the four constituents of all life—have previously been part of my body, part of my substance.

I must therefore always cultivate the practice of liberating sentient beings." This precept promulgates from the viewpoint of the transmigration of life that we should not eat meat. To be sure, it is important to view the transmigration of life in light of the ethical foundation of Buddhism.

However, we must consider the fact that human beings and other animals can sustain life only by eating living things. Plants greatly differ from animals on this point. On the other hand, if there is Buddha Nature in all things, a plant could also possess Buddha Nature. Then, even eating vegetables becomes conduct that tramples on the respect-worthy Buddha Nature.

The last thing to be considered is the statement "restricting a transmi-gration of life to a sentient being." We generally draw the line between sentient and insentient beings at the level of animals. However, since there are also animals without a brain, we can not come to a definite conclusion that all animals have sentiments (consciousness).

Moreover, a plant without a brain is independently equivalent to various situations and its environment. For example, a plant changes direction of a leaf to light and stretches a root to water or nutrients. That is, a plant recognizes the environment and acts to that as an animal recognizing the environment by the five sense organs (the five consciousnesses of Buddhism) of an eye, an ear, a nose, a tongue, and a body and acting to that. Therefore, from a broad perspective, a plant is considered to have sentiment. If we were to follow this logic, however, we would have little left to rightly eat.

This dilemma can be addressed using the doctrine of dependent origination. As described previously, the historical relation of a living thing, including inorganic matter, can be considered to be a transmigration of life. The sentence "all elements, earth, water, fire and air—the four constituents of all life—have previously been part of my body, part of my substance" in the "twentieth light precept" suggests that the transmigration of life include inorganic substance.

Judging from this frame of reference, it will be evil to destroy any relationships within an ecosystem. Therefore, if an ecosystem is destroyed by taking wildlife from its habitat, it will be necessary to admonish against such behavior. However, since human beings manage agriculture or livestock farming, eating these animals would not destroy the ecosystem, i.e., the historical relationship of the animal, and the elemental cycle. Therefore, the act of eating meat will be allowed in Buddhism.

Thus from the viewpoint of ecological and historical relationships (transmigration of life) derived from the concept of dependent origination, Buddhism regards the existence of human beings and living things, as well as the future lives of human beings and other living things, as of equal importance.

CONCLUSION

The view of Buddhist ethics with regards to living things, as I have mentioned, depicts actions based on wisdom of dependent origination and of the middle way. The pursuit of profit has been discussed as being neither confirmed nor dinied. However, as living things are usually only beneficial for human beings, we have to examine what we are able to give in return. First, since a valuable life is lost by eating, we need to have a sense of obligation. Since human beings survive through consuming living things, we also have to have a sense of gratitude.

Also, human beings can not only be born because of the ecosystem, but also continuously gain from the circulation of substances in such a system. According to Buddhism, this means that we should have a sense of obligation, as well as appreciation towards other living things. In Buddhism there are various forms for obligation: obligation to a parent, to a sentient being, to a king, and to the three treasures as expounded in the "Meditation on the Mind-base Sutra (HRdayabhEmidhyana- sutra)."

For the purpose of our discussion here, I will elaborate on the meaning of "the obligation to a sentient being." According to Shigeo Kamata, this obligation is categorized as "close relationships" and "distant relationships." Specifically, a close relationship includes family relations, social relations, state relation, and other living things closely related to human beings, such as a horse or a cow. A distant relationship is considered to include not only all living things but also even inorganic matter. Therefore, Buddhism elucidates one's obligation to all things.

Let us consider what this means in concrete terms. As stated previously, even if we assert that deforestation, the capturing of living things, and the eating of animals are necessary acts to support human beings, we can not deny that these acts are regarded as evil in Buddhism, and that "the meat-eater forfeits the seed of Great Compassion."

Moreover, eating animals, felling trees, and capturing wildlife are expressions of desire. Naturally overeating and excessive-drinking, the thoughtless felling of trees, and over-hunting should be condemned from a moral point of view. It is, however, important not only to condemn such evil acts, but also to accumulate much good karma by doing good acts.

The "twentieth light precept" stresses the importance of cultivating "the practice of liberating sentient beings" as described above. That is, we should seek to refrain from restraining a living thing and instead aim to provide it with freedom. Considering this from the precept of "notstealing", the notion of granting enough space for living things to thrive is necessary. Such actions as releasing fish into rivers or lakes, reforesting, and developing methods for riverbank construction suitable to the habitation of marine life and others, are examples of habitat development for living things.

Reforestation and proper riverbank construction methods are especially important affirmative actions that contribute to recreating habitat for animals. It is also important to construct policies that are based on an understanding of ecosystem management. Such well-thought out policies are equivalent to the practice of donation of the six practices mention in the introduction. We should aim to act "with mercy," and should strongly admonish acts "with evil intention." This is also stressed by many of the other light precepts.

8

Moral Pluralism, Skillful Means, and Environmental Ethics

Since the simultaneous spread of awareness concerning environmental challenges and Buddhism in North America during the 1960's, it has been a widely held belief that among world religions, Buddhism is uniquely attuned to the natural environment. In an oft-cited article, Lynn White, Jr., argued that the root cause of the ecological crisis was the devaluation of nature and anthropocentrism of Western religious and philosophical traditions.

In contrast, he suggested, Asian traditions are more holistic and conceive of humans as interdependent with the environment. Succeeding scholarship has led to more nuanced views of both Western and Eastern traditions and their relations with non-human nature. Nevertheless, the association of Buddhism and ecology, as evidenced in an extensive literature, has continued to be popular among scholars, Buddhist practitioners, and environmental activists.

Donald Swearer has constructed a five-fold taxonomy with which to order the vast literature on Buddhism and ecology: eco-apologists, eco-critics, eco-constructivists, eco-ethicists, and eco-contextualists. According to Swearer, eco-apologists argue that Green Buddhism is a "natural extension of the Buddhist worldview."

Eco-critics, on the other hand, claim that Buddhism, with its emphasis on liberation and world negation, is incompatible with environmental ethics. Eco-constructivists, Swearer says, are those who believe that Buddhist traditions contain resources for constructing an environmental ethic. Eco-ethicists argue that any authentically Buddhist environmental ethic must be evaluated according to Buddhist ethics, not simply derived from Buddhist metaphysics. And finally, eco-contextualists insist that Buddhist environmental ethics that actually engage with the environment are necessarily embedded in local practices and traditions.

While this paper is a contribution to the discourse on Buddhism and ecology, it does not fall into any of Swearer's categories, or Ian Harris's earlier taxonomy. Though I am sympathetic to what Swearer terms eco-constructivism, I will not draw on conceptual resources from Buddhist traditions to construct a metaphysics of nature or a Buddhist environmental ethic. Rather, my purpose here is to argue that South Asian Buddhist moral traditions, with their moral pluralism, offer an appropriately pragmatic model of moral reasoning for contemporary environmental ethics.

I will begin with a sketch of the debate on monism and pluralism in environmental ethics. Some environmental philosophers argue that moral pluralism is necessary to respond to all our various moral responsibilities. In defense of monism, J. Baird Callicott claims that pluralism leads to relativism, skepticism, and the undermining of moral obligations. In the second part of my paper, I will argue that Buddhist ethics provides a counterexample to Callicott; it is a robust tradition of moral pluralism. Focusing on one of the most significant texts in Buddhist ethics, Sântideva's Bodhicaryâvatâra, I show how it draws on a multiplicity of moral principles determined by context and skillful means (upâya kauúalya). In contrast to Callicott's description of pluralism as detrimental to moral life, I suggest that South Asian Buddhist traditions provide a model of moral reasoning that is both robust and flexible, a model appropriate for the many kinds of moral obligations that arise in the context of environmental ethics.

Monism, Pluralism, and Environmental Ethics

One method of categorizing moral theories is according to their relation to moral principles. Utilitarianism and natural law theory, for instance, share a formal structure in that each is grounded in a supreme moral principle. In utilitarianism, for example, all moral reasoning must be derived from the principle of utility. Such theories, founded upon one overarching moral principle that provides unity and coherence, are monistic.

Some theorists reject moral monism, arguing instead for a pluralism that acknowledges the legitimacy of a multiplicity of independent, basic moral principles. These principles may well be in tension, or even mutually incompatible; but, it is said, they can be consistent with the phenomena. Pluralists argue that there is no one monistic theory that can encompass the whole moral realm, with all its complexities; there are, however, moral theories that can provide principles that are true for some kinds of moral acts, intentions, or states of affair.

Moral pluralism, they claim, is not a form of relativism, but an appropriate and necessary response to the multiple kinds of moral concern in our lives. A third kind of moral theory, moral particularism, associated with David McNaughton, Jonathan Dancy, and perhaps illustrated in some existentialist ethics, rejects the need for any moral principles. Instead of deriving judgments from a supreme moral principle or a plurality of self-justifying moral principles, particularists argue that the moral features of acts, agents, and states of affair arise contextually and cannot be grasped by universal principles. Instead of following moral principles, particularists claim, moral agents must cultivate the discernment of specific, contextualized moral landscapes.

The debate between monists and pluralists has been particularly pertinent in environmental ethics.10 During the 1960's and 1970's, faced with growing evidence of environmental degradation, some scholars attributed the state of the environment not just to destructive environmental practices, but to the traditional moral and metaphysical frameworks that seemed to justify these practices. Motivated in large part by concern for the environment, some philosophers called, in the words of Richard Sylvan, for "a new, an environmental, ethic."

This environmental ethic would lead us to be more responsive to the needs and values of non-human nature. A variety of theories were proposed and debated that recognize not just the value and moral standing of human subjects, but also of animals, non-sentient natural beings, and even ecosystems and the earth itself. In the early years of environmental ethics, philosophers generally sought to achieve a monistic theory that could encompass all our moral responsibilities.

According to Christopher Stone, in their quest for a monistic theory, environmental philosophers were caught in internecine, theoretical debates that lost sight of engaging practical policy questions. To move beyond abstract doctrines, Stone advocates moral pluralism in environmental thought so that philosophical debates could be more applicable, to better respond to the original motivation of environmental ethics.

Moral pluralism in the context of environmental ethics has been developed by Andrew Light, Bryan Norton, Anthony Weston, and others, who promote an environmental philosophy that can be applied to practical environmental policies. Moral pluralists, who generally see themselves as environmental pragmatists, do not look for one supreme principle that will cover all questions of environmental practice. Rather, they admit that in some instances, for example questions concerning the treatment of farm animals, animal rights or sentientism might be the best theory.

However, when considering what to do about an invasive species that is degrading an ecosystem, an ecocentric ethic that is not as attentive to the suffering and needs of individual animals might be the most prudent to follow. Moral pluralists acknowledge that we have moral obligations to salmon, pets, mountains, children, elms, works of art, fellow-citizens, and watersheds. However, they argue, we possess different moral obligations derived from different principles for these distinct entities.

When theories such as animal rights and ecocentrism lead to incompatible results, instead of rejecting one theory wholesale in the pursuit of monism, pluralists and environmental pragmatists argue, we should prudently determine which moral principle to apply to a particular situation. Instead of debating the one, right, univocal metaphysics of morals – ecocentrism versus anthropocentrism, biocentrism versus sentientism, deep ecology versus social ecology, etc. – pluralists and pragmatists seek agreement on practical policies that can be derived from a variety of moral principles. In "The Case Against Moral Pluralism" and "Moral Monism in Environmental Ethics Defended," J. Baird Callicott argues that moral pluralism weakens our moral obligations. "With a variety of theories at our disposal, each indicating different, inconsistent, or contradictory courses of action," Callicott writes, "we may be tempted to espouse the one that seems most convenient or self-serving in the circumstances."

Even if sincere, Callicott claims, pluralism provides no basis for determining which one of multiple incompatible principles to follow in any given circumstance. Finally, according to Callicott, moral pluralism results in the dissolution of moral responsibility in general for it leads to the skepticism and nihilism he associates with "deconstructive postmodernism." Without a unitary and systematic metaphysics of morals, Callicott insists, we lose both our moral and intellectual coherence and any foundation from which to argue for an environmental ethic.

Moral Pluralism in Santideva's Bodhicaryavatara

As with other internally diverse and rich traditions, Buddhism can be characterized as morally pluralistic in part, because there are so many different kinds of moral reasoning and teaching. Indeed, scholars have recognized the contours of eudaimonistic virtue ethics, utilitarianism, and Kantian ethics in Buddhist moral traditions. Additionally, it has been argued, some Buddhist moral strategies constitute a form of ethical particularism, for they emphasize context and do not follow any general principles.

As I have argued elsewhere, it is a mistake to believe that Buddhist ethics can be characterized as a whole – it is simply too diverse – and assimilating Buddhist ethics to Western moral principles loses the complexity and uniqueness of Buddhist moral traditions. Nevertheless, characterizations of Buddhist traditions in Western categories can be helpful in sketching the contours of Buddhist ethics; taken together they support the claim that Buddhist ethics is a form of moral pluralism.

In what follows, I will argue that even within one text, Úântideva's Bodhicaryavatara, there is a pluralistic approach to ethics. I believe that the Bodhicaryâvatâra provides a good counterexample to Callicott's claim that pluralism leads to moral skepticism and nihilism, because Úântideva's text is one of the most significant texts in the history of South Asian and Tibetan Buddhism.

There is widespread agreement with Frank Reynolds and Charles Hallisey, who claim that the Bodhicaryavatara's perhaps the best single source for the study of classical Mahayana ethics." Indeed, many discussions of Mahayana ethics in South Asia focus on the Bodhicaryavatara. The current high regard for Santideva's work is not new or unique to Western scholars. Shortly after it was composed, the Bodhicaryavatara spread quickly amongst Indian monastics, with whom it remained popular until the demise of Mahayana Buddhism on the sub-continent.

In Tibet, the popularity of the Bodhicaryavatara seems to have increased. The famous "Prajñâpâramitâ-pariccheda" was employed as a philosophy textbook in Tibetan scholastic curricula. The various Tibetan schools produced their own commentaries with very different interpretations of Santideva's text, but they all agreed on its significance as an authoritative exposition of what doxographers termed "Prasangika" Madhyamaka.

The Bodhicaryavatara was also popular outside scholastic environs. Variations on Santideva's presentation of the anuttara-puja (Supreme Worship) were widely practiced in Tibetan traditions. And his elaboration of the bodhisattva path became a primary inspiration for two important genres of Tibetan literary production: lam rim (stages of the path) and blo sbyong (mind training).

Moreover, Santideva's psychologically astute moral advice and often powerful and evocative language have had a broad appeal to lay practitioners. At the beginning of the fourteenth century, the Bodhicaryavatara was the first Buddhist text translated for the newly converted Mongolians, an indication of the high status of Santideva's work in Tibet. Though there may be other candidates, it is not without reason that some contemporary scholars claim that the Bodhicaryavatara "has been the most widely read, cited, and practiced text in the whole of the Indo-Tibetan Buddhist tradition."

Santideva employs a plurality of ethical strategies in the Bodhicaryavatara. However, one is tempted to interpret it as a form of eudaimonistic virtue ethics because the text is structured according to the development of the six virtues, or perfections (paramitas), of the bodhisattva. Chapter V treats the perfections of generosity (danaparamita) and moral discipline (silaparamita). Chapters VI through IX address the remaining perfections respectively: patience (ksantiparamita), vigor (viryaparamita), meditative contemplation (dhyanaparamita), and wisdom (prajnaparamita).

Santideva provides an account of the nature of the virtues and how they are to be cultivated. His presentation of the Middle Way is a map of the bodhisattva path oriented towards the telos of bodhicitta, the awakened mind characterized by great compassion (mahakaruna) and the perfection of wisdom (prajnaparamita).

Santideva further seems to endorse a virtue ethic with his understanding that there are no universal rules applicable to all situations. Rather, one must attend to each singular situation and then determine the proper course of action. Thus, Santideva argues, a bodhisattva motivated by compassion and guided by wisdom, should transgress general rules, such as the precepts and the monastic rules of conduct. Instead of following rules at all times, even the proscriptions against killing, stealing, and lying, a bodhisattva ought to determine what is best in a particular context.

Santideva does not treat skill in means as a unique perfection, as is done in many Mahayana accounts of ten, instead of six, perfections. Nevertheless, the Bodhicaryavatara clearly states that one who is skillful in strategy, method, or means (upaya) ought to do those actions which are generally proscribed, if it will diminish suffering in the world. Santideva addresses skillful means in the context of his presentation of moral discipline, as if to emphasize that rules of conduct are designed to make the practitioner mindful and aware, and not conceived as unchanging laws determining every action.

Santideva's commitment to relieving suffering through any means, including the transgression of prohibitions against violence, might lead one to interpret the Bodhicaryavatara as a form of utilitarianism. Santideva takes it as a given that suffering is to be avoided as such, regardless of whose suffering it may be. At times, Santideva does recognize a positive value in suffering.

However, this positive value is only justified when it serves to diminish overall suffering, as when it motivates the aspiring bodhisattva. Indeed, Santideva makes the calculation that it is appropriate to sacrifice oneself for someone who is equally or more compassionate, but not for someone who is less attentive to the sufferings of others, "That way, there is no overall loss." Clearly, there are elements of utilitarianism functioning in the Bodhicaryavatara.

In contrast to utilitarianism, however, like Kant, Santideva believes that motivation is a primary locus of moral significance. Ṣantideva is committed to dependent origination (pratitya-samutpada), the doctrine that no single causal power, including individual moral agents, can be regarded as solely responsible for external states of affair.

Thus, we cannot be held solely responsible for the consequences of our actions in the world; we are only responsible for our own states of mind. Santideva argues: "the perfection is the mental attitude itself," and "since I cannot control external events, I will control my own mind." While there is a family resemblance to Kantian ethics, Santideva does not share the Kantian understanding of moral responsibility for an autonomous will. According to Santideva, the activity of our minds is also dependently originated and thus not free in the Kantian sense.

The attempt to reduce Santideva's ethics to a monistic Western moral category would make his writings appear inconsistent and confused. It would also be a mistake to interpret the Bodhicaryavatara as a uniquely Buddhist moral monism. Rather, grounded in the doctrine of dependent origination, Santideva provides rich descriptions of the moral significance of intention and consequence, character and action, without seeking to circumscribe all moral activity under one principle.

In contrast to Callicott's claim that pluralism leads to moral skepticism and nihilism, the Bodhicaryavatara, with its central place in more than a millennium of Indo-Tibetan Buddhist ethics, suggests that pluralism, with its flexibility, can provide a robust ethic applicable in daily life.

Conclusion: Moral Pluralism, Skillful Means, and Environmental Ethics

In response to a series of metaphysical questions in the Cûlamalunkya Sutta' such as whether or not the world is spatially or temporally finite, whether the self is identical to the body, etc.' the Buddha tells a parable about a man wounded by a poisoned arrow. If prior to allowing the surgeon to remove the arrow, the wounded man were to insist upon knowing the caste, name, physical characteristics, and native place of the shooter, or the kind of bow and arrow employed, he would die.

This story is often interpreted as the Buddha, whose teaching began with an account of the pervasiveness of dissatisfaction, claiming that, instead of concerning oneself with metaphysical speculation irrelevant to liberation, one should pursue practices that are liberating from the mental defilements that cause suffering. The Buddha's response is read by some contemporary scholars as an anticipation of Kant's employment of antinomies and the Kantian critique of metaphysics; others interpret the Buddha's silence on metaphysical questions as Wittgensteinian. According to this reading, the Buddha regarded philosophy as a therapy and found metaphysical speculation to be dangerous and not simply useless.

Gadjin Nagao notes that the Buddha employed silence in a variety of different ways depending on his interlocutor and the context of their conversation.49 Because elsewhere the Buddha makes specific claims concerning the very questions about which he is silent in the Culamalunkya a Sutta, regarding the Buddha's silence as primarily an anticipation of Kant or Wittgenstein is inadequate.

Instead, it seems that the Buddha practices skillful means, and recognizes that metaphysical frameworks are sometimes beneficial and sometimes detrimental. Moreover, the Buddha may provide different metaphysical frameworks, guided by what he thinks is best for the particular audience. According to Mahayanists, all the Buddha's very different teachings were geared towards the different capacities of the student. Some Indian Buddhist texts even advocate teaching non-Buddhist doctrines, such as Saivism, to those who lack the capacity to understand the Buddha dharma. What all teachings could agree on, however, was the importance of removing the arrow of suffering.

Global climate change, pollution overload, resource depletion, the degradation of the land where we live, work, and play, and the various other environmental challenges we face, are conditions that lead to enormous suffering for sentient beings; they constitute an immense poisoned arrow we have unleashed upon ourselves and our fellow creatures in the web of life.

Santideva and other Mahayanists in South Asia did not consider all views to be equally valid or equally true. Mahayanists constructed detailed doxographic hierarchies; full liberation, they believed, was only possible with the correct understanding situated at the top of the hierarchy of doctrines.

According to Santideva, the proper understanding of the lack of inherent existence of all conventionally constructed phenomena was necessary to fully relinquish attachments that cause suffering. Nevertheless, he shared many views with others regarding the kinds of actions, traits, intentions, and states of affair that alleviate suffering.

Similarly, there is much agreement that can be reached on practical policy matters amongst environmental philosophers. Indeed, not only can agreement be reached among those who advocate ecocentrism and biocentrism, deep ecology and animal rights, but more importantly, between non-anthropocentrists and those who disregard non-human values, or those inspired by eco-kosher practices, or members of the Creation Care movement. Forging this agreement would be the task of what Andrew Light calls "metaphilosophical environmental pragmatism." Light characterizes metaphilosophical environmental pragmatism as a pragmatic compatibilism amongst thinkers with competing metaphysical commitments working together on practical policy issues.

I am not suggesting that all theoretical debates be set aside, for practical policy determinations are inevitably grounded in metaphysical systems. Nevertheless, when environmental philosophy takes place primarily at the level of metaphysics and abdicates the realm of policy to the social and natural sciences, it abandons much of its capacity to contribute to a more sustainable future.

Buddhist ethics provides a model of pluralistic moral strategies that are compatible with competing metaphysical frameworks. The doctrine of skillful means would suggest that we should be more pluralistic and pragmatic; the reception of the Bodhicaryâvatâra and other historically significant approaches to Buddhist ethics suggest that pluralism can augment moral commitments without leading to skepticism and nihilism.

9

In Search of Buddhist Foundation for Environmental Ethics

Environmental problems are among those urgencies pressing us for timely solutions. And, like many others, environmental crisis gives rise to the question whether Buddhism can contribute anything to the attempt to alleviate the situation. The question is apparently clear. However, a consideration of answers commonly given shows us that it is too broad and therefore prompts us to redefine it. Many who give an affirmative answer raise a famous example in which Buddhist monks lead local people in the activities of 'tree ordination' and also of other environmental movements led by local monks. However, monks' activities do not comprise a good answer because there are a lot of counterexamples. Some popular monks, for instance, had a big area of forest cleared so that 'forest temples' could be constructed as peaceful places for meditation retreat.

This points out that we should not understand by the term, 'Buddhism,' a religious institution with its members. The above examples pose us a question which of those activities by monks is in accordance with the true Buddhist spirit. To distinguish Buddhist from non-Buddhist activities, 'Buddhist worldview' therefore needs to be understood. As a result, the question should be so refined as to inquire whether Buddhist worldview can be utilized as a basis to tackle the environmental crisis.

Ways to answer this redefined question can be classified into two:

(1) The Buddhist way of world understanding should be used as the foundation on which appropriate environmental

framework is constructed. It is anticipated that this approach will yield a characteristically Buddhist solution;

(2) Conditions that environmentalists believe to be necessary for environmental protection should be used as a framework for which Buddhism needs to provide a foundation.

Apparently, answers to these questions do not seem to diverge. Yet, they bear an asymmetrical relationship. The answer to the first question may not be accepted by those who prefer to approach the problem with the second question while it can be sure that the answer to the second question will be endorsed by those who work with the first question. The reason is that the conditions posed by the environmentalists are more restrictive. We shall see below that there are cases in which Buddhism can support some environmental practice, but still fails to meet the environmentalist criteria.

Before we proceed, there is a possible objection to the above consideration that it leaves out some other alternative to deal with the question. That is, some argue that Buddhism can not provide any foundation for environmental ethics whose aim is to protect this world. That is because it rather teaches people to renounce this world. However, this does not seem to be really problematic because it is not difficult to see that, despite that sort of teaching, Buddhism does not reject the mundane level of reality (lokiya).

The instruction of renunciation belongs to the 'religious' order having as its goal spiritual development, which concerns the relationship between an individual and the transcendental reality (lokuttara). At the same time, Buddhism also gives instruction in what one ought or ought not to do, which belongs to the 'moral' order embedded in the mundane realm. More than that, in order to renounce this world through enlightenment, one need to start with moral practice as prescribed in the threefold training (sikkhattaya). Therefore, Buddhism does not only accept this world—the mundane reality—but also prescribed moral orientation in the realm.

Another related point is that some suggest that fruits of spiritual development be utilized as the basis of environmental movement.

Nevertheless, this can not be considered to be a general framework since it implies that environmental protection depends on spiritual development in each individual, which is not timely—the insight development is difficult and not something for which people in general are happy to endeavor. The proper environmental ethics should provide a rationale for people with different spiritual progress to take care of the environment.

Distinguishing between the two levels of teachings e.g. moral and religious, we are aware that moral principles are prescribed for all whereas religious goals depend on each individual. This however does not completely exclude an ethical consideration that refers to the spiritual development. Apart from their practical aspect, spiritually developed individuals also have the aspect that can be loosely termed, 'cognitive'— they have more access to the truth about absolute reality. Granted that practice is based on understanding, the environment-friendly conduct purportedly observed in those with well-developed mind should have its root in their understanding of the absolute truth. If that truth is discovered, the question about Buddhist contribution should be answered.

Next are the environmentalist conditions, after which proposed Buddhist solutions are critically considered against the background of these conditions.

The basic conditions that the environmentalists use as criteria for judging adequacy of proposed theories comprise the followings.

(1) Nature and things in nature have value in themselves. They have value neither because they can satisfy human needs nor because human existence depends on them.

(2) Diversity in nature has value in itself.

(3) Nature does not consist only of particular things but also holistic entities such as forest, species, and ecosystem. In other words, holism is endorsed.6 Any proposed ethical theories need to be able to accommodate all these three elements.

Those important points are below which Buddhist scholars raise in support of the thesis that there is something in Buddhism that can provide an environmental ethical foundation. In the Discipline (Vinaya), proscriptions are found that seem to bear the tone of environmental concern. For example, it is forbidden that monks damage plants, cut a tree, or pass waste into a water resource. However, the Discipline is not sufficient for two reasons. First, the rationale behind some of these is not related to environmental care, but others such as respectability of the monastic order.

Second, though some other proscriptions was motivated by the perception of value in things in wilderness e.g. animals' lives7, the rationale is not sufficient because it does not cover holistic entities as indicated in the third environmentalist condition. For example, when the Buddha barred his disciple, Moggallna, from turning the earth surface upside down with his psychic supernatural power to provide starved people with a sort of edible soil, he gave a reason that particular animals would be harmed, not their species.

Suppose we grant that the third condition was met—that the whole species were taken into account, those particular and holistic entities without sentience such as trees and forest are still left out. Of course, it will not do to explain that they should be preserved for the sake of living animals because that implies they have no internal value, which is against the first condition.

In Aggañña Sutta, the relationship between human moral condition and state of the world is related. When human morality decreases, the world becomes less and less livable. This implies that human beings should conduct themselves morally in order to preserve the good condition of the world. This should become a basis for environmental ethics. However, the problem is that human happiness is used as the criterion for judging the state of the world. This violates the first principle.

Loving-kindness (mett), non-violence (ahimsa), and identification with other living beings as fellows in the birth-and-death cycle (samsra) are raised in support of Buddhist environmental relevance. Although they run into the same kind of problem in a consideration of this point will lead us to some other crucial aspects. Lovingkindness is broader than abstinence from infliction and killing. For instance, in cases that some type of animals is so overcrowded that the ecosystem is badly affected, the teaching to avoid taking life does not permit us to solve the problem by culling. But, it is possible that the principle of loving-kindness dictates otherwise in order to benefit the greater number of other living beings in the effected ecosystem.9 Even though it seems the principle allows a consideration of ecosystem e.g. a holistic thing, it is precisely in the view of each living beings' well-being, and thus violates the first and the third condition—ecosystem is treated as means to animals' happiness and it is particular animals that are the objects of concern, not their whole species.

Neungnoi Boonyanetra suggests that 'mett' and 'chanda' (aspiration) as states of mind are opposite to 'taGh' (craving). These former states are realized '...in individuals who see the truth that everything is under the law of dependent origination (paraiccasamuppda)...They are motives free from the idea of self...the wish to see everything exists in their valuable conditions, ones in which their perfect values are maintained..."

This suggestion seems to enable us to satisfy those environmentalist conditions. The appreciation that everything has value in themselves satisfies the first condition; the wish that everything remains in their valuable conditions satisfies the second condition (since diversity is implied); and, despite the ambiguity of the term, 'everything,' in relation to the holistic concept, it should be save to infer that the acceptance of everything as they are should allow a Buddhist support to the idea of holistic entities together with their internal value. Nevertheless, the crucial point is the connection between the insight into the dependent origination and 'mett/chanda.' What makes those people with the insight see value in all things. The knowledge of interdependence does not seem to have anything to do with value.

The idea of dependent origination seems to make Buddhism a viable candidate for the foundation of environmental ethics, especially because it seems to imply holism, which in turn connotes equality among all things and is also linked to the idea of lessening attachment to self and self-interest.

These mean that anthropocentric stance is avoided. Human beings are no longer the source or attributers of value; and nature and its diversity have value in themselves. However, 'holism' so implied has a sense different from that endorsed by the environmentalists. As for Buddhism, the holism in question is in the ontological level while that of the environmentalists is in the ethical level.

According to Buddhism, holism refers to interdependence of all that exist. A particular thing is what it is because of the other things. On the other hand, according to the environmentalists, holism means the approach of ethical consideration that does not include only particular things but also holistic entities. The crucial point is that, as for Buddhism, particular and holistic entities are not ontologically distinct. They are equally constituted by the web of interdependent factors. However, the distinction is required by the environmentalists.

Moreover, to some extent, anyone, even those anthropocentric ethicists, accepts the interdependence in the ecosystem since it can be scientifically explained. And yet, not all of them see that it is necessary to construct an ethical theory that meets the environmentalist criteria. Therefore, it is still questionable why the doctrine of dependent origination should lead to that sort of ethical theory. Perhaps, the answer can be found if we return to the connection between the insight into the interdependence and the result of lessened self-attachment.

The more a person sees things have no essence, the less she becomes selfish and so is less likely to exploit nature. Nevertheless, selfishness is not the sole factor of environmental depletion. Selfless individuals can cause natural damages too, say for the sake of others. Thus, it is necessary to go further as to explicate that, when the self-attachment is lessened, that person has 'mett/chanda' developing in her, and consequently sees the value in all things. The problem that remains is the aforementioned lack of explanation about the connection between the insight and 'mett/chanda.'

In addition, it is not evident whether the perceived value has objective existence as the environmentalists require. It seems to be only a subjective consequence. One possible answer is the idea that the mind free from self-attachment can better perceive objective values. The Venerable Payutto once raised this in response to the question of how to accept the teaching that, in a sense, 'heaven' and 'hell' are in the mind when it is clear that many wicked persons enjoy mental well-being.

He clarified that the wicked could not perceive inner dissatisfactions because their mind was too coarse due to the density of self-attachment. Ignorance made their mind insensitive to values that occurred in it. His response shows that values occur in the mind when deeds are done, but their existence may not be evident if the mental faculty is not adequately refined. These values are identified with mental qualities e.g. wholesome (kusala) and unwholesome (akusala).

Therefore, although the basis for objectivity of value is found, it can not be understood how the value of things in nature and the nature itself can share this sort of ontological status. In fact, if Buddhism could provide an ontological basis for these things in the first place, there would be no need for the above considerations. From the above, it can be concluded that Buddhism can satisfy the environmentalist criteria only if it can answer the following questions.

Is there anything in the Buddhist doctrine that allows us to indicate the existence of value-in-itself that belongs to nature and natural entities—something just like wholesome and unwholesome qualities that provide the ethical foundation? Is there anything that allows the assertion that holistic entities exist really as something whole? Buddhism seems to allow some sort of holistic entities. For example, we may classify 'society' as something holistic. But that is simply because we refer to the minds of people in that collectivity. This approach does not seem effective when it comes to the cases of species, forest, or ecosystem.

Is there anything that supports the value of natural diversity without the need to refer to benefits of humans or animals?

Ontological inquiry appears to be hopeless because it is generally held in Theravāda Buddhism that there exist only four types of things e.g. mind (citta), mental qualities (cetasikas), forms (rkpas), and Nibbāna. It is not imaginable how things indicated in the three environmentalist conditions are related to these types. It is questionable if we should simply turn back on the environmentalist criteria and resort to the approach of deriving from Buddhism its own foundation of environmental ethics.

That is because it is believed that, developed by those who closely study environmental crisis, the criteria have a firm root in the reality of the situation. Another possible way out is for Buddhism to set a new set of criteria that can respond to the needs to preserve holistic entities and diversity while the reference to the internal value and the existence of holistic entities as belonging to distinct ontological types are at the same time avoided. Of course, all anthropocentric stances must be avoided. However, this seems to be desperate.

To sum up, the environmentalist criteria utilized in environmental ethics to judge adequacy of proposed ethical theories are very restrictive and therefore pose a challenge that Buddhism can not easily overcome if it aspires to give an environmental ethical foundation. Actually, this is an impregnable challenge to all other religions with the same aspiration.

10 Buddhist Ethics and Social Criticism

Moral conduct for Buddhists differs according to whether it applies to the laity or to the Sangha or clergy. A lay Buddhist should cultivate good conduct by training in what are known as the "Five Precepts". These are not like, say, the ten commandments, which, if broken, entail punishment by God. The five precepts are training rules, which, if one were to break any of them, one should be aware of the breech and examine how such a breech may be avoided in the future. The resultant of an action (often referred to as Karma) depends on the intention more than the action itself. It entails less feelings of guilt than its Judeo-Christian counterpart. Buddhism places a great emphasis on 'mind' and it is mental anguish such as remorse, anxiety, guilt etc. which is to be avoided in order to cultivate a calm and peaceful mind. The five precepts are:

(1) To undertake the training to avoid taking the life of beings. This precept applies to all living beings not just humans. All beings have a right to their lives and that right should be respected.

(2) To undertake the training to avoid taking things not given. This precept goes further than mere stealing. One should avoid taking anything unless one can be sure that is intended that it is for you.

(3) To undertake the training to avoid sensual misconduct. This precept is often mistranslated or misinterpreted as relating only to sexual misconduct but it covers any overindulgence in any sensual pleasure such as gluttony as well as misconduct of a sexual nature.

(4) To undertake the training to refrain from false speech. As well as avoiding lying and deceiving, this precept covers slander as well as speech which is not beneficial to the welfare of others.

(5) To undertake the training to abstain from substances which cause intoxication and heedlessness. This precept is in a special category as it does not infer any intrinsic evil in, say, alcohol itself but indulgence in such a substance could be the cause of breaking the other four precepts.

These are the basic precepts expected as a day to day training of any lay Buddhist. On special holy days, many Buddhists, especially those following the Theravada tradition, would observe three additional precepts with a strengthening of the third precept to be observing strict celibacy. The additional precepts are:

(6) To abstain from taking food at inappropriate times. This would mean following the tradition of Theravadin monks and not eating from noon one day until sunrise the next.

(7) To abstain from dancing, singing, music and entertainments as well as refraining from the use of perfumes, ornaments and other items used to adorn or beautify the person. Again, this and the next rule.

(8) To undertake the training to abstain from using high or luxurious beds are rules regularly adopted by members of the Sangha and are followed by the layperson on special occasions.

MAHAYANA TRADITION

Laypersons following the Mahayana tradition, who have taken a Bodhisattva vow, will also follow a strictly vegetarian diet. This is not so much an additional precept but a strengthening of the first precept; To undertake the training to avoid taking the life of beings. The eating of meat would be considered a contribution to the taking of life, indirect though it may be. The Buddhist clergy, known as the Sangha, are governed by 227 to 253 rules depending on the school or tradition for males or Bhikkhus and between 290 and 354 rules, depending on the school or tradition for females or Bhikkhunis. These rules, contained in the Vinaya or first collection of the Buddhist scriptures,, are divided into several groups, each entailing a penalty for their breech, depending on the seriousness of that breech. The first four rules for males and the first eight for females, known as Parajika or rules of defeat, entail expulsion from the Order immediately on their breech. The four applying to both sexes are: Sexual intercourse, killing a human being, stealing to the extent that it entails a gaol sentence and claiming miraculous or supernormal powers. Bhikkhunis' additional rules relate to various physical contacts with males with one relating to concealing from the order the defeat or parajika of another. Before his passing, the Buddha instructed that permission was granted for the abandonment or adjustment of minor rules should prevailing conditions demand such a change. These rules apply to all Saṅgha members irrespective of their Buddhist tradition.

The interpretation of the rules, however differs between the Mahayāna and Theravāda traditions. The Theravadins, especially those from Thailand, claim to observe these rules to the letter of the law, however, in many cases, the following is more in theory than in actual practice. The Mahayana Saṇgha interprets the rule not to take food at an inappropriate time as not meaning fasting from noon to sunrise but to refrain from eating between mealtimes. The fasting rule would be inappropriate, from a health angle, for the Sangha living in cold climates such as China, Korea and Japan. When one examines the reason that this rule was instituted initially, the conclusion may be reached that it is currently redundant. It was the practice in the Buddha's time for the monks to go to the village with their bowls to collect food.

To avoid disturbing the villagers more than necessary, the Buddha ordered his monks to make this visit once a day, in the early morning. This would allow the villagers to be free to conduct their day to day affairs without being disturbed by the monks requiring food. Today, of course, people bring food to the monasteries or prepare it on the premises so the original reason no longer applies. As many of you would be aware, in some Theravadin countries, the monks still go on their early morning alms round, but this is more a matter of maintaining a tradition than out of necessity. Also, a rule prohibiting the handling of gold and silver, in other words-money, is considered by the Mahayāna Sangha a handicap were it to be observed strictly in today's world. They interpret this rule as avoiding the accumulation of riches which leads to greed. Theravadin monks tend to split hairs on this rule as, although most will not touch coins, many carry credit cards and cheque books. Let me now deal briefly with the Buddhist attitude to violence, war and peace. The Buddha said in the Dhammapada:

* Victory breeds hatred. The defeated live in pain. Happily the peaceful live giving up victory and defeat.(Dp.15,5) and

* Hatreds never cease by hatred in this world; through love alone they cease. This is an eternal law. (Dp.1,5)

The first precept refers to the training to abstain from harming living beings. Although history records conflicts involving the so-called Buddhist nations, these wars have been fought for economic or similar reasons. However, history does not record wars fought in the name of propagating Buddhism. Buddhism and, perhaps, Jainism are unique in this regard. His Holiness, the Dalai Lama has never suggested armed conflict to overcome the persecution and cruelty perpetrated by the Communist Chinese occupation forces. He has always advocated a peaceful and non-violent solution. Venerable Maha Ghosananda, the Supreme Patriarch of Cambodia has urged Cambodians to put aside their anger for the genocide of the Khmer Rouge and to unify to re-establish their nation.

He has written: The suffering of Cambodia has been deep. From this suffering comes great compassion. Great compassion makes a peaceful heart. A peaceful heart makes a peaceful person. A peaceful person makes a peaceful family. A peaceful family makes a peaceful community. A peaceful community makes a peaceful nation. A peaceful nation makes a peaceful world. Going back to the early history of Buddhism, Emperor Asoka, who, after a bloody but successful military campaign, ruled over more than two thirds of the Indian subcontinent, suffered great remorse for the suffering that he had caused, banned the killing of animals and exhorted his subjects to lead kind and tolerant lives. He also promoted tolerance towards all religions which he supported financially. The prevalent religions of that time were the sramanas or wandering ascetics, Brahmins, Ajivakas and Jains. He recommended that all religions desist from self praise and condemnation of others. His pronouncements were written on rocks at the periphery of his kingdom and on pillars along the main roads and where pilgrims gathered. He also established many hospitals for both humans and animals. Some of his important rock edicts stated:

1. Asoka ordered that banyan trees and mango groves be planted, rest houses built and wells dug every half mile along the main roads.
2. He ordered the end to killing of any animal for use in the royal kitchens.
3. He ordered the provision of medical facilities for humans and beasts.
4. He commanded obedience to parents, generosity to priests and ascetics and frugality in spending.
5. All officers must work for the welfare of the poor and the aged.
6. He recorded his intention to promote the welfare of all beings in order to repay his debt to all beings.
7. He honours men of all faiths.

Seeds of Peace

Not all Buddhists follow the non-violent path, however. A Buddhist monk, Phra Kittiwutthi of the Phra Chittipalwon College in Thailand, is noted for his extreme right-wing views. He said that it was not a breech of the first precept to kill communists. He said that if Thailand were in danger of a communist takeover, he would take up arms to protect Buddhism. Sulak Sivaraksa, a Thai peace activist, reports in his book, "Seeds of Peace" that Phra Kittiwutthi has since modified his stance by declaring "to kill communism or communist ideology is not a sin". Sulak adds that the monk confessed that his nationalist feelings were more important than his Buddhist practice and that he would be willing to abandon his yellow robes to take up arms against communist invaders from Laos, Cambodia or Vietnam. By doing so, he said, he would be preserving the monarchy, the nation and the Buddhist religion. In contrast to the views of Phra Kittiwutthi, Sulak Sivaraksa reports that the Vietnamese monk, Thich Nhat Hanh is of the view that 'preserving Buddhism does not mean that we should sacrifice people's lives in order to safeguard the Buddhist hierarchy, monasteries or rituals. Even if Buddhism as such were extinguished, when human lives are preserved and when human dignity and freedom are cultivated towards peace and loving kindness, Buddhism can be reborn in the hearts of human beings. In conclusion, I will briefly mention some other issues mentioned in the Syllabus.

Theravadin Tradition

The third precept on training in restraint of the senses includes sexuality. A Buddhist should be mindful of the possible effects on themselves and on others of improper sexual activity. This precept would include adultery because this also breeches the precept of not taking what does is not freely given. A relationship with someone who is committed to another is stealing. Similarly in cases of rape and child abuse, one is stealing the dignity and self respect of another. One is also the cause of mental pain, not to mention physical pain so one is causing harm to another living being.

Therefore, such behaviour is breaking several precepts. Marriage is not a sacrament in Buddhism as it is in other religions. Marriage is governed by civil law and a Buddhist is expected to observe the prevailing law in whatever country they live. In the Theravadin tradition, monks are prohibited by their Vinaya rules to encourage or perform a marriage ceremony. The rule states: Should a Bhikkhu engage to act as a go-between for a man's intentions to a woman or a woman's intentions to a man, whether about marriage or paramourage, even for a temporary arrangement, this entails initial and subsequent meeting of the Sangha. In many Theravadin countries, the couple will, following their marriage in a civil ceremony, invite the monks to their home to perform a blessing ceremony.

They will offer food and other requisites to the monks and invite their family and friends to participate. In the Mahayana tradition the same rule conveys an entirely different meaning. It reads: Should a Bhikkshu, seek to establish a conducive situation by means of which a man and a woman engage in sexual misconduct, either by himself, by order, or by means of messages, and as a result of his activities the man and woman should meet, he has committed an offence. This rule does not preclude marriage but, rather, deals with the monk assuming the role of a procurer for immoral purposes.

In Western countries, following the Christian precedent, many Mahayana monks become registered marriage celebrants so that, if called upon, a marriage ceremony can be performed in the temple. Generally, in countries where the law allows, Buddhists accept de-facto relationships. Promiscuity would be frowned upon as sexual misconduct but an ongoing relationship between two people, either within or outside of marriage would be considered moral conduct. As one of the essential Buddhist teachings is that everything is impermanent and subject to change, the irrevocable breakdown of a relationship between a couple would be understood in this light, so divorce would not be considered improper. As far as bioethical questions are concerned, it is mainly a matter of the attitude of the different traditions or schools of Buddhism. This is tied to the concept of rebirth and when it occurs.

According to the Theravādin tradition, rebirth occurs immediately upon death. The body of the deceased is no longer considered as a part of the former being, so such things as autopsies, organ transplants etcetera are allowable. In fact, many Theravādins, especially in Malaysia, encourage the donation of human organs as being the highest form of giving. Often, especially at Vesak, the celebration of the birth, enlightenment and passing away of the Buddha, blood donations are performed in the temple grounds. The Mahayana, on the other hand, believes that there is an intermediate state between incarnations, known as Antarabhava. Most people following this tradition try to avoid touching or moving the body for, at least eight hours after death. This, of course, means that the organs would by then be useless for transfer to another human being. The Buddhist work ethic and business and professional ethics would, ideally be closely tied to respect for the environment. It is well described in E. F. Schumacher's book "Small is Beautiful": "While the materialist is mainly interested in goods, the Buddhist is mainly interested in liberation. But Buddhism is the Middle Way and therefore in no way antagonistic to physical well being. The keynote of Buddhist economics is simplicity and non-violence. From an economist's point of view, the marvel of the Buddhist way of life is the utter rationality of its pattern-amazingly small means leading to extraordinarily satisfying results."

Ken Jones in a paper called "Buddhism and Social Action" comments: "Schumacher outlines a 'Buddhist economics' in which production would be based on a middle range of material goods (and no more), and on the other a harmony with the natural environment and its resources. The above principles suggest some kind of diverse and politically decentralised society, with co-operative management and ownership of productive wealth.

It would be conceived on a human scale, whether in terms of size and complexity or organisation or of environmental planning, and would use modern technology selectively rather than being used by it in the service of selfish interests. In Schumacher's words, 'It is a question of finding the right path of development, the Middle Way, between materialist heedlessness and traditionalist immobility, in short, of finding Right Livelihood'". Despite the theory surrounding Buddhist business practice, greed still seems to be the order of the day in many Buddhist countries.

In Thailand, a monk in the north, Acharn Ponsektajadhammo, has been leading a campaign against the environmental vandalism of the timber industry. Tree felling in Northern Thailand has caused erosion, flooding and has economically ruined small farmers. For his environmental efforts, Acharn Ponsektajadhammo has had death threats and was recently arrested. In Japan, another country where the majority of the population is Buddhist, the killing of whales and dolphins is still prevalent. Animals seem to find no place in the group culture of Japanese society. As may be seen from the foregoing, Buddhist ethical principles are very noble and in an ideal world their practice would lead to peace and harmony but, unfortunately, as the Buddha has taught, people are motivated by greed hatred and delusion-even Buddhists.

THE ETHICS OF BUDDHISM

It is well-known that Buddhism is the most ethical of "religions". An important part of the Noble Eightfold Path relates to the development of ethical conduct; for many a layperson Buddhist practice consists mainly in the "keeping of the precepts"; many Bhikkhus see in the Vinaya rules the essence of the religious life; and even many of the paramitas expected of those aspiring to Buddhahood are ethical in nature. Yet to present the teaching of the Buddha as being solely and exclusively concerned with ethics could serve as a detraction from the real objective of the Buddha-Dhamma, which is to serve as a path or vehicle leading to Enlightenment. While conforming to the norms of Buddhist ethics is essential for this purpose this alone will not guarantee the elimination of ignorance (avijja), which is the real meaning of Enlightenment. The tendency of some exponents of the Dhamma to represent Buddhism as just another ethical system is misleading, especially when put before a newcomer to the Dhamma who may not be able to distinguish between Buddhist ethics and the precepts of other ethical teachers, and may conclude that Buddhism has nothing new to offer. All religions inculcate some basic ethics, whether relating to individual or to social conduct.

Indeed the advocacy of an ethical system does not need a religious framework, and some: of the great ethical teachers of the world (e.g. Socrates or Confucius) did not feel the need for one. The religion-surrogates of the modern world, like Humanism, rationalism, or Communism, have all evolved their own norms of ethics, however inadequate we may consider them to be. Wherein, then, lies the uniqueness of Buddhist ethics? This question could be answered in many ways, but here we shall look at it from the standpoint of three criteria. First of all there are the ethical rules themselves.

When we consider what actions are considered "good" and what are deemed to be "bad", it might appear that there is a great deal of agreement between the different ethical Systems. Such actions like killing, theft, sexual misconduct, and falsehood seem to be condemned universally. The differences emerge when we examine the question more closely, e.g. when we investigate the rationale for these rules, whether they are absolute or are relative to some other end, and so on. The rule against killing could be taken as an example. Many ethical systems proscribe only the killing of humans (i.e. murder), but Buddhism applies the rule to all sentient existence.

Furthermore even in the case of humans, exceptions are sometimes allowed, e.g. for "holy" or "just" war. Buddhism admits of no such exemptions. In Buddhism the ethical quality of actions depends on the mental factors associated with their commission or even contemplation, and on the impact they have on the well-being of others. If action is committed with greed, aversion or delusion it is unwholesome (akusala), but the degree of moral reprehensibility (and karmic consequence) depends on a whole host of factors. Even an "accidental" killing could have adverse consequences if it was caused through negligence and unmindfulness, which is a kind of "Delusion" (moha). What has been said of the rule regarding killing, may also be extended to the other ethical precepts as well. Furthermore Buddhist ethics does not stop at the Five Precepts (panca siila), which provides only the very minimum for the proper conduct of lay persons. The second criterion that could be adduced for the evaluation of ethical Systems relates to the motivation for adhering to the ethical rules of the system, religious or secular.

In Buddhism the goal of ethical conduct is self-control, self-understanding, and self-development. It is an essential prerequisite for the training of the mind, the elimination of ignorance and the attainment of Enlightenment. Theistic religions usually require the adherence to their ethical precepts as a means to the union with God, whether in an abstract metaphysical sense or more directly as entry into a kingdom ruled by God, or even the enjoyment of pleasures in a heavenly paradise. In such a system the most important rule, precept or commandment is not usually an ethical one, but belief in, love of, submission and obedience to, and veneration of God. This is thus placed at the head of the Judeo-Christian decalogue, with the ethical rules coming subsequently. When we look at "secular" ethics, such as those embodied in legal systems, the objective is usually the avoidance of social conflict, the regularization of property rights, and the like. Of course, some secular laws (e.g. those relating to the so-called "victimless crimes") are more directly "moral" in nature, but these too usually are indirect social objectives. The pursuit of Buddhist ethics too leads to social harmony, but this harmony is achieved through individual perfection, rather than through the compulsory observance of legalistic rules. But because of the non-compulsive nature of Buddhist ethics, they are not intended to replace the laws of society, but neither are those of other ethical systems erected on religious and philosophical foundations. The third aspect of the question relates to the way in which "good" and "bad" conduct results in appropriate consequences.

This is the question of the "policing of the rules". Here two approaches may be distinguished. One is where some kind of trial and punishment (or reward) is instituted individually for each person. The supreme judicial authority could be God to the theist; or simply the normal judicial processes of society in the case of the secularist and the materialist. The second approach relies on the workings of an impersonal law (like the Law of Karma in its Buddhist and Hindu-Jam forms). The legal model of trial-and-punishment is best suited to the enforcement of the laws of society, such as are necessary for the preservation of the authority of the State and the well-being of society. When this model is used to evaluate personal moral conduct and behaviour, as in the theory of divine judgement, several curious features arise. One that could be mentioned is the doctrine of the "forgiveness of sins". According to this doctrine the exercise of divine grace could wipe out "sins" and negate the principle that actions bring their own reward. In such a system the ultimate factor which determines the destiny of an individual is not the scrupulous observance of the ethical rules of the system, but the element of blind faith in its dogmas. In Buddhism the operation of the law of kamma (karma) is all-pervasive and universal.

Its exact modus operandi is not detailed, and may not be immediately obvious. Unlike in some other versions of the karmic hypothesis, in Buddhism there is no mechanical equivalence between action and result (vipaka). As mentioned above the karmic quality of an act depends on a whole host of circumstances. In the accumulation of kammas, good and bad, the fruiting of some may be postponed or delayed while that of others could be immediate. What is certain is that the law of kamma makes divine authority, divine grace, etc. redundant. Thus in spite of superficial similarities, Buddhist ethics differs from other ethical systems when analysed in detail. In the Noble Eightfold Path the elements corresponding to morality and ethics are Right Speech, Right Action and Right Livelihood.

These three together constitute siila. The cultivation of siila normally proceeds alongside progress in the other two great constituents of the Path, namely mental training (bhavana) and wisdom-insight (panna). Because of the mutually supportive nature of the three components of morality, mental development and wisdom, it is difficult to argue about the relative importance of these three components. Nonetheless it has long been the generally accepted view that panna is both the threshold as well as the culmination of Buddhist practice, with the other two components of sila and bhavana being the chief means to the realization of this great objective. The distinction between ends and means is very important in the understanding of the true place of ethics in Buddhism. For the ordinary person (putujjana) ethical conduct may appear to be an end in itself, but for the adept (sekha) it is a means to the realization of a greater end. Because of the Buddha's custom of proclaiming the Dhamma according the varied capacities of his listeners, there are diverse references to the importance of siila in the Buddha's discourses which at first sight might appear to be inconsistent or even contradictory. This apparent inconsistency, however, disappears when the actual context is considered. By way of illustration we can consider two places in the Pali Cannon of Buddhism which seem to attach different degrees of importance to morality (sila) in the Buddha's system. "The first of these comes from the Brahmajala Sutta. This is the first discourse in the Sutta Pitaka (the section dealing with Buddhist doctrines), and this exalted position accorded to it reflects its importance to the early Buddhists, perhaps to the Buddha himself. This discourse was occasioned by a report brought to the Buddha of derisive comments made on him, his Doctrine and the Sangha by a wandering teacher called Suppiya, and the equally unfounded praise bestowed on him by Brahmadatta a follower of Suppiya. This had led to conflict between teacher and pupil, and disquiet amongst the followers of the Buddha. The Buddha commences the discourse by advising his followers to consider all statements made about him, whether favourable or unfavourable, in an objective manner, with equanimity and even-handedness, and then to reject what was wrong, whether it be unfounded blame or unfounded praise, and to point out these errors in a calm and reasoned manner.

The Buddha anticipated that much of the praise heaped on him would be for the wrong reasons: "It is in respect only of trifling things (appamattakam) or matters of little value (oramattakam), or mere morality (silamattaka.m) that an unconverted man (puthujjana) when praising the Buddha would speak". What is interesting from our point of view is that the Buddha considers the mere keeping of ethical rules to be a matter not worthy of any real praise.

In this sutta the Buddha groups ethical rules into three categories. The first of these (the cula sila) contains the basic ethical precepts (like the "killing of living things") which are usually included amongst the Five Precepts laid down for the guidance of lay persons. The other two categories (the majjhima and maha silas) contain, ethical rules of lesser importance or those specially laid down for monks. As against these "moralities", none of which is deserving of real praise, the Buddha describes those things that are deserving of real praise. These are the "things profound difficult to realize, hard to understand, tranquillising, sweet, not to be grasped by mere logic, subtle, comprehensible only to the wise". More specifically they turn out to be the realization of Right View (sammaditthi), and the refutation of wrong views, in which connection the Buddha outlines the famous list of sixty-two schools of thought, ranging from theism to materialism, which then as now, were the main contenders with the Dhamma. Even though the Brahmajala was mainly concerned with what was praiseworthy in a Buddha, it does provide a clear statement of the principle that wisdom-insight (panna) ranks above sila and bhavana in the accomplishments necessary for the realization of the Buddhist goal of Nibbana. The second extract from the Dhamma which we shall consider seems to paint a slightly different picture. This is probably the best known stạnza in the Dhammapada, itself the best-known of the Buddhist books. This Stanza (No.183) with its usual translation is as follows:

Sabbapapassa akaranam, kusalassa upasamapda,

sacittapariyodapanam etam Buddhana sasana.m

Not to do any evil, to do good,

To purify one's mind, this is the teaching of the Buddhas.]

The ethical import of this Stanza is obvious. It seems to claim that the Buddha's teaching is threefold: avoid unethical conduct, cultivate good deeds, and train one's mind. There is no question of the ethical purport of the first two postulates. "Training the mind" could also be interpreted as an ethical postulate, especially when we consider the Buddhist view that evil thoughts generated by an unguarded mind are karmically effective. The last phrase of this Stanza is usually taken to mean that the three ethical postulates constitute the whole (or at least the most important part) of the Dhamma.

However it could be taken to mean that these ethical principles are part of the teachings of the Buddha, and not necessarily the part that constitutes the Buddha's unique discovery. In the Commentary to the Dhammapada it is stated that this and the two following Stanzas constituted the admonition (ovadagata) delivered by the previous legendary Buddhas to bhikkhus on the uposatha days. In the explanation of the meaning of the terms in this Stanza, the Commentator says that "to do good" really means the "generation and development of skillful acts from ordination until the realization of the path of Arahat-hood", while "purifying the mind" means the elimination of the five "hindrances" which are obstacles to the realization of jhanic states during meditation. All this is in keeping with the general purpose of these stanzas, which was to serve as exhortations to Bhikkhus on the uposatha day, and not to serve as a summary of the Buddha-Dhamma. The uniqueness of Buddhist ethics lies in its many outstanding qualities.

It is all-embracing and comprehensive without being impractical or impossible to follow. It is free from taboos relating to diet, dress, behaviour etc. which very often pass as ethical principles. It serves the needs of the worldling as well as those of the recluse. It is useful to the rich and to the poor; to the powerful as well as to the powerless. To conform to Buddhist ethics one need not have to be a "buddhist"; and it serves as a norm to measure the ethical standard of other teachings. But Buddhist ethics is only the threshold for those who wish to pursue the Buddha's path to Enlightenment and the end of all ill.

BUDDHIST ETHICS AND SOCIAL CRITICISM

Buddhism arose in India during a period of intense intellectual and social ferment. It was a period during which the authority of the Vedas had been placed in doubt, the concept of god as a supreme being and creator was in question, the hereditary restrictions on caste mobility were under attack, and the efficacy of Brahminical rituals was being challenged. The authors of the Upanishads had opened the door for various heterodox currents to emerge in society, and amongst the most significant of these were the Lokayatas who polemicized against religious charlatans, and the Nyayavadis whose rational epistemology created the foundation for intense philosophical debate and encouraged the investigation of the real world based on reason and logic, freed from the burden of superstition and irrational adherence to burdensome rituals. Various ideological sects competed for the attention and acceptance of the ruling elites and the public.

The most important amongst these were the Jains and the Buddhists. Although each of the various sects made original and interesting contributions to philosophy, it was the early Buddhists who attempted to provide a unified philosophical system where ethical conduct and social criticism lay at the very core of their ideological system. Although today, Buddhism is viewed as a religion by many of its followers, the early Buddhists sects were either strongly atheistic or agnostic. The atheists believed that rather than "God having created man in his own image" it was man who had created "God" in his image. In their view, the liberation of humanity was contingent upon humanity shedding the delusion that "God" existed. Other parables from surviving Buddhist texts indicate agnosticism.

For instance, there is a suggestion that Buddhist followers ought not to waste their time on unsolvable metaphysical questions such as "does god exist". The search to identify the "one true god" or to speculate on the nature of god was seen as an exercise in futility. But the most frequently cited argument against god by the Buddhists was that if an omnipotent and omniscient being such as "God" truly existed, and who was also all good, there could not be the kind of dukkha (suffering) that was so widespread in the real world.

These shlokas (verses) from the Bhuridatta Jataka illustrates this point: If the creator of the entire world they call "God" be the lord of every being, why does he order such misfortune, and not create concord? If the creator of the entire world they call "God" be the lord of every being, why let prevail deceit, lies and ignorance, why create such inequity and injustice? If the creator of the entire world they call "God" be the lord of every being, then an evil master is he, knowing what's right did let wrong prevail!

Unlike religions that ascribed earthly miseries to human sinfulness that brought upon the wrath of a vengeful god who needed to be feared, Buddhism saw the root of human suffering in ignorance that could only be ended through the acquisition of wisdom. Rather than expect some supernatural entity to end human suffering, the Buddhists argued that it was in human hands to end their sorrows through conduct and action driven by knowledge and correct understanding of human nature and the physical world. Hence, the aspiration for knowledge was seen as the answer to blind faith. Although the Buddhists were not alone in developing this view, the elaboration of this point of view became pivotal to early Buddhist philosophy. Central to Buddhist philosophy was an understanding of human nature and what caused dukkha—i.e. human suffering. They saw human personality as constituting five attributes, i.e. body, feeling, perception, disposition and consciousness, and used this framework to develop their understanding of human suffering.

Citing examples of conditions that led to human suffering, such as aging, sickness and death, or association with the unpleasant, (or separation from the pleasant), or the inability to get what one wished-they concluded that suffering was a condition of stress and conflict inherent within human existence and interaction with the world. They also connected suffering to the very impermanence of things. They observed how people lamented over the loss of a loved one, or experienced sorrow when something or someone that had once given them happiness became separated from them. They noted that even human pleasures were not immune from suffering because they didn't last forever, and the loss of pleasure inevitably left people feeling deprived. Seeing as how clinging to things (that were necessarily impermanent) was one of the primary causes of dukkha, they cautioned against excessive attachment. At the same time, they recognized a recurring and more general type of existential unease and anxiety (cinta) that arises from the very transience of life, and our inability to control or comprehend all worldly phenomenon, which they characterized as viparinama-dukkha. But the Buddhists did not see dukkha only emanating from the difficulties of an individual. They also saw suffering emerge on a much larger scale from hostile social conditions such as poverty, war, and social oppression which they described as dukkha-dukkha.

As a formula for addressing these different types of suffering, the Buddhists advocated a four-fold scheme of (a) recognizing the problem i.e. suffering (dukkha); (b) identifying the cause of the suffering (samudaya) such as craving stemming from ignorance; (c) establishing the goal of ending the problem (nirodha)-i.e. the cessation of suffering (nirvana); (d) conducting life in a manner that was consistent with the cessation of suffering-following the right path or engaging in the right practice (marga). Followers were thus goaded into developing both a sense of personal ethics and a social conscience:

> "He who has understanding and great wisdom does not think of harming himself or another, nor of harming both alike. He rather thinks of his own welfare, of that of others, of that of both, and of the welfare of the whole world. In that way one shows understanding and great wisdom." Anguttara Nikaya (Gradual Sayings)

> "By protecting oneself (e.g., morally), one protects others; by protecting others, one protects oneself." Samyukta

Nikaya (Kindred Sayings) Human actions (kamma, or karma) in the Buddhist framework were to be judged based on both the intention or motive (chetana) and the consequences (vipaka) of the action. Altruistic actions which helped in the establishment and promotion of a just society were encouraged in the dharmaniyama (moral duty code). {The discourses, or suttas in the Digha Nikaya, illustrate how there was deep concern with the creation of social conditions favourable to the cultivation of Buddhist values and the expansion of social equity and justice. These views undoubtedly influenced the creation of a "welfare state" during the reign of emperor, Ashoka (B.C. 274-236)}

In their theories of causality Buddhists challenged the view that human destiny was unaffected by the ethics or morality of human actions. They countered the doctrine of amoral causation (akriyavada) whose adherents argued that there was no merit in doing good and no demerit for doing evil. (An extreme expression of such thinking was seen in philosophers who denied all morality and saw no crime in the killing of any person.) Realizing that such a world-view could lead to the rejection of moral distinctions and personal responsibility for ones actions, they argued strenuously against such beliefs.

They also argued against the theory of Makkhali Gosala who believed that human fate was predetermined, and therefore denied that human actions had any bearing on the results of things (ahetuvada) and maintained that human intention and effort were essentially powerless in changing human destiny, and therefore advocated fatalism (niyati). They also countered philosophers from the school of "absolute skepticism" who doubted everything and never committed themselves to any specific position in doctrinal debates.

Philosophers from this school such as Sanjaya Belatthiputta (who was known as a theorist of endless equivocation or an equivocationist (amravikkhepavadin)) were criticized in the Brahmajaala Sutta as "eel-wrigglers" who were incapable of taking a definitive stance on the vital philosophical questions of the day.

Such skepticism was seen as emanating from both the fear of being in error and the lack of knowledge (or inability) to provide reasonable answers to question put forward for discussion. Such all-pervading doubt coupled with a cynical skepticism (vichikiccha) was viewed as a serious mental hindrance, a fetter in the path to wisdom. Other theories that contradicted the notion that human actions mattered were theories of accidentalism (ahetu-apaccayavada), theistic determinism (ishvaranimmanavada) and past-action determinism (purvaketavaada or purvekatahetu). All of these were opposed by the Buddhists. Accidentalism was an indeterminist theory which held that whatever was experienced was uncaused and unconditioned by human intervention. Theistic determinism was a determinist theory, which held that whatever was experienced was due to God's will or by plan of a "Supreme-Being". Past-action determinism was also a determinist theory, but it held the belief that whatever was experienced, whether pleasurable or painful or indifferent was entirely due to ones past actions (from a previous life), and ones present actions had no relevance. The danger in each of these theories was highlighted in these words: "Thus for those who fall back on these three erroneous views as essential dogma, there is neither the will to do what is ought to be done, or not to do what is ought not to be done, nor necessity to do this deed or abstain from that deed. No moral improvement or intellectual culture can be expected from them." Some of the theories in circulation at that time built on a germ of truth but generalized to the point of absurdity. For instance the accidentalists were correct only to the extent that certain things did indeed appear to happen by random chance or accident. But they failed to recognize that sometimes what may have seemed to be accidental was more due to inadequate understanding or improper or incomplete perception, and that other activities had a clearly discernible cause. To deal with the extreme generalizations of such theorists, they introduced a middle standpoint for their epistemology and ethics.

They thus rejected the theory admitting that everything exists (sabba atthii ti) and in permanence-i.e. the extreme of eternalism (sassatavada), and its opposite which advocated that nothing actually exists (sabban natthi ti) i.e. nihilism (the denial of all reality in real-world phenomenon) or the extreme of annihilationalism (ucchedavada). Related to their critique of the eternalist and nihilist philosophies was their rejection of both hedonism and self-mortification (attakilamathanuyoga) which they viewed as painful, fruitless, unprofitable and ignoble. Buddhist texts also expressed suspicion about claims by heretical teachers of being constantly "all-knowing" and "all-seeing" and in possession of "all-embracing knowledge-and-vision."

Such claims were countered with arguments relating to the actual behaviour of such charlatans in different situations. For instance, they wondered why such "all-knowing" and "all-seeing" spiritual teachers lost their way in an unfamiliar place or why they were unable to escape from trouble while countering a fierce animal such as dog, elephant, horse or bull. Moreover, if they were really omniscient, they wouldn't need to ask for people's names, clans, or the name of a village or market town or make enquiries about anything. That they did such things indicated that their knowledge was evidently limited just like that of any average worldly person (puthujjana). Unlike religions that were based on revealed truth or the sanctity of every word in a holy textbook, the Buddhist belief system prescribed reasoning based on investigation as the means of determining ones dhamma, (or dharma as in Hindu practise).

In a parable in the Kalama Sutta, followers of Buddhism are advised not to accept any moral codes on the following ten grounds: (1) Vedic authority (anussava), (2) tradition (parampara), (3) hearsay or report (itikira), (4) textual authority (pitakasampada), (5) apparent agreebility of the view (sama o no garu), (6) authority of the holder of the view (takkahetu), (7) apparent logicality of the view (nayahetu), (8) the fact that the view is an accepted standpoint (akaraparivitakka), (9) inadequate reflection on reasons (bhabbarupata), or (10) the fact that the view agrees with one's own. In this manner, the Buddhism developed a very sophisticated philosophical system in which social ethics were integrated with rational investigation of human nature, social organization and the physical world.

Buddhist ideas and concepts left a powerful impression on other Indian philosophical and religious belief systems, and over time, many commonalities developed amongst the competing ideologies. However, there were also certain problems with the Buddhist world view which prevented its complete acceptance by intellectuals committed to the scientific method.

For instance, although the Buddhists rejected the theory of past action determinism, they did posit the existence of a soul which survived a person's death and carried with it the merits and demerits of a person's past lives. Presumably this concept was essential to the Buddhist goal of encouraging right conduct but it was rejected by those who considered the soul as inseparable from the body and did not believe that the soul survived death. Those who rejected the concept of transmigration of the soul naturally couldn't accept the idea that human destiny had anything to do with merits and demerits accumulated in previous incarnations of the "soul". In their view, morality and ethics were entirely social constructs and had to be dealt with accordingly. The realists (such as the Nyayavadis) who shared the Buddhist concern for morals and ethics in society argued that while morals and ethics ought to be encouraged, they could only be enforced through societal laws and judicial codes. Another problem facing the Buddhists was that in many ways, their views were too **advanced for their** times.

Society had not yet developed to the point where education was universal, and knowledge of the real world sufficient to prevent superstitions and irrational beliefs from being completely abandoned by the masses. In an era where society had only limited control over nature, it was inevitable that sections of society would continue with beliefs in deities and supernatural phenomenon in the hope that they may be spared from natural disasters or that their crops might withstand attacks from pests and disease.

Thus although the Buddhists had a very important and salutatory effect on Indian society, the most advanced Buddhist concepts could be understood and practised by only a minority in society. Over time, the spirit of inquiry and rational investigation that had spurred the early Buddhist scholars towards dialectical thinking and critical social analysis became more and more replaced by narrow and literalist interpretations of the earlier texts.

For instance, advice against accepting something that appeared "logical" without personal verification was taken to mean that logic could be rejected. Advice against wasting ones time on unsolvable metaphysical questions was also taken too literally and many Buddhist scholars remained aloof from the metaphysical debates pursued by other philosophical schools such as those of the Jains and the Nyaya Vaisheshikas. What they didn't anticipate was that some of these debates might lead to useful advances in mathematics or deeper understanding of human thought processes and new insights on human memory and psychology. These led to valuable advances in the interpretation of moods and emotions-thus benefiting Indian art, literature and music. In addition, later Buddhist monks lapsed into some of the very things that had been attacked by the early Buddhists such as indulgence in unnecessary and elaborate rituals, belief in supra-natural phenomenon, and alienation of the priests from the masses.

Activities such as meditation which were encouraged as a means to gaining wisdom became ends in themselves, and were turned into idealistic fetishes. Although Buddhist monks dutifully delivered sermons on right conduct and right action, they often failed to engage in relevant and timely social criticism-and did not always connect the textual suggestions to concrete practice. Intra-Buddhist disputes developed around less significant details, even as some of the most important ideas that had initially shaped the philosophy were pushed into the background. As a result Buddhism as it was practised came to be associated with idealism and inaction. Whereas the early Buddhists saw no merit in worshipping god or its images, later Buddhism developed a pantheon of deities not very different from other Indian religions. Thus even as Buddhism had spread almost throughout Asia by the 5th-6th C AD, it gradually began to lose its distinct edge and liberating influence on much of Indian society. Within the Indian subcontinent, strains of Buddhism survived in Sri Lanka, Bengal, Bhutan, Sikkim, parts of Bihar and Nepal, and parts of Sindh, Punjab, Kashmir and Afghanistan. In parts of Orissa and adjoining regions (such as Chhattisgarh and Telengana), Tantric (and other) influences reshaped the practice of Buddhism. Yet, Buddhism continued to have an impact outside India and developed pockets of influence as far West as Syria, as well as in much of Central Asia (including what is now Uzbekistan, Tajikistan, Kyrgyzia, Kazakhstan) and Tibet. In the East, its influence was felt on virtually every nation including Burma, Thailand, Malaya and Indonesia, Laos, Cambodia, Vietnam, China, Korea and Japan. As noted earlier, the vast literature of Buddhism (like much of Hindu or Jain literature) was not a literature of revelation and authority.

Its essays on social ethics and moral responsibilities, its treatises on philosophy and science, its art and poetry were but pointers to a path to wisdom. This gave Buddhism both flexibility and adaptability. Owing to its non-hegemonic character and humanist appeal, Buddhism was adopted without coercion or force. It was also successfully fused with Hinduism in many parts of South East Asia just as elements of it had been integrated into Hindu practices in India. In China, it was integrated with Taoism and Confucian principles; in Japan with Shinto beliefs. For several centuries, within India and outside, several people followed multiple faiths and identified as both Buddhists and Hindus, or as both Buddhists and Tantrics, (or Buddhists and Taoists) and so on. During the Gupta period (and in other reigns), philosophers from various schools of thought received royal patronage and temple grants were conferred for the construction of Buddhist and Hindu monuments alike. It is also important to recognize that the form of Buddhism that was embraced in each nation was often quite different.

For instance, in Western and Central Asia, it was not the philosophical or intellectual aspects of Buddhism that were popularized, but rather, its personal moral codes. Buddhist prosletysers imbued their stories of the Buddha with examples of miraculous healing and super-natural compassion so as to win more followers. While such tendencies were also to be seen as Buddhism travelled within India or outwards, in Burma, Sri Lanka and Thailand, Buddhism developed organizational structures that appear to have been much more resilient.

It was perhaps realized that the development of Buddhist virtue would require leadership and constant interaction with the community. In these nations, Buddhism did not degenerate into the extremes of mysticism or retreatism that became commonplace in certain parts of India (such as in the foothills of the Western Himalayas). Burmese and Thai monks maintained a practical and benevolent connection with the community, and thus retained a measure of respect within the community. This also appears to be the case in Japan. In Korea, the emphasis on gaining wisdom was taken very seriously, and Buddhist monks took the lead in promoting mass literacy. This propelled the growth of technologies associated with the production of paper, writing instruments, inks, and furniture. And unlike in India, (where due to Upanishadic influences, "inner" wisdom came to be favoured over outer wisdom), Buddhist concern for disseminating the writings of the Buddha had significant positive secular impact. In Korean (and other Eastern) Buddhism, there was the correct realization that a Buddhist mindset, or that a Buddhist society could not be constructed overnight. There was thus the emphasis on the (helical) upgradation of individuals and society towards greater "Buddhahood". This philosophical element was perhaps signficant in that it prevented the sort of philosophical stagnation that occurred in India, where followers too often sought immediate succuor, and thus not only became divorced from reality, but also lost sight of the strategic potential of the philosophy. In addition, it ought to be noted that Buddhism in India also had to contend with strongly anarchic and ultra-democratic tendencies.

Precisely because its philosophical structure emphasized the relative and changing nature of truth, different tendencies under the Buddhist mantle competed for leadership through argument and debate. Initially, this led to important advances in democratic practices within the Sanghas. But over time, it also led to clashes of egoes, hair-splitting and deadlock. While some Buddhist sects compromised and fused with other tendencies (even alien tendencies), others remained fiercely autonomous. To survive, Buddhism had to confront both the tendency to be co-opted, as well as the tendency to atomize. However, the catastrophic demise of Buddhism in India was triggered by the onslaught of Islam which first obliterated the remnants of Buddhism in Central Asia, and then later in Afghanistan and India.

By and large, Buddhism survived only in those countries that escaped invasions by Islamic conquerors. As a gentle faith that encouraged its followers to abjure violence, it was perhaps unable to protect itself from iconoclasts and proselytizers who intended to enforce a new religio-political order. Accustomed to centuries of peaceful co-existence, India's Buddhists had not anticipated the need to develop viable strategies for self-defence that could have combated the violence of India's Islamic conquerors who virtually obliterated Buddhism from the land of its birth. Yet, it also appears that (in large part) later Buddhism had deviated considerably from the rational principles outlined in the early texts.

Monasteries often became isolated from mainstream society, and monks who focused exclusively on meditative practices and idealistic or esoteric philosophical speculation contributed little to social progress. Some have even argued that the monastic orders had degenerated into sheer parasitism and were becoming a heavy social drain. Consequently, value judgements on the demise of Buddhism and the rise of Islam in India need to be made with a measure of caution. Nevertheless, it must be acknowledged that the ascent of Islam was concomitant with the eclipse of Buddhism, and since the influence of Buddhism was greatly dependant on the existence of the monastic orders, the destruction of monasteries and their conversion to mosques and institutions of Quranic learning simply lead to mass conversions to Islam. In the long term, this could have had the effect of stunting India's future intellectual development, since the destruction of important institutions of Buddhist learning also led to a notable decline in the opportunity (and social sanction) to study secular subjects such as logic and epistemology (which were also taught at Buddhist universities-such as Bhagalpur). It might also be observed that the destruction of Buddhist centres of learning coincided with the destruction of extremely valuable textual materials-which could have been potentially rediscovered, and revived or reinterpreted by future generations of Indians so as to achieve a society that was more thoughtful and learned.

Islamic texts did not offer anything comparable in terms of causality or epistemology. Nor did they offer the psychological, sociological, or moral insights that had been developed under the ambit of Buddhism. Nor was there any comparable stress on seeking knowledge or constantly updating ones understanding of nature and human society. One can, therefore, only speculate as to the full consequences of this profound sociolgical and cultural loss (and discontinuity).

But East of India, Buddhism did survive, and in countries such Korea, Thailand and Burma, it continued to enjoy a loyal popular following. Philosophical innovations also took place, and as noted earlier, Buddhist scholars in China, Korea and Japan offered their own commentaries and somewhat individual interpretations of Buddhist concepts and formulations outlined in later (5-7th C.) Indian texts. And although the sacking of monasteries and centres of learning (such as Nalanda and Vikramshila in Bihar) led to records of the original Buddhist texts being permanently destroyed, it has been possible to reconstruct some of them from translations that survived outside India such as in Thailand and Tibet. Notwithstanding the virtual erasure of Buddhism in India, it is possible to infer from these reconstructed texts and other archaeological records (and surviving monuments and artifacts) that Buddhism had a very powerful impact in shaping the destiny of India, and in triggering a social and cultural renaissance that would take Indian and other Asian civilizations to a higher level of social, cultural and material development.

BUDDHIST ETHICS

PAI LU-TIEN, a famous Chinese poet, author, and statesman who lived in the thirteenth century of the Christian era, once went to see an eminent Buddhist monk whose saintly life was known far and near, and asked him if he would instruct him in the essentials of Buddhist doctrine. The monk assented and recited the following gatha:

"Commit no wrong, but good deeds do,

And let thy heart be pure,

All Buddhas teach this truth,

Which will for aye endure."

The statesman-poet was not at all satisfied with this simple moral teaching, for he expected to have something abstruse, recondite, and highly philosophical from the mouth of such a prominent and virtuous personality. Said the poet, "Every child is familiar with this Buddhist injunction. What I wish to learn from you is the highest and most fundamental teaching of your faith." But the monk retorted, "Every child may know of this gatha, but even a silvery-haired man fails to put it into practice." Thereupon, it is said, the poet reverentially bowed and went home meditatively. If we are requested today to state what is the most fundamental in Buddhist ethics, we have to make the same assertion.

But it is not a negative condition, for the most essential postulate of Buddhism is that in each of us there abide the indwelling reason of the universe, which, when released from the temporal bondage of ignorance and self-will, becomes the master of itself by reducing everything to subjection and restoring it to its right place. In a pure heart, therefore, the universal reason manifests itself in its full glory and works its own destiny unmolested. What one with such a heart wills is what makes the bird sing and the flower smile, what has raised the mountain and makes the water flow. He is hungry and the universe wishes to eat; he is asleep and all the world hybernates. This sounds extraordinary, but the enlightened understand it perfectly well. We cannot make the blind see what we ourselves see. The blind may protest that we are deceiving them; but could we do otherwise, inasmuch as they are deprived of the sense we have, or they have not yet learned how to make use of it? It is declared by Buddhists, therefore, that to realize fully the sanctity of religious life one must have Buddha-wisdom awakened from its unconscious slumber in which it is indulging from time out of mind. Analytically, purity of heart consists of sympathy and intelligence, and on this groundwork the structure of practical Buddhism is founded.

Sympathy is the tremulation of the spiritual cord which unites the hearts of all sentient beings; and it is intelligence that discovers the presence of the sacred cord in every one of us and keeps it from being entangled. The cord freely responds to cries of suffering. The heart contrives to effect all the possible means to relieve sentient beings from misery and ignorance. The ten deeds of goodness, the eightfold path, the six virtues of perfection, and many other good things all flow from this one source of pure-heartedness. It is, then, of unqualified importance in the ethics of Buddhism to have one's heart perfectly cleansed and free from the dust of egotism which has been accumulating through the want of enlightenment.

In this sense "blessed are the pure in heart"; they may not see God as he is superficially and superstitiously understood, but they will surely come into personal touch with the ultimate authority of conduct and also perceive that the author is not residing outside of their being but within themselves. We read in the Dharmapada:

"Manopubbangama dhamma, manosettha, manomaya;

Manasa, ce padutthana bhasati va karoti va,

Tato nam dukkham anveti, cakkara va vahato padam.

"Manopubbangama dhamma, manosettha, manomaya;

Manasa ce pasannena bhasati va karoti va,

Tato nam sukhara anveti, chaya va anapayinî."

In this respect Buddhism can be said to have a decidedly idealistic tendency, since it fully recognizes the paramountcy of ideas in the moral realm. But we must not lose sight of the fact that Buddhism is not a system of metaphysics, but a religion which is practical more than anything else. What it teaches is the profound spiritual experience of every enlightened man, while the philosopher and theorist will speculate on the facts and offer whatever interpretation they may please or feel compelled to give to account adequately for them. Buddhism is often charged with passiveness and quietism, lacking the "push" of some other religions; and the backwardness of Asiatic nations in the general march of humanity is sometimes ascribed to the influence of Buddhism.

Bibliography

Arthur Miller: *As a Critic of Drama,* New Delhi, Anmol, 2004.

Batchelor, Martine and Kerry Brown: *Buddhism and Ecology,* London, Cassell, 1992.

Bell, Sir Charles: *Portrait of a Dalai Lama: The Life and Times of the Great Thirteenth,* Boston, Wisdom Publications, 1987.

Cook, Elizabeth: *Holy Places of the Buddha,* Berkeley, Dharma Publishing, 1994.

Eppsteiner, Fred: *The Path of Compassion: Writings on Socially Engaged Buddhism,* Berkeley, Parallax Press, 1988.

Gonda, Jan: *Vedic Literature: Samhitas and Brahmanas,* Wiesbaden, 1975.

Hogan, Robert Goode: *The Modern Irish Drama: a Documentary History,* NJ: Humanities Press, 1975.

Ireland, John D.: *The Udana: Inspired Utterances of the Buddha,* Buddhist Publication Society, Kandy, 1990.

Jones, Ken: *Beyond Optimism: A Buddhist Political Ecology,* Oxford, Jon Carpenter, 1993.

Keown, Damien: *The Nature of Buddhist Ethics,* New York, St. Martin's Press, 1992.

Mookerjee, Satkari: *Buddhist Philosophy of Universal Flux,* Delhi, Motilal Banarsidass, 1980.

Morrell, Robert: *Early Kamakura Buddhism: A Minority Report,* Berkeley, Asian Humanities Press, 1987.

Payutto, Prayudh: *Buddhist Economics: A Middle Way for the Marketplace,* Bangkok, Buddhadhamma Foundation, 1994.

Powers, John: *Wisdom of Buddha: The Samdhinirmocana Sutra,* Berkeley, Dharma Publishing, 1994.

Titmuss, Christopher: *The Green Buddha,* Devon, Insights, 1995.

Index

□□□